Kenneth [illegible]

INTRODUCTION TO GENERAL EQUILIBRIUM THEORY AND WELFARE ECONOMICS

ECONOMICS HANDBOOK SERIES
SEYMOUR E. HARRIS, EDITOR

THE BOARD OF ADVISORS

Neil W. Chamberlain
Columbia University—Labor
John M. Culbertson
University of Wisconsin—Monetary Theory
Seymour E. Harris
Harvard University—International Economics, Social Security; all other areas
Franco Modigliani
Massachusetts Institute of Technology—Economic Theory
Richard A. Musgrave
Harvard University—Public Policy
Marc Nerlove
Yale University—Econometrics and Mathematical Economics

Burns · SOCIAL SECURITY AND PUBLIC POLICY
Carlson · ECONOMIC SECURITY IN THE UNITED STATES
Duesenberry · BUSINESS CYCLES AND ECONOMIC GROWTH
Fisher · THE IDENTIFICATION PROBLEM IN ECONOMETRICS
Hansen · A GUIDE TO KEYNES
Hansen · THE AMERICAN ECONOMY
Hansen · THE DOLLAR AND THE INTERNATIONAL MONETARY SYSTEM
Hansen · ECONOMIC ISSUES OF THE 1960s
Hansen · MONETARY THEORY AND FISCAL POLICY
Harrod · THE BRITISH ECONOMY
Henderson and Quandt · MICROECONOMIC THEORY
Hoover · THE LOCATION OF ECONOMIC ACTIVITY
Johnston · STATISTICAL COST ANALYSIS
Kindleberger · ECONOMIC DEVELOPMENT
Lebergott · MANPOWER IN ECONOMIC GROWTH
McKean · PUBLIC SPENDING
Phelps · FISCAL NEUTRALITY TOWARD ECONOMIC GROWTH
Quirk and Saposnik · INTRODUCTION TO GENERAL EQUILIBRIUM THEORY AND WELFARE ECONOMICS
Taylor · A HISTORY OF ECONOMIC THOUGHT
Theil, Boot, and Kloek · OPERATIONS RESEARCH AND QUANTITATIVE ECONOMICS
Tinbergen and Bos · MATHEMATICAL MODELS OF ECONOMIC GROWTH
Vanek · ESTIMATING FOREIGN RESOURCE NEEDS FOR ECONOMIC DEVELOPMENT
Walton and McKersie · A BEHAVIORAL THEORY OF LABOR NEGOTIATIONS

INTRODUCTION TO GENERAL EQUILIBRIUM THEORY AND WELFARE ECONOMICS

JAMES QUIRK
Professor of Economics
University of Kansas

RUBIN SAPOSNIK
Professor of Economics
University of Kansas

McGRAW-HILL BOOK COMPANY
New York
St. Louis
San Francisco
Toronto
London
Sydney

INTRODUCTION TO GENERAL EQUILIBRIUM THEORY AND WELFARE ECONOMICS

Library of Congress Catalog Card Number

51076

1234567890MAMM7432106987

to
SHIRLEY
and
MARLENE

PREFACE

The primary purpose of this book is to make available to students relatively recent developments in general equilibrium analysis. Much of the work that has been done in general equilibrium theory during the past fifteen years or so has used rather advanced mathematics. We have attempted, in this volume, to present this material in a way that would require little mathematical knowledge on the part of the reader and yet would not sacrifice unduly the logical rigor inherent in the subject matter. It is our hope that an introductory work such as this will be useful as a reference tool for practicing social, behavioral, and managerial scientists as well as for providing text material.

This book is not intended to be an encyclopedic treatise such as Professor Kuenne's *The Theory of General Economic Equilibrium;* the aim of this book is largely heuristic. To the extent that we have used mathematics, we have attempted to present it, as needed, in the text, rather than in appendixes.

As for the detailed contents of this volume, briefly, Chapters 1 and 2 deal with the general equilibrium framework, beginning with the behavior of individual economic agents and culminating in the multimarket environment. Chapter 3 deals with the problem of the existence of competitive equilibrium, the central exposition following most closely Debreu's *Theory of Value*. Chapter 4 is concerned with welfare economics, taking up Arrow's possibility theorem as well as his two theorems relating competitive equilibrium and Pareto optimality. Chapter 5 takes up the problem of the stability of competitive equilibrium, and Chapter 6 is concerned with the relationship between competitive equilibrium and comparative statics analysis.

We wish to acknowledge the aid and encouragement afforded us in the development of this volume by E. T. Weiler and J. S. Day of the Krannert School of Purdue University. We are indebted to several "generations" of graduate students at Purdue who were subjected to this material in various stages of its development. There have been any number of helpful suggestions and corrections forthcoming from members of the economics profession. In this connection, we are particularly indebted to James Murphy of the University of North Carolina and Richard Ruppert of the University of Kansas. In addition, the Department of Economics at the University of Kansas has been extremely helpful in the last stages of the writing of this volume.

Finally, we are indebted to Mrs. Divona Donaldson, Mrs. Melody Shaeffer, Mrs. Sandra Meyer, and Mrs. Carole Weeks for their patience and skill in preparing the manuscript.

James Quirk
Rubin Saposnik

CONTENTS

ONE

THE SETTING: INDIVIDUAL ECONOMIC AGENTS

1-1 MACROECONOMICS, MICROECONOMICS, AND GENERAL EQUILIBRIUM THEORY

Traditionally a distinction has been drawn in economic theory between microeconomics, the study of the behavior of isolated economic entities such as individual consumers or firms or industries, and macroeconomics, the study of the behavior of the economy as a whole, as measured by such aggregates as the level of output, the price level, and the level of employment. General equilibrium theory forms a bridge between these two branches of economic theory, using the tools of microeconomics to analyze the behavior of the entire economy. In common with macroeconomics, general equilibrium theory is concerned with the interrelationships that exist among the markets for goods and services in the economy; in common with microeconomics, the analysis in general equilibrium theory is carried out in terms of individual decision makers and commodities rather than in terms of aggregates. The fundamental questions that general equilibrium theory attempts to answer are the same as those posed in macroeconomic theory: given different economic environments, what goods will the economy produce, how will these be produced, and who will obtain them? But, where macroeconomics provides answers in terms of aggregates, general equilibrium theory provides answers in terms of the individual consumers, producers, and commodities making up these aggregates.

In fact, from the point of view of the formal logical structure of the analysis, macroeconomics may be regarded as a highly specialized form of general equilibrium theory in which the decision makers in the economy consist of one consumer, one producer, and "the government." The consumer makes decisions with respect to the allocation of his income between consumption and saving, the amount of labor he is to supply, and the form in which he will hold his wealth (money holdings versus securities). The producer decides on the number of units of labor to hire to produce a single physical commodity which is used either as a consumption or as a capital good, and in addition determines the number of units of output to allocate to investment. The resulting interactions among these consumption, wealth-holding, and production decisions then determine such magnitudes as the price of the commodity, the interest rate (the inverse of the price of securities), the number of units of labor employed, and the number and distribution of units of output of the commodity, given exogenous decisions on government purchases and determination of the size of the money supply. Needless to say, the importance of macroeconomics as a tool in policymaking arises from an interpretation of the variables of macroeconomic models in terms of index numbers and aggregates rather than in terms of the behavior of hypothetical individual economic units.

Thus, through the use of aggregates that have a relatively straightforward interpretation in terms of data available to the economist, macroeconomics is able to provide simplified answers to the questions of which goods will be produced, how they will be produced, and who will obtain them. General equilibrium theory has a considerably more ambitious goal—that of analyzing the operations of the economy, explicitly taking into account the diversity of consumption and capital goods and the varying tastes and wealth and income positions of consumers as well as the differences in technological possibilities available to firms. The analytical framework of general equilibrium theory is that of microeconomics. Consequently, it has the same faults and virtues as microeconomics, perhaps to an exaggerated degree. These faults and virtues both stem from a common source, the economist's lack of precise knowledge concerning the characteristics of individual tastes and the technological possibilities available to producers. In the absence of such detailed information on these aspects of the economy, economists have found it necessary to construct theories that hold under very general conditions. Because of the relative weakness or generality of the assumptions that are employed in microeconomics, theories are developed that apply to a wide range of possible "worlds," an outstanding virtue of economic theory. The price that is paid for this wide applicability is that the theorems of economics are correspondingly nonspecific; what we can say about economies characterized by the assumptions employed by economists is extremely limited. In addition, the weakness of the assumptions and the generality of the analyses in turn lead to abstract theorizing that often more closely resembles formal logic or mathematics than the empirically oriented specific theorizing of the physical sciences.

The highly abstract nature of economic theory is particularly evident in general equilibrium analysis, at least partially because in this branch of economic theory the number of variables taken into account is arbitrarily large. It has been said with some truth that in two dimensions, economic theory is trivial, but in three (or more) it is impossibly difficult. To some extent, the difficulties encountered in generalizing the concepts we are familar with in two dimensions to higher dimensions can be accounted for by the problem of visualizing relations in higher-dimensional spaces; there are, however, other substantive grounds for the increased complexity of the more general case. For example, it turns out that every two-commodity competitive economy possesses a certain kind of dynamic stability, but this result does not carry over into economies with more than two goods. Similarly, a whole host of problems arises in attempting to evaluate the relative desirability of different patterns of production and consumption for an economy with two or more consumers as compared with an economy of only one consumer. In international trade theory, the complexities that arise in attempting to generalize the discussion from two to three countries are well known, and anyone who has attempted to graph indifference curves in two-dimensional space in such a way that the two commodities are complements (in the Hicksian sense) will be aware of the fact that not all of economic theory can be handled within the confines of the plane. Once we go from a single market to the multimarket context of general equilibrium analysis, two-dimensional graphs have, at most, heuristic value. The economic theoretic difficulties associated with the dimensionality of the model used typically become apparent in going from two to three dimensions, while going from three dimensions to an arbitrary finite dimension presents no real difficulties. In general, however, it should be kept in mind that economic theory is simply more complicated once more than two variables are involved.

1-2 VECTORS AND EUCLIDEAN SPACE

With only one or two minor exceptions, this book will be concerned with problems of general equilibrium theory in which the number of variables is finite. Consequently, the mathematical setting for the analysis is euclidean space. Without attempting to give a formal definition of euclidean space, it may simply be noted that the real line (the set of all real numbers) is euclidean one-dimensional space, while the plane (the set of all pairs of real numbers) is euclidean two-dimensional space, and similarly for higher-dimensional euclidean spaces.

It will be recalled from analytical geometry that there is a one-to-one correspondence between points in the plane and pairs of real numbers.

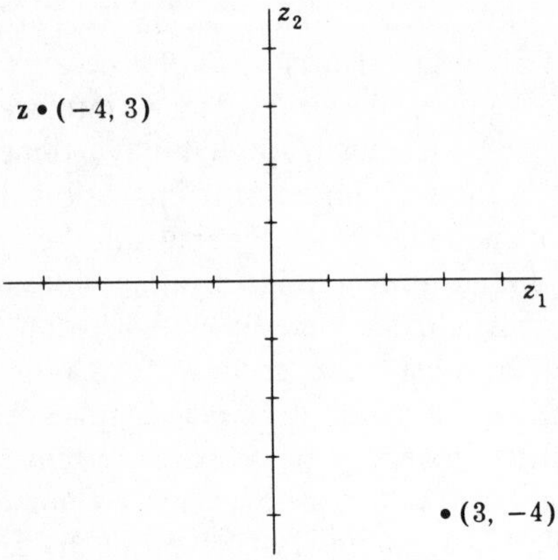

FIGURE 1-1

For example, in Fig. 1-1, the point **z** may be defined by plotting, or it may be equally unambiguously defined by the pair of numbers (—4,3). More precisely, **z** is defined by the *ordered pair* (—4,3), since the order of the numbers is important, and (—4,3) is clearly a different point than (3,—4).

Any point in the plane may then be defined by a pair of numbers (z_1,z_2). Sometimes it is convenient to think of a point $\mathbf{z} = (z_1,z_2)$ as the end point of a *vector* starting at the origin and terminating at the point **z**. Then (z_1,z_2) may be thought of as identifying a two-dimensional vector having components z_1, z_2. Although conceptually the situation is essentially unaltered in going to higher dimensions than two, graphic representations are of limited use beyond three dimensions. Therefore a point (or a vector) in n-dimensional euclidean space will be denoted by an n-tuple of real numbers, $(z_1, z_2, \ldots, z_n)$, each number denoting the corresponding coordinate in n-dimensional space.

Certain operations defined with respect to vectors will be used in our later discussions and may be conveniently summarized here. We define scalar multiplication of a vector as follows: Let $\mathbf{z} = (z_1, z_2, \ldots, z_n)$ be an n-dimensional vector, and let a be a real number. Then multiplying a by **z**, written $a\mathbf{z}$, is defined as multiplying each component of **z** by the real number (scalar) a, that is,

$$a\mathbf{z} = (az_1, az_2, \ldots, az_n)$$

is the scalar multiplication of a and **z**.

In two dimensions, scalar multiplication is illustrated by the multiplication of $\mathbf{z} = (-4,3)$ by the scalar -1, giving the vector (4,—3), as shown in Fig. 1-2.

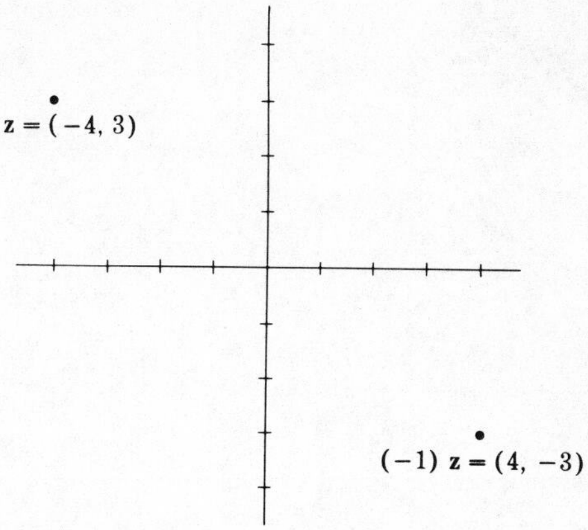

FIGURE 1-2

Two vectors may be added together by adding corresponding components. Thus, if $\mathbf{z} = (z_1, z_2, \ldots, z_n)$ and $\mathbf{y} = (y_1, y_2, \ldots, y_n)$ are two n-dimensional vectors, we define the sum of the vectors $\mathbf{z}$ and $\mathbf{y}$, written $\mathbf{z} + \mathbf{y}$, by

$$\mathbf{z} + \mathbf{y} = (z_1 + y_1, z_2 + y_2, \ldots, z_n + y_n)$$

In two-dimensional space, addition of vectors may be accomplished graphically by using the "parallelogram law," as illustrated in Fig. 1-3 for the two vectors $\mathbf{z} = (2,1)$ and $\mathbf{y} = (1,2)$.

The product of two vectors will be defined by $\mathbf{z} \cdot \mathbf{y} = z_1y_1 + z_2y_2 + \cdots + z_ny_n$, for any n-dimensional vectors z and y. Using the product-of-vector concept, we may denote the length of a vector $\mathbf{z}$ by $\sqrt{\mathbf{z} \cdot \mathbf{z}}$.

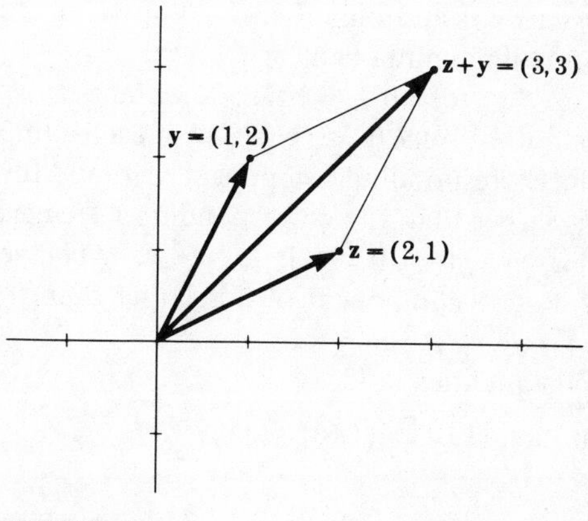

FIGURE 1-3

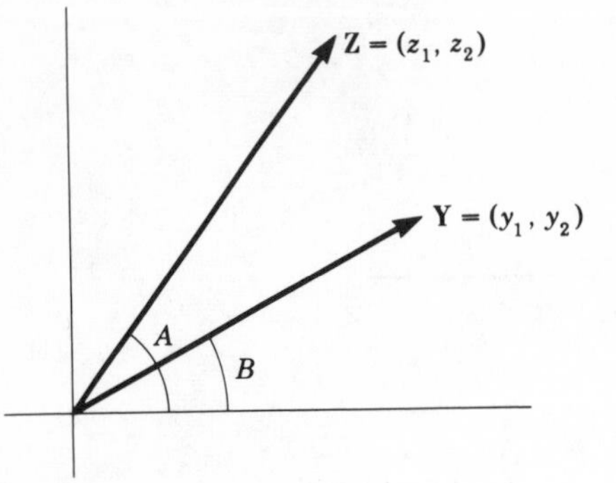

FIGURE 1-4

Figure 1-4 illustrates how the product of two vectors may be interpreted in two dimensions. A denotes the angle formed by the vector **z** and the horizontal axis, and B denotes the angle formed by the vector **y** and the horizontal axis. It is obvious then that the angle formed by the two vectors themselves is $A - B$. We recall the trigonometric formula $\cos(A - B) = \cos A \cos B + \sin A \sin B$. Letting $|\mathbf{z}|$ denote the length of **z**, we have, by inserting the values of $\cos A$, $\cos B$, $\mathbf{z} \cdot \mathbf{y} = |\mathbf{z}|\,|\mathbf{y}| \cos(A - B)$. Thus we see that a positive, zero, or negative value for the product of two vectors is associated with the angle formed by the vectors being acute, right, or obtuse, respectively.

Finally, two n-dimensional vectors **z** and **y**, the components of each vector being real numbers, may be compared for size as follows:

$\mathbf{z} = \mathbf{y}$ if and only if $z_i = y_i$ for all $i = 1, 2, \ldots, n$. (The vectors **z** and **y** are said to be *equal* if and only if all of the corresponding components of **z** and **y** are equal.)

$\mathbf{z} \geqq \mathbf{y}$ if and only if $z_i \geqq y_i$ for all $i = 1, 2, \ldots, n$. (The vector **z** is said to be *at least as large as* **y** if and only if each component of **z** is at least as large as the corresponding component of **y**.)

$\mathbf{z} \geq \mathbf{y}$ if and only if $z_i \geqq y_i$ for all $i = 1, 2, \ldots, n$, and $z_i > y_i$ for some i. (The vector **z** is said to be *weakly larger than* **y** if each component of **z** is at least as large as the corresponding component of **y**, and for some component the z element is larger than the corresponding y element.)

$\mathbf{z} > \mathbf{y}$ if and only if $z_i > y_i$ for all $i = 1, 2, \ldots, n$. (The vector **z** is said to be *larger than* **y** if each component of **z** is larger than the corresponding component of **y**.)

Thus the following inequalities hold:

$(1,0) \geqq (1,0)$ [in fact, $(1,0) = (1,0)$]

$(1,1) \geq (1,0)$

$(1,1) > (0,0)$

In particular, the set of vectors larger than the zero vector is said to comprise the *positive orthant* of the space. Similarly, the set of vectors smaller than the zero vector is said to comprise the *negative orthant* of the space. In two-space, the positive orthant is the first quadrant and the negative orthant is the third quadrant.

1-3 ECONOMIC AGENTS

It is common practice in microeconomic theory to distinguish among individuals according to the economic functions that they perform or on the basis of the kinds of decisions they make. Thus a *consumer* is an individual (or unit such as the family) that consumes commodities and supplies inputs in production. The role of the consumer may be defined as that of choosing from among the alternative commodity bundles available to him. Similarly, a *producer* is an individual (or group) that utilizes inputs to produce commodities. The role of the producer may be characterized as that of choosing from among the alternative input-output patterns available to him. It is clear that the same individual might appear in the economy both as a consumer and as a producer, so that any distinction drawn between the set of consumers and the set of producers is not to be interpreted as the separation of individuals comprising the economy into nonoverlapping sets. Because of this, we must take pains that our theory of individual behavior is consistent with the dual role of the individual as both consumer and producer. In particular, it is sometimes thought that the notions of *utility maximization* by consumers and *profit maximization* by producers embody an inconsistency when applied to an individual who is both consumer and producer. This problem will be discussed in greater detail in Sec. 1-7. Suffice it to say here that, when properly interpreted, the theories of decision making postulated for consumers and for producers are logically consistent with one another.

Following most of the recent work in general equilibrium theory, it will be assumed that consumers hold title to existing resource stocks such as land, minerals, inventories, etc., as well as being the owners of the productive units of the economy, i.e., consumers are stockholders. A producer is then regarded as an employee of the firm (productive unit) whose job it is to determine the optimal method of producing whatever it is that he decides the firm should produce.

1-4 STATES OF THE ECONOMY

Once each consumer chooses from among the commodity bundles available to him, and each producer, acting for the firm, chooses from among the input-output patterns available to him, we could summarize the condition or state of the entire economy by cataloging the choices made. By a *state of the economy*, then, will be meant a listing of the commodity bundle chosen by each consumer and the input-output combination chosen by each producer. Since the state-of-economy concept will be basic to our study of general equilibrium theory, we proceed to formalize this notion.

We assume that the economy contains n goods and services (commodities), m consumers, and l producers. Let x_{ij} denote the quantity of the ith commodity consumed by the jth consumer, where the subscript i runs over the integers $1, 2, \ldots, n$ and the subscript j runs over the integers $1, 2, \ldots, m$. If we arrange the $n \times m$ x_{ij} terms in a rectangular array or matrix, it is clear that the commodity bundle chosen by the jth consumer will show up as the jth column of the matrix: the commodity bundle chosen by the jth consumer is $\mathbf{x}^j = (x_{1j}, x_{2j}, \ldots, x_{nj})$. A commodity bundle thus may be represented as an n-dimensional vector or, equivalently, as a point in n-dimensional space. We adopt the usual convention that a positive x_{ij} means that the jth consumer is consuming the ith commodity, while a negative x_{ij} means that the jth consumer is supplying the ith commodity as an input for production.

Similarly, let y_{ik} denote the quantity of the ith commodity produced by the kth producer, where again the i subscript runs over the integers $1, 2, \ldots, n$ and the k subscript runs over the integers $1, 2, \ldots, l$. If we arrange the $n \times l$ y_{ik} terms in a matrix, it is clear that the input-output pattern chosen by the kth producer for his firm will show up as the kth column of the matrix: the input-output pattern chosen by the kth producer is $\mathbf{y}^k = (y_{1k}, y_{2k}, \ldots, y_{nk})$. Thus an input-output pattern may be represented as an n-dimensional vector or a point in n-dimensional space. Again we adopt the usual convention that a positive y_{ik} means that the kth producer has the ith commodity as output of his firm, while a negative y_{ik} means that the kth producer has the ith commodity as input to his firm. Clearly, the assumption so often made in the usual discussions of the firm concerning the single output of each firm (no joint production) translates in this framework to the presence of not more than one positive component in the input-output pattern chosen by the producer. Permitting more than one would correspond to the possibility of joint production in that firm.

Letting $\mathbf{X}$ be the matrix of $n \times m$ elements describing the commodity bundles chosen by the m consumers, and letting $\mathbf{Y}$ be the matrix of $n \times l$ elements describing the input-output pattern chosen by the producers, we may represent a state of the economy as the matrix

$$\mathbf{Z} = [\mathbf{X};\mathbf{Y}] = \begin{bmatrix} x_{11} & x_{12} & \cdots & x_{1m} & y_{11} & y_{12} & \cdots & y_{1l} \\ x_{21} & x_{22} & \cdots & x_{2m} & y_{21} & y_{22} & \cdots & y_{2l} \\ \cdots & \cdots & \cdots & \cdots & \cdots & \cdots & \cdots & \cdots \\ x_{n1} & x_{n2} & \cdots & x_{nm} & y_{n1} & y_{n2} & \cdots & y_{nl} \end{bmatrix}$$

A state of the economy [**X**;**Y**] is thus an array with n rows and $m + l$ columns, where the first m columns describe the behavior of consumers and the remaining l columns describe the behavior of producers.

Returning to the **X** matrix itself, we note that the elements of the ith row describe the allocation of the ith good among the m consumers. Consequently, adding together the elements of the ith row yields the net claims made by all consumers on the ith commodity. Similarly, considering the **Y** matrix, we note that the elements of the ith row describe the pattern of output of the ith commodity among the firms. Consequently, adding together the elements of the ith row yields the net output of all firms of the ith commodity. At this point a condition of viability of any state of the economy is suggested, namely, that the sum of the first m elements of any row in the [**X**;**Y**] matrix be no greater than the sum of the remaining elements of that row. In down-to-earth terms this condition merely asserts that the net consumption of any commodity cannot exceed the net output of the commodity in a viable state of the economy.

1-5 THE CHOICE CRITERION OF THE CONSUMER

We have discussed the manner in which the choices made by the individual economic agents give rise to a state of the economy, without explicit consideration of how the choices are made. In order to understand the decision-making process of consumers and producers, economic theory starts out by postulating that individual economic agents behave in a purposive manner, in accordance with certain choice criteria. We first deal with the choice criterion of the consumer.

Each consumer is assumed to have "tastes" or "feelings" concerning alternative states of the economy. These tastes or feelings are expressed through the ability of the consumer to decide, as between any two states of the economy, which he likes better or whether he likes them equally well. We note that since the tastes of the consumer are expressed entirely with respect to states of the economy, and since states of the economy have to do with the allocation and production of commodities, monetary phenomena influence the behavior of the consumer only by way of their effect on the production or allocation of goods and services. In particular, there is no place in this theory for preference rankings based on money prices of commodities: we exclude the possibility of the consumer having "money illusion" in this framework.

We summarize the assumptions made about the ability of the consumer to rank states of the economy by introducing the notion of a *ranking*, R_j. R_j is a relation between states of the economy, and "state of the economy number one R_j state of the economy number two" is synonymous with "state of the economy number one is at least as preferred by the jth consumer as state of the economy number two." R_j is assumed to satisfy the following three conditions, where S denotes any set of states of the economy.[1]

1. Completeness property: If $\mathbf{Z}', \mathbf{Z}'' \in S$, then $\mathbf{Z}' \, R_j \, \mathbf{Z}''$ or $\mathbf{Z}'' \, R_j \, \mathbf{Z}'$.
2. Transitivity property: If $\mathbf{Z}', \mathbf{Z}'', \mathbf{Z}''' \in S$, and if $\mathbf{Z}' \, R_j \, \mathbf{Z}''$ and $\mathbf{Z}'' \, R_j \, \mathbf{Z}'''$, then $\mathbf{Z}' \, R_j \, \mathbf{Z}'''$.
3. Reflexivity property: If $\mathbf{Z}' \in S$, then $\mathbf{Z}' \, R_j \, \mathbf{Z}'$.

The completeness property states that between any two states of the economy the consumer is able to assert that the first is at least as preferred as the second, the second is at least as preferred as the first, or each is at least as preferred as the other, in which case the consumer is said to be indifferent between the states.

The transitivity property is a type of consistency condition on R_j, asserting that if the consumer ranks state of the economy one as being at least as preferred as state two, and state two as being at least as preferred as state three, then he should rank state one as at least as preferred as state three.

The reflexivity property says that any state of the economy is at least as preferred by the consumer as itself. In this respect the relation R_j is like the relation $\geq$ as applied to real numbers as opposed to the relation $>$. $\geq$ is often referred to as the "weak" ordering of the real numbers, while $>$ is often referred to as the "strong" ordering of the real numbers. By analogy, we refer to R_j as a *weak* ranking and to the relation "strictly preferred to" as a *strong* ranking.

As a further matter of notation we use P_j to denote strict preference on the part of the jth consumer, and I_j to denote indifference. Formally, these symbols are defined as follows:

Given $\mathbf{Z}', \mathbf{Z}'' \in S$, $\mathbf{Z}' \, P_j \, \mathbf{Z}''$ if $\mathbf{Z}' \, R_j \, \mathbf{Z}''$ and not $\mathbf{Z}'' \, R_j \, \mathbf{Z}'$. ($\mathbf{Z}'$ is preferred to $\mathbf{Z}''$ by the jth consumer if $\mathbf{Z}'$ is at least as preferred as $\mathbf{Z}''$ but $\mathbf{Z}''$ is not at least as preferred as $\mathbf{Z}'$.)

Given $\mathbf{Z}', \mathbf{Z}'' \in S$, $\mathbf{Z}' \, I_j \, \mathbf{Z}''$ if $\mathbf{Z}' \, R_j \, \mathbf{Z}''$ and $\mathbf{Z}'' \, R_j \, \mathbf{Z}'$. ($\mathbf{Z}'$ and $\mathbf{Z}''$ are said to be indifferent from the point of view of the jth consumer if each is at least as preferred as the other.)

In terms of the weak ranking R_j, we now state the choice criterion of the consumer postulated by our theory:

Given freedom of choice among any set S of states of the economy,

[1] By a set is meant any collection of elements. The notation $z \in S$ is to be read as "z is a member (element) of S" or "z belongs to S."

the consumer chooses a state, say $\mathbf{Z}^*$, where $\mathbf{Z}^* \in S$, such that $\mathbf{Z}^* \, \mathrm{R}_j \, \mathbf{Z}$ for all $\mathbf{Z} \in S$, if such a state $\mathbf{Z}^*$ exists.[1]

The postulated choice criterion thus asserts that the consumer's tastes among the states of the economy may be represented by a weak ranking defined on states of the economy and that he chooses among the alternatives in a manner consistent with his tastes by choosing a state as least as preferred as any available state, if such a state exists.

The relation I_j, by its very definition, suggests that the consumer may very well "feel the same" about two quite distinct states of the economy. Such is not the case in considering the relation as applied to real numbers. For in this case, clearly $X \geq Y$ and $Y \geq X$ imply $X = Y$. A relation that satisfies conditions 1, 2, and 3, and for which the relation going both ways for two elements implies equality of the elements, is called a complete (linear, simple, total) *ordering*. A complete ordering thus may be considered a ranking in which "indifference" reduces to equality.

A particular example of an ordering that may be defined on *n*-dimensional vectors is the so-called *lexicographic ordering*. Let $\mathbf{V}' = (V'_1, V'_2, \ldots, V'_n)$ and $\mathbf{V}'' = (V''_1, V''_2, \ldots, V''_n)$ be any two n-dimensional vectors. Using the symbol L to mean "is lexicographically less than," the lexicographic ordering on points in *n*-space is defined by $\mathbf{V}' \, \mathrm{L} \, \mathbf{V}''$ if and only if $V'_k < V''_k$ for the smallest integer k $(0 < k \leq n)$ for which $V'_k \neq V''_k$. L is clearly a complete strong ordering. The modifier "lexicographic" is used to describe this ordering so as to point up the similarity between this way of establishing a "chronology" or "hierarchy" among points and the way in which words are arranged in a lexicon or dictionary.

Suppose now that we define a relation "lexicographically at least as great as." Denote this relation by G. Then G may be defined by $\mathbf{V}' \, \mathrm{G} \, \mathbf{V}''$ if and only if not $\mathbf{V}' \, \mathrm{L} \, \mathbf{V}''$. It is easy to see that G is a complete weak ordering. The fact that G is an ordering rather than merely a ranking, as we have defined these terms, will be of some interest in our subsequent discussion.

[1] There are some difficulties associated with ensuring that a most preferred state $\mathbf{Z}^*$ (or a set of equally most preferred states) exists in an arbitrary set of states of the economy S. To illustrate, assume that a consumer prefers more money to less, that money is infinitely divisible, and that the consumer is permitted to choose any amount of money less than \$1. (In this case S is the set consisting of all real amounts of money less than \$1.) It is easy to verify that no most preferred choice exists in this case. Similarly, if the consumer is permitted to choose any real number as the amount of money he obtains under the same assumption that more is preferred to less, there does not exist a most preferred choice in the set of alternatives. In the first example, S is not closed, while in the second example, S is not bounded. Problems associated with these conditions will be discussed subsequently.

We have stated the choice criterion of the consumer simply in terms of the consumer choosing the most preferred state of the economy available to him, provided, of course, that such a state exists. Typically, in the literature the choice criterion of the consumer is not stated quite this way, but rather in terms of utility maximization. We proceed to show that, under appropriate circumstances, the two ways of stating the choice criterion of the consumer are equivalent.

By a utility function or utility indicator for a consumer is meant an assignment of real numbers to states of the economy in such a way that the ordering of the numbers by $\geq$ preserves the ranking of the corresponding states according to the consumer's preferences. Notationally, let u^j denote the utility indicator of the jth consumer. Then for any states $\mathbf{Z}', \mathbf{Z}'' \in S$, the following must hold:

$$u^j(\mathbf{Z}') \geq u^j(\mathbf{Z}'') \qquad \text{if and only if } \mathbf{Z}' \mathrm{R}_j \mathbf{Z}''$$

$$u^j(\mathbf{Z}') = u^j(\mathbf{Z}'') \qquad \text{if and only if } \mathbf{Z}' \mathrm{I}_j \mathbf{Z}''$$

$$u^j(\mathbf{Z}') > u^j(\mathbf{Z}'') \qquad \text{if and only if } \mathbf{Z}' \mathrm{P}_j \mathbf{Z}''$$

In terms of the utility function, then, the choice criterion of the consumer asserts that, given freedom of choice, the consumer chooses a state $\mathbf{Z}^* \in S$, if $\mathbf{Z}^*$ exists such that $u^j(\mathbf{Z}^*) \geq u^j(\mathbf{Z})$ for all $\mathbf{Z} \in S$. Given the existence of a utility function for the consumer, it is clear from its definition that utility maximization leads the consumer to a state of the economy such that this state is at least as preferred as any available state. Consequently, if it is possible for the consumer to assign real numbers to states of the economy in the "order-preserving" way defined above (if the consumer's utility indicator exists), then the two ways of stating the choice criterion of the consumer are indeed equivalent. There is some difficulty associated with the existence of a utility function for the consumer: the ranking of the consumer must be assumed to be sufficiently "well-behaved" to permit the existence of a utility function. The fact that the consumer has a ranking of the states of the economy *per se* is not sufficient to guarantee the existence of a utility function. In particular, if the consumer ranks states in terms of the lexicographic ordering in the manner that will be discussed subsequently, it is not possible to define a utility function for the consumer.

We use the phrase *ordinal utility* to refer to the real number associated with a state of the economy by a utility indicator as defined above. *Ordinal* refers to the fact that only the ranking of states of the economy by the consumer is involved in determining the values assigned to particular states. To illustrate, assume S consists of three states, $\mathbf{Z}'$, $\mathbf{Z}''$, and $\mathbf{Z}'''$, where $\mathbf{Z}' \mathrm{P}_j \mathbf{Z}'' \mathrm{P}_j \mathbf{Z}'''$. Then a set of real numbers satisfying our definition of utility numbers would be 1,000 assigned to $\mathbf{Z}'$, 0 assigned to $\mathbf{Z}''$, and

-1 to $\mathbf{Z}'''$. The point, of course, is that any numbers would have done so long as the number assigned to $\mathbf{Z}'$ was greater than the number assigned to $\mathbf{Z}''$, which in turn was greater than the number assigned to $\mathbf{Z}'''$. Technically, this characteristic of ordinal utility indicators is summarized in the statement that a utility indicator is ordinal if any increasing transformation of a utility indicator is also a utility indicator. (By an increasing transformation is meant any change in the set of utility numbers assigned to states of the economy such that if the numbers are arranged in ascending or descending order, each number has the same position before and after the change.)

A more restricted concept of utility is sometimes employed in the theory of consumer behavior—that of a *cardinal* utility function or indicator. When the consumer's ranking over states of the economy, as well as the intensity with which he prefers one state to others, is taken into account in describing the tastes or preferences of the consumer, then an arbitrary assignment of real numbers to states of the economy in an order-preserving manner will not completely reflect the consumer's tastes. For example, assume the consumer feels very strongly that state $\mathbf{Z}'$ is preferred to state $\mathbf{Z}''$, but that he "barely" prefers state $\mathbf{Z}''$ to state $\mathbf{Z}'''$. To reflect accurately the preferences of the consumer, the difference between the real number ("utility") assigned to $\mathbf{Z}'$ and that assigned to $\mathbf{Z}''$ should be greater than the difference between the utilities of $\mathbf{Z}''$ and $\mathbf{Z}'''$. When utility numbers are assigned in this manner, the utility indicator is said to possess cardinal properties; the numbers assigned to states of the economy reflect not only the ranking of the alternatives, but also the intensities with which a consumer prefers one alternative to others. It seems but a minor and completely defensible step to include in our assumptions concerning consumers that they not only can rank states of the economy according to their preferences, but also can judge as to the intensity of their preferences among such states. Despite this, the modern theory of consumer behavior is based solely on ordinal, not cardinal, utility. Why is this the case? The answer is that in order to explain or describe the behavior of consumers as reflected, for example, in the characteristics of consumer demand and supply functions, the assumption of cardinal utility adds nothing to our knowledge that ordinal utility does not already provide. By the principle of Occam's razor, since the cardinality assumption is not needed, we use the simpler, less restrictive assumption of ordinal utility. It should be pointed out, however, that in the theory of welfare economics, the cardinal and ordinal utility postulates lead to quite different results, to be discussed in detail in Chap. 4.

From a purely formal point of view, the difference between ordinal and cardinal utility is expressed in the statement that any increasing transformation of an ordinal utility indicator is an ordinal utility indicator, but only transformations of cardinal utility indicators that preserve the order of *differences* in utility are cardinal utility indicators. An illustration is provided by linear-increasing transformations. For example, assume we assign utilities to states $\mathbf{Z}'$, $\mathbf{Z}''$, and $\mathbf{Z}'''$ by a utility indicator u^j such that $u^j(\mathbf{Z}') - u^j(\mathbf{Z}'') > u^j(\mathbf{Z}'') - u^j(\mathbf{Z}''')$, where $u^j(\mathbf{Z}') > u^j(\mathbf{Z}'') > u^j(\mathbf{Z}''')$. Let v^j be a transformation of u^j such that $v^j(\mathbf{Z}) = a + bu^j(\mathbf{Z})$ for all $\mathbf{Z}$, where a is an arbitrary real number and b is a real number satisfying $b > 0$. Such a transformation preserves the order of differences in intensities of preference, as a substitution in $v^j(\mathbf{Z}') - v^j(\mathbf{Z}'')$ and $v^j(\mathbf{Z}'') - v^j(\mathbf{Z}''')$ will verify.[1]

A separate but related problem arises in connection with interpersonal comparisons of utility. Assume two persons, Mr. *A* and Mr. *B*, order the three states $\mathbf{Z}'$, $\mathbf{Z}''$, and $\mathbf{Z}'''$, and that utility numbers are assigned to the three states for Mr. *A* and Mr. *B* separately in such a way that the intensities of preferences among states are represented by differences in utilities. Thus we can say, for example, that Mr. *A* prefers state $\mathbf{Z}'$ to $\mathbf{Z}''$ more intensely than he prefers $\mathbf{Z}''$ to $\mathbf{Z}'''$. If utilities are to be comparable on an interpersonal basis, it must be possible, by examining the utility numbers assigned to states, to determine whether Mr. *A*'s intensity of preference of $\mathbf{Z}'$ over $\mathbf{Z}''$ is greater than (less than) Mr. *B*'s intensity of preference of $\mathbf{Z}''$ over $\mathbf{Z}'$. In short, there must be some common unit of measurement of intensity of preference that can be applied both to Mr. *A* and to Mr. *B* in characterizing their tastes. It should be made clear that the question of whether such a measuring rod of intensity of preferences can be devised is strictly an empirical matter—it is not a question of value judgment. While it seems highly unlikely at the present time that such a

[1] A distinction should be drawn between cardinal utility, as discussed above, and measurable utility of the von Neumann–Morgenstern variety. Cardinal utility in our sense refers to utility numbers associated with states of the economy under the implicit assumption that, given a choice from any set *S*, the consumer knows with certainty what the outcome of his choice will be, i.e., there is no uncertainty associated with the choice mechanism. Measurable utility, on the other hand, refers to utility numbers assigned to uncertain alternatives in situations in which the consumer must choose from among "lottery tickets" or probability distributions over alternatives. The lack of any formal connection between cardinal utility and measurable utility is evidenced by the fact that the only axiom of measurable utility theory concerned with preferences defined on outcomes with certainty simply states that such preferences must be representable by a ranking; the other axioms are concerned entirely with the preferences of the consumer with respect to probability distributions over alternatives. For discussions of measurable utility see J. von Neumann and O. Morgenstern, *Theory of Games and Economic Behavior*, Princeton University Press, Princeton, N.J., 1944; J. Marschak, Rational Behavior, Uncertain Prospects, and Measurable Utility, *Econometrica*, vol. 18, pp. 111–140, 1950; I. N. Herstein and John Milnor, An Axiomatic Approach to Measurable Utility, *Econometrica*, vol. 21, pp. 291–297, 1953.

measuring device could be constructed, there is no *a priori* reason for excluding the possibility of such a psychometric invention at some time in the future. Certainly the literature of the neoclassical school of economics contains many assertions based on the assumption that interpersonal comparisons (at least among individuals of the same general social class) are not unreasonable. It is of course a further step, and one that is purely and simply a matter of value judgment, to argue that if interpersonal comparisons of utility were possible, then that state should be judged best that ranks highest in terms of "net intensity of preference" relative to all others. Therefore, if, as in our example, Mr. *A* prefers $\mathbf{Z}'$ to $\mathbf{Z}''$ more intensely than Mr. *B* prefers $\mathbf{Z}''$ to $\mathbf{Z}'$, then $\mathbf{Z}'$ is judged a "better" state than $\mathbf{Z}''$. The trouble with such conclusions is that there is really no way of justifying the assignment of equal weights to Mr. *A* and Mr. *B* in determining "social preference"—without introducing value judgments.

We shall return to the issue of cardinal versus ordinal utility and interpersonal comparisons of utility in Chap. 4. For the remainder of this and the following chapter, we shall accept only the more general assumption that tastes of any consumer can be represented by a ranking, or alternatively, by an ordinal utility function. Even the relatively weak axioms underlying the existence of an ordinal utility function for each consumer, however, are not necessarily "realistic." For example, in experiments involving choices by individuals among complex alternatives, the crucial axiom of transitivity is often violated by the subjects involved in the experiments. It is true, however, that when this is brought to the attention of the subjects, there is the reaction of "having made a mistake," such as incorrectly answering a problem in mathematics.[1] It might then be safer and more realistic to regard the transitivity axiom as a normative rule of consumer behavior rather than as a description of the actual choice patterns of consumers. [In descriptive studies, the concept of *stochastic preference* is sometimes used to preserve at least the minimum shreds of transitivity. In terms of this framework, an individual is said to prefer $\mathbf{Z}'$ over $\mathbf{Z}''$ if the probability of choosing $\mathbf{Z}'$ over $\mathbf{Z}''$ is greater than $\frac{1}{2}$; transitivity of stochastic preference asserts that if $\mathbf{Z}'$ is stochastically preferred to $\mathbf{Z}''$ (chosen over $\mathbf{Z}''$ more than half the time) and $\mathbf{Z}''$ is stochastically preferred to $\mathbf{Z}'''$, then $\mathbf{Z}'$ is stochastically preferred to $\mathbf{Z}'''$. This axiom is also occasionally violated in experimental studies.[2]]

[1] A discussion of experiments involving choices among alternatives under certainty is contained in A. G. Papandreou, O. H. Sauerlander, O. H. Brownlee, Leonid Hurwicz, and William Franklin, *A Test of a Proposition in the Theory of Choice*, University of Minnesota, Minneapolis, 1954 (unpublished).

[2] For a discussion of the theory of stochastic preferences see R. Duncan Luce and Howard Raiffa, *Games and Decisions*, pp. 371–384, John Wiley & Sons, Inc., New York, 1957. Note references on p. 374.

An even more fundamental objection to the axiom of transitivity by consumers arises when choices are made by groups (husband and wife, entire family, etc.), rather than by individuals. Arrow's famous *paradox of majority voting* points out that when the rule for making choices by a group is that of choosing the alternative with more votes over that with fewer votes (the "majority voting" rule), then even if each individual in the group has a ranking over alternatives, the group might fail to have a ranking because the transitivity condition might fail to hold. The following example illustrates this problem: Let Mr. A, Mr. B, and Mr. C be members of a group that uses the majority voting principle for making decisions, and let $\mathbf{Z}'$, $\mathbf{Z}''$, and $\mathbf{Z}'''$ be three alternatives ranked by the members of the group as follows:

Mr. A: $\mathbf{Z}'$ preferred to $\mathbf{Z}''$ preferred to $\mathbf{Z}'''$
Mr. B: $\mathbf{Z}''$ preferred to $\mathbf{Z}'''$ preferred to $\mathbf{Z}'$
Mr. C: $\mathbf{Z}'''$ preferred to $\mathbf{Z}'$ preferred to $\mathbf{Z}''$

Thus, in paired comparisons using the majority voting rule, the group prefers $\mathbf{Z}'$ to $\mathbf{Z}''$ (2 votes to 1), and $\mathbf{Z}''$ to $\mathbf{Z}'''$ (2 votes to 1), but prefers $\mathbf{Z}'''$ to $\mathbf{Z}'$ (2 votes to 1). While each individual's preference ranking satisfies the transitivity axiom, the group ranking based on majority voting violates this axiom.[1]

It will be noted that throughout our discussion we have assumed the existence of rankings by consumers defined over states of the economy, rather than over own commodity bundles as in the usual treatments of consumer behavior. This approach reflects, in its most general form, the current concept of rationality as applied to consumers; however, the specification of assuming rankings defined with respect to own commodity bundles turns out to be virtually impossible to avoid if any interesting theorems concerning the operation of the economy are to be formulated. This extremely important restriction on the preferences of consumers is referred to as the condition of *selfishness of preferences*. We formalize this condition as follows:

Let $\mathbf{Z}'$, $\mathbf{Z}''$, $\mathbf{Z}'''$, and $\mathbf{Z}$ be any four states of the economy with the characteristics that $\mathbf{x}'^j = \mathbf{x}''^j$ and $\mathbf{x}'''^j = \mathbf{x}^j$. ($\mathbf{Z}'$ and $\mathbf{Z}''$ are states of the economy in which the jth consumer has the same commodity bundle, and similarly for states $\mathbf{Z}'''$ and $\mathbf{Z}$.) Then the jth consumer is said to be *selfish* (or to possess a selfish ranking) if for all such states $\mathbf{Z}'$, $\mathbf{Z}''$, $\mathbf{Z}'''$, and $\mathbf{Z}$, if $\mathbf{Z}' \mathrm{R}_j \mathbf{Z}'''$, then $\mathbf{Z}'' \mathrm{R}_j \mathbf{Z}$ (if $\mathbf{Z}''' \mathrm{R}_j \mathbf{Z}'$, then $\mathbf{Z} \mathrm{R}_j \mathbf{Z}''$). (When a consumer is selfish, his preferences depend only upon the commodity

[1] See Kenneth J. Arrow, *Social Choice and Individual Values*, Cowles Foundation Monograph 12, John Wiley & Sons, Inc., New York, 1951.

bundles that he receives, not upon the pattern of production or the commodity bundles assigned to other consumers in the economy.)

The assumption that each consumer's preferences satisfy the selfishness condition excludes, in particular, the practice of judging quality by price, since a consumer following such a practice will be influenced by the commodity bundles held by other consumers and the pattern of production, through the effect of aggregate demand and aggregate supply on price. Similarly, Veblen's "conspicuous consumption" is excluded from our analytical framework when the selfishness condition is assumed to hold.

Given the selfishness assumption, the consumer ranks states of the economy entirely on the basis of a comparison of the n-dimensional vectors representing his commodity bundles in the various states. One ranking that the consumer might have is the lexicographic ordering discussed above: R_j, the jth consumer's ranking, could be the ordering G defined above. The meaning of this would be that the consumer feels so strongly about commodity 1 that he chooses between any two commodity bundles solely on the basis of which contains more of commodity 1, regardless of what else is in the bundles. If the two bundles have the same amount of commodity 1, then he chooses on the basis of which has more of commodity 2. If again there is equality, he proceeds to check the amounts of the third commodity, and so on. If this process terminates by the time the consumer has checked the nth commodity, then that bundle having the greater amount of the commodity at the termination point (and hence the state associated with it) is preferred to the other bundle (and the state associated with it). If the process does not terminate by the time the consumer reaches the nth commodity, then the two bundles are the same.

The lexicographic ordering was singled out because if the consumer ranks states of the economy by lexicographically ordering his commodity bundles and if commodities are infinitely divisible, then a utility indicator for the consumer does not exist.[1] If one tends to be skeptical about the difficulties introduced if the consumer ranks states by lexicographically ordering his own commodity bundles in the states, one can begin to overcome this skepticism by attempting to assign real numbers to different commodity bundles for the jth consumer in accordance with the definition of a utility indicator, where the ranking of the jth consumer is the lexicographic ordering and there are only two commodities in the economy.

At this point we might use the lexicographic ordering to find a clue as to what might be added to the already assumed conditions of completeness, transitivity, and reflexivity so as to guarantee the existence of a

[1] For a proof of this see Gerard Debreu, *Theory of Value*, p. 72, n. 2, Cowles Foundation Monograph 17, John Wiley & Sons, Inc., New York, 1959.

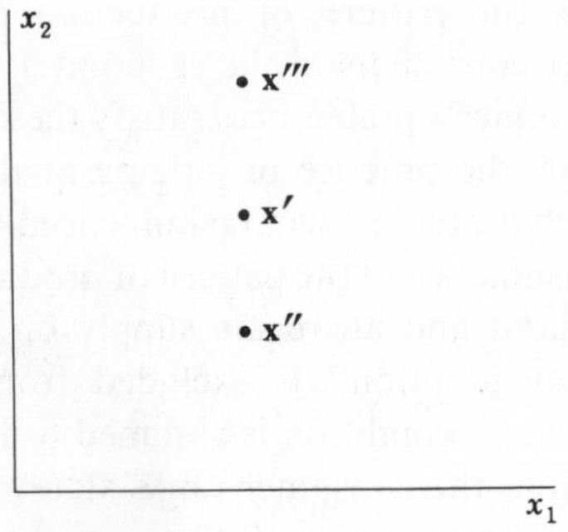

FIGURE 1-5

utility indicator. That is, cognizance of what is "wrong" with the lexicographic ordering might lead us to a set of conditions on the individual's ranking that are sufficient for the existence of a utility indicator.

In Fig. 1-5 the points are chosen such that $x_1' = x_1'' = x_1'''$ and $x_2''' > x_2' > x_2''$. Therefore, $\mathbf{x}'' \text{ L } \mathbf{x}'$ and $\mathbf{x}' \text{ L } \mathbf{x}'''$. If we consider two additional points $\bar{\mathbf{x}} = (x_1'' + \epsilon, x_2'')$ and $\mathbf{x}^* = (x_1''' - \delta, x_2''')$, where ϵ and δ are arbitrarily small positive numbers, we have $\mathbf{x}' \text{ L } \bar{\mathbf{x}}$ and $\mathbf{x}^* \text{ L } \mathbf{x}'$. Thus we have $\mathbf{x}'' \text{ L } \mathbf{x}'$ and $\mathbf{x}' \text{ L } \bar{\mathbf{x}}$, where $\bar{\mathbf{x}}$ and $\mathbf{x}''$ are arbitrarily close to each other. Similarly $\mathbf{x}' \text{ L } \mathbf{x}'''$ and $\mathbf{x}^* \text{ L } \mathbf{x}'$, where $\mathbf{x}^*$ and $\mathbf{x}'''$ are arbitrarily close to each other. It is precisely this "discontinuous" behavior of the lexicographic ordering that causes difficulty in attempting to define a utility indicator. A way of circumventing the difficulty introduced by "discontinuities" in the preferences of the consumer is to assume explicitly that preferences must be "continuous." Roughly speaking, "continuity" of preferences means that any commodity bundle very close to a commodity bundle that is preferred to some given bundle must be at least as preferred as the given bundle.[1]

To summarize, if the consumer has a complete, transitive, and reflexive ranking and preferences are "continuous," then we may impute a utility indicator to him.

[1] As we shall see later, "continuity" of preferences may be formalized by asserting that the sets $\{\mathbf{x}' \mid \mathbf{x}' \text{ R } \mathbf{x}\}$ and $\{\mathbf{x}' \mid \mathbf{x} \text{ R } \mathbf{x}'\}$ are closed sets for every commodity bundle $\mathbf{x}$. For a proof of the existence of a utility function given this condition along with completeness, transitivity, and reflexivity, see Debreu, *op. cit.*, pp. 56–59. For other proofs, which relax the transitivity assumption, deriving it in part from the structure of the commodity space, see Trout Rader, Existence of a Utility Function to Represent Preferences, *Review of Economic Studies*, vol. 30, pp. 229–233, 1963, and Hugo Sonnenschein, The Relationship between Transitive Preference and the Structure of the Choice Space, *Econometrica*, vol. 33, pp. 624–635, 1965. Moreover, these authors have established continuity of utility functions under conditions that guarantee existence.

1-6 CONSUMPTION SETS AND CONVEXITY OF PREFERENCES

We shall assume throughout the remainder of our discussion, unless it is specifically stated to the contrary, that consumers are selfish and that their preferences are expressed in terms of "well-behaved" rankings, in particular excluding the lexicographic ordering. Then each consumer's ranking may be expressed in terms of n-dimensional vectors representing his own commodity bundles, and there exists an associated utility indicator. It is convenient to think of commodity bundles as points in euclidean n-dimensional space. Certain such points involve economic absurdities; for example, any point such that more than 24 hr of labor is supplied per day by an individual consumer would represent a physical impossibility. Consequently, we shall restrict our attention to proper subsets of euclidean n-space for each consumer. With each consumer there will be associated a set of commodity bundles called the *consumption set* of that consumer, designated by $\bar{X}_j$ for the jth consumer, $\bar{X}_j$ being a proper subset of euclidean n-dimensional space. The ranking of the jth consumer, R_j, is then defined with respect to elements of $\bar{X}_j$. Or, equivalently, with each point (commodity bundle) $\mathbf{x}^j \in \bar{X}_j$ is associated the real number $u^j(\mathbf{x}^j)$, the ordinal utility of that point. [More completely, we can write $u^j(\mathbf{x}^j)$ as $u^j(x_{1j}, x_{2j}, \ldots, x_{nj})$, it being recalled that x_{ij} is the amount of the ith good or service consumed (supplied) by the jth consumer.]

In the neoclassical theory of consumer behavior, as has been mentioned, cardinal utility functions were assumed for each consumer. Under such an assumption, the marginal utility associated with any commodity for a consumer is a meaningful concept, the marginal utility of commodity i to consumer j being the increase in utility associated with an increase of one unit in the amount of commodity i consumed by consumer j, the amounts of all other goods and services consumed (or supplied) being held constant. A basic assumption of neoclassical economics, introduced independently by Walras, Menger, and Marshall, is the law of diminishing marginal utility of consumption. This states that the marginal utility of any commodity decreases with additional units of the commodity consumed, at least after consumption has reached some sufficiently large amount. It is, of course, the exact counterpart for consumer theory of the law of diminishing returns in production. Various justifications of a physical or psychological nature were offered in the neoclassical literature for the law of diminishing marginal utility; for example, given a commodity with multiple uses, it is clear that the "rational" consumer would allocate the first units of such a commodity to those uses fulfilling the most pressing needs, and succeeding units to successively less pressing needs, so that marginal utility of the commodity would fall as consumption increased. More generally, it was assumed that for any specific commodity there exists a *saturation point*, i.e., a level of consumption such that any further consumption would lead to a fall in utility, as expressed in the statement that any specific want can be completely satisfied, again ensuring diminishing marginal utility of consumption. (It should be mentioned that this position taken by the neoclassical economists was coupled with the belief that the existence of bliss points was highly unlikely, where a *bliss point* is defined as a commodity bundle such that an increase in any component representing consumption of goods and services would lead to a fall in utility.)

Whatever the validity of the physical or psychological justifications offered for the law of diminishing marginal utility, the logical role it plays in the neoclassical theory of consumer behavior is that of acting as a device to exclude (or at least render less likely) "corner" solutions to the problem of allocating a fixed budget among commodities, e.g., solutions in which the consumer ends up purchasing only one commodity. On precisely the same grounds, the modern theory of consumer behavior has introduced assumptions relating to the convexity of consumer preference orderings as illustrated, for example, by what Hicks terms the *law of diminishing marginal rate of substitution between commodities.* For the two-commodity case, this law states that as the amount consumed of either commodity increases, the consumer remaining at the same utility level, the amount of the other commodity consumed decreases at a decreasing rate.[1]

In arguing the need for assuming diminishing rates of substitution between commodities, Hicks does not appeal to human nature or empirical evidence.[2] Rather, having implicitly ruled out the possibility of "corner" solutions to the consumer's choice problem, he points out that, in the absence of diminishing rates of substitution, those points that satisfy the usual first-order (tangency) conditions would correspond to utility-minimizing rather than utility-maximizing commodity bundles and would not be "stable" positions in this sense. Further, since any commodity bundle could conceivably be a solution to the choice problem of the consumer, diminishing rates of substitution must hold throughout the consumer's consumption set.

We may illustrate certain of the concepts of this section by considering the case in which there are two commodities, labor and wheat.

[1] It is easy to verify that no necessary logical relation exists between the law of diminishing marginal utility and the law of diminishing marginal rate of substitution. If, however, as was often assumed in the neoclassical literature, the marginal utility of any commodity is independent of the amounts of other commodities consumed, the law of diminishing marginal utility implies the law of diminishing marginal rate of substitution, but not conversely.

[2] J. R. Hicks, *Value and Capital*, 2d ed., pp. 20–25, Oxford University Press, London, 1946

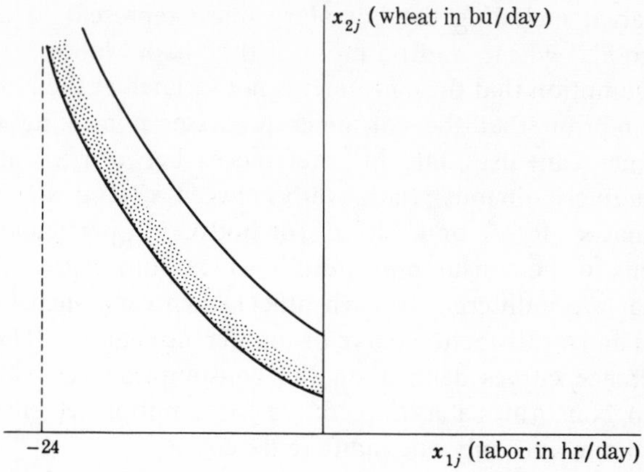

FIGURE 1-6

The consumption set of the jth consumer, $\bar{X}_j$, is taken to be the set of points shown in Fig. 1-6, where x_{2j} is wheat consumption by the jth consumer per day and x_{1j} represents labor services supplied by the jth consumer per day.

The justification for graphing $\bar{X}_j$ as in Fig. 1-6 is based on the following assumptions: the amount of labor supplied as an input for production is nonpositive (labor services are not consumed by the jth consumer); no more than 24 hr of labor may be supplied per day; and a minimum amount of wheat must be consumed per day for survival, this amount increasing as the amount of labor supplied per day increases.

If we regard wheat consumption as "good," and labor supplied as "bad," then intuitively we might expect all points in the shaded area of Fig. 1-7 to be "at least as preferred as" the point $\mathbf{x}'^j$, since all the points

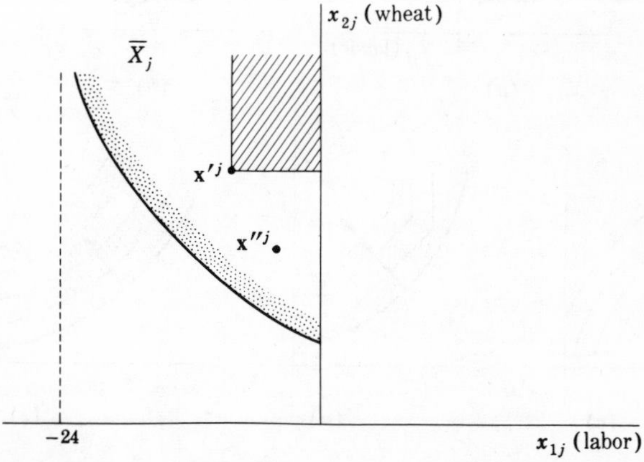

FIGURE 1-7

in the shaded area, including the boundary lines, represent at least as much of the "good," wheat, and no more of the "bad," labor. (This is based on the assumption that the consumer is not satiated at the point $\mathbf{x}'^j$.)

The assumption that the consumer possesses a ranking implies that the consumer can also state his preferences between $\mathbf{x}'^j$ and $\mathbf{x}''^j$. There is no intuitively obvious relationship between $\mathbf{x}'^j$ and $\mathbf{x}''^j$, but the assumption is that $\mathbf{x}'^j \, R_j \, \mathbf{x}''^j$ or $\mathbf{x}''^j \, R_j \, \mathbf{x}'^j$ (or both). In particular, if we connect all points in the consumption set for which both of the relations hold (points that are indifferent to each other), then each such locus of points is termed an isosatisfaction curve or indifference curve. The set of all such indifference curves defined on the consumption set, called an indifference map, constitutes a *partition* of the consumption set, since each point must lie in one and only one indifference curve.

Figure 1-8*a* is the usual depiction of some elements of the indifference map of an individual with respect to the two commodities wheat and labor. (The arrow denotes the direction of increasing preference.)

Other possible ways of depicting the individual's indifference map for two commodities are shown in Fig. 1-8*b* to *e*. In Fig. 1-8*b* we note that the point $\bar{\mathbf{x}}^j = (\bar{x}_{1j}, \bar{x}_{2j})$ is a point of complete satiety (point of bliss) for the consumer, because any change in the amounts consumed (supplied) of either wheat or labor drives the consumer to a lower level of satisfaction. In Fig. 1-8*c* the curvature of the set of points comprising the indifference

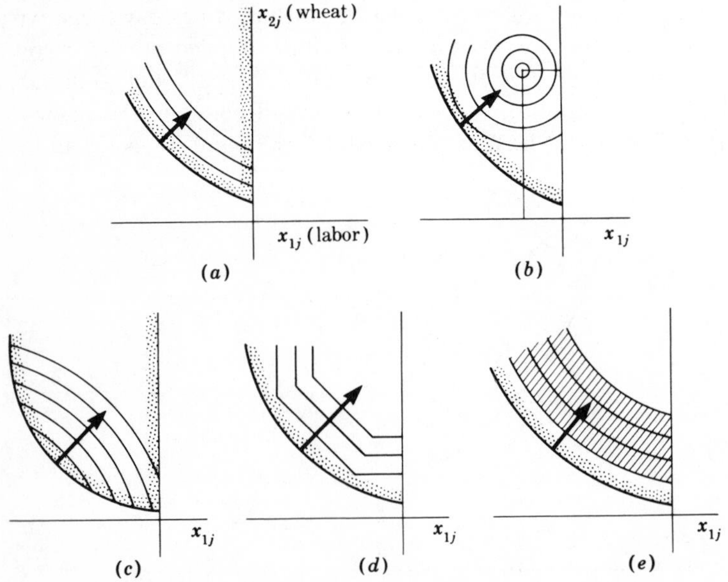

FIGURE 1-8

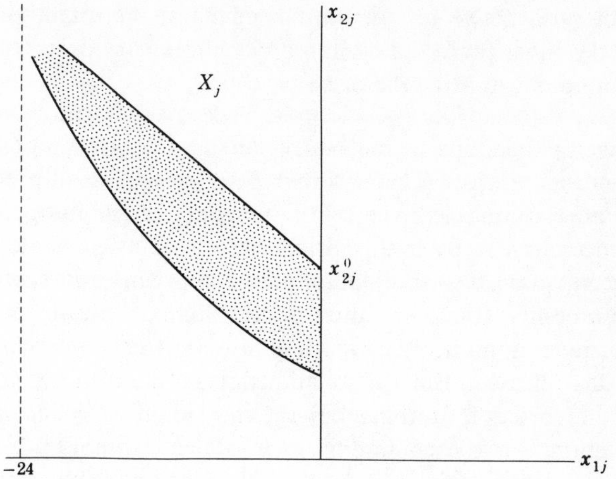

FIGURE 1-9

curves is "reversed" from Fig. 1-8*a*. In Fig. 1-8*d* the indifference sets contain straight line segments. In Fig. 1-8*e* the indifference sets are "thick," in that the entire shaded area shown between two indifference curves belongs to the same indifference set as the lower curve itself.

If we assume that prices for labor services and wheat are given by p_1 and p_2, respectively, then $p_1x_{1j} + p_2x_{2j}$ represents the amount, net of income earned by supplying labor services, that the *j*th consumer spends on wheat. If he has initial holdings of wheat x^0_{2j}, and he treats prices as fixed, the *j*th consumer is constrained in his choices by the inequality $p_1x_{1j} + p_2x_{2j} \leq p_2x^0_{2j}$. This constraint defines a certain region of the consumption set as attainable. The attainable set—the set of points in $\bar{X}_j$ satisfying $p_1x_{1j} + p_2(x_{2j} - x^0_{2j}) \leq 0$—is the shaded area in Fig. 1-9. The straight line boundary of the attainable set is called the *budget line*.

Superimposing Fig. 1-9 on Fig. 1-8, we are in a position to analyze the implications of satisfaction-maximizing behavior of the consumer. Superimposing Fig. 1-9 on Fig. 1-8*a*, we get the usual two-dimensional depiction of consumer equilibrium, shown in Fig. 1-10.

If the indifference sets are as depicted in Figs. 1-8*a* and 1-10, we note that at the tangency point of the budget line and indifference curves, the following conditions hold:

1. The consumer is consuming the most preferred commodity bundle that he can afford.

1′. There is only one such commodity bundle.

2. If the consumer had a lower income (budget line shifted to the left) he would be forced to settle for a less preferred commodity bundle.

3. As the price ratio between commodities changes, the quantities comprising the most preferred commodity bundle vary in a "smooth" or continuous way with the price ratio.

A change in the slope of the budget line in Fig. 1-10 represents a change in the price ratio. There would be a new "most preferred" commodity bundle attainable given by the tangency of the budget line to some indifference curve. By letting prices vary we may generate a relationship between quantities of commodities comprising most preferred attainable commodity bundles and prices. Since "most preferred attainable" is quite a mouthful, we shall use the term *optimum* as a synonym for this phrase. But this relationship between the quantity of a commodity and prices is nothing but the individual's *demand function* (or *supply* function) for the commodity. It is clear from Fig. 1-10 that a change in the budget line from B_1 to B_2 is brought about by an increase in the ratio of p_1 to p_2, that is, by a fall in the price of wheat relative to the price of labor services. Figure 1-10 shows that such a change in prices is accompanied by an increase in the amount of wheat in the consumer's optimum commodity bundle. In this case, since there is only one "good," the consumer will never become a supplier of wheat, but if we momentarily enlarge the system to include another "good," corn, it seems clear that, for certain prices, the consumer might very well get rid of some of his initial holdings of wheat to acquire more corn. This would make him a supplier of wheat. By the very construction of Fig. 1-10, the consumer is consuming negative amounts of labor services, making him a supplier of labor services. In fact the way the indifference map has been set up in Fig. 1-10

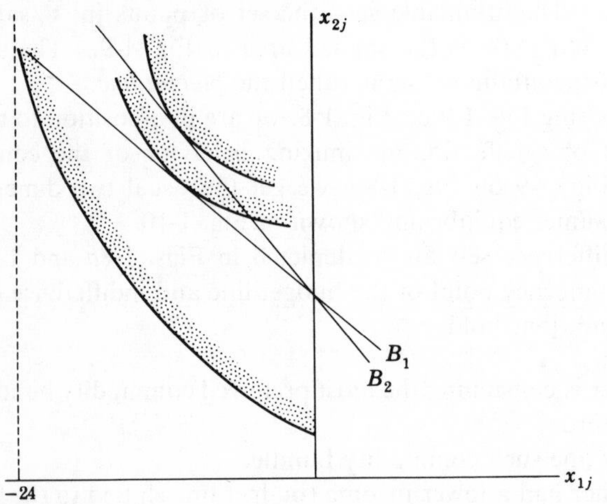

FIGURE 1-10

we see that the consumer is going to have a supply curve for labor services that is "backward-bending." It follows from Fig. 1-10 (or Fig. 1-9) that if all prices are multiplied by any positive constant, then the optimum commodity bundle is unaltered.[1] This illustrates the familiar "homogeneity of degree zero in prices" property of demand (or supply) functions.

The status of conditions 1, 1′, 2, and 3 under the alternative types of indifference sets as pictured in Fig. 1-8 should be noted. If Fig. 1-8*b* is an accurate depiction of the consumer's indifference map, then for any budget line lying above the point $\bar{\mathbf{x}}$, (2) will not be satisfied. If Fig. 1-8*b* depicts the indifference map of the consumer, then by drawing in various budget lines it is easy to verify that the consumer will always have a "corner" rather than tangency optimum, i.e., the consumer's optimum commodity bundle will lie on the boundary of $\bar{X}_j$.† Furthermore it is clear that a slight change in price may alter the consumer's optimum commodity bundle from one corner extreme to another in such a way that the "smoothness" property (condition 3) is violated. If thick indifference curves as depicted in Fig. 1-8*e* are permitted, we again find condition 2 violated. Finally, if straight line segments as in Fig. 1-8*d* are permitted, the budget line can be "tangent" to an indifference set at many points. Consequently we would generally have multiple optima, rather than a unique optimum, i.e., condition 1′ is violated. Indifference sets as in Fig. 1-8*d* lead to demand (or supply) correspondences (set-valued functions) rather than single-valued functions.

It might be useful to summarize the properties of the indifference map as it appears in Fig. 1-8*a*.

1. There is no bliss point shown. ($\bar{\mathbf{x}}^j$ in Fig. 1-8*b* is a bliss point.)
2. Each indifference set consists entirely of a boundary, i.e., is not thick. (The indifference sets depicted in Fig. 1-8*e* are thick.)
3. For any commodity bundle $\mathbf{x}'^j$, the set of all commodity bundles at least as preferred as that commodity bundle is a convex set. (This property does not hold for the indifference map pictured in Fig. 1-8*c*.)

Property 3 introduces the notion of a convex set. The notion of convex sets is a simple one and is very important in the modern treatment of economic theory, as well as in programming and game theory.

[1] For any positive constant k, the relationship $p_1x_{1j} + p_2x_{2j} \leq p_2x_{2j}^0$ obviously defines precisely the same set of points as $kp_1x_{1j} + kp_2x_{2j} \leq kp_2x_{2j}^0$.

† It is easy to see in Fig. 1-8*b* that the usual condition of tangency between the indifference sets and the budget line gives the consumer's least preferred commodity bundle, given the assumption that all of his income is spent.

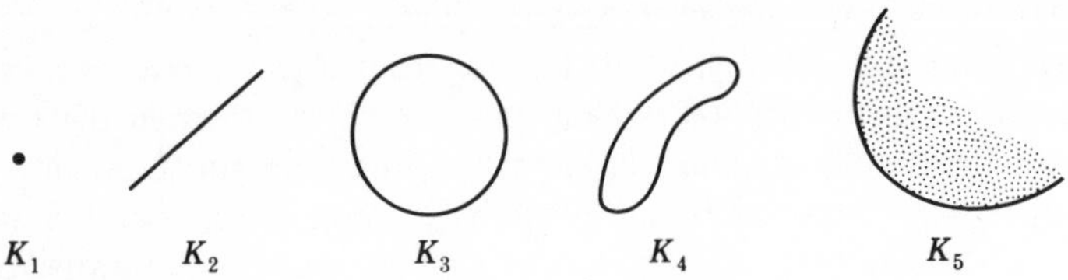

FIGURE 1-11

A *convex set* is simply a set of points such that, given any two points in the set, all points on the line segment connecting the two points are also in the set. In two dimensions, the sets K_1, K_2, K_3, and K_5 are convex sets, while K_4 is not. Formally, a set K is said to be a convex set if for any real number t such that $0 \leq t \leq 1$, $\mathbf{x}'$, $\mathbf{x}'' \in K$ implies $t\mathbf{x}' + (1 - t)\mathbf{x}'' \in K$. [Remembering the rules for scalar multiplication and addition of vectors given in Sec. 1-2, it is easy to verify that in two dimensions any point of the form $t\mathbf{x}' + (1 - t)\mathbf{x}''$ for $0 \leq t \leq 1$ is on the straight line segment joining the points $\mathbf{x}'$ and $\mathbf{x}''$.]

It will be noted that each of the sets bounded by indifference curves from below in Fig. 1-8 is convex, except for those shown in Fig. 1-8*c*. In terms of our notation for preference rankings, this means that, with the exception of Fig. 1-8*c*, given any point $\mathbf{x}^j \in \bar{X}_j$, the set of $\mathbf{x}'^j$ such that $\mathbf{x}'^j \in \bar{X}_j$ and $\mathbf{x}'^j \mathrm{R}_j \mathbf{x}^j$ is a convex set. Such a set is referred to as the *preference set* of the *j*th consumer relative to the bundle $\mathbf{x}^j$ and contains all commodity bundles at least as preferred as the bundle $\mathbf{x}^j$.†

A further exploitation of the notion of convexity will enable us to distinguish the situations shown in Fig. 1-8*a*, *c*, and *e* from each other in a rigorous manner. To this end we introduce the notion of convexity of preferences.[1] Three variations of the notion of convexity as applied to the preference ordering of the consumer will be stated. (In all of the following, it is assumed that $\mathbf{x}'^j$, $\mathbf{x}''^j \in \bar{X}_j$.)

We define *convexity of preferences* by the condition that if $\mathbf{x}'^j \mathrm{P}_j \mathbf{x}''^j$, then for all $0 < t < 1$, $(t\mathbf{x}'^j + (1 - t)\mathbf{x}''^j) \mathrm{P}_j \mathbf{x}''^j$. The indifference map depicted in Fig. 1-8*e* does not satisfy this condition.

We define *strong convexity of preferences* by the condition that if $\mathbf{x}'^j \mathrm{I}_j \mathbf{x}''^j$, then for all $0 < t < 1$, $(t\mathbf{x}'^j + (1 - t)\mathbf{x}''^j) \mathrm{P}_j \mathbf{x}''^j$. The indifference maps depicted in Fig. 1-8*d* and *e* both fail to satisfy this condition.

We define *weak convexity of preferences* by the condition that if $\mathbf{x}'^j \mathrm{R}_j \mathbf{x}''^j$, than for all $0 < t < 1$, $(t\mathbf{x}'^j + (1 - t)\mathbf{x}''^j) \mathrm{R}_j \mathbf{x}''^j$. The indifference maps depicted in Fig. 1-8*b*, *d*, and *e* all satisfy this condition.

† It will also be noted that under the assumptions made with respect to $\bar{X}_j$, $\bar{X}_j$ is also a convex set.

[1] For a comprehensive discussion of convexity of preferences, see Debreu, *op. cit.*.

Briefly, the condition of weak convexity of preferences simply states that sets bounded from below by indifference curves (preference sets) are convex sets. The condition of strong convexity of preferences states that such convex preference sets can contain no straight line segments along the indifference curve boundaries and that thick indifference curves are ruled out. Convexity of preferences permits straight line segments in indifference curves, but excludes thick indifference curves. As we shall see, strong convexity is not needed in most of the modern theory (except possibly in stability and comparative statics analysis), while weak convexity is not restrictive enough to permit certain results in the theory of existence of equilibrium of a competitive system. Therefore we shall generally find ourselves working with the assumption of convexity of preferences. It might be noted that in the usual interpretation of the Hicksian law of diminishing marginal rate of substitution, both strong convexity of preferences and the absence of bliss points are assumed, making this assumption stronger than any of the convexity conditions listed above.

To summarize our discussion of the principles of consumer behavior, we have assumed that each consumer's tastes can be represented by a ranking over states of the economy; that tastes are "selfish" in the sense that consumers are concerned only with the commodity bundles that they receive and not with the commodity bundles assigned to other consumers; that each consumer's preferences are defined with respect to a restricted subset of euclidean n-dimensional space, termed the consumer's consumption set; and that preferences are convex in one of the senses defined above and are "continuous." The rational consumer, when presented with choices from some available set of commodity bundles, chooses that bundle that is most preferred or, equivalently, that bundle that has the highest ordinal utility number associated with it, if such a bundle exists.

1-7 PRODUCTION AND PROFIT MAXIMIZATION

Production of goods and services in the economy takes place in productive units called *firms*. A *producer* is an individual (or group) that manages a firm, converting inputs into outputs. In general, each firm will produce several commodities, using several inputs in the production process. The activities of any firm, say the kth, can be summarized by a concept termed the *input-output vector of the kth firm*, defined as follows:

Let y_{ik} denote the number of units of the ith good or service produced (or used up as an input in production) by the kth firm, where $i = 1, 2, \ldots, n$. Then the input-output vector of the kth firm, denoted by $\mathbf{y}^k$, is defined as

$$\mathbf{y}^k = (y_{1k}, y_{2k}, \ldots, y_{nk})$$

Following the convention adopted in Sec. 1-4, we shall treat outputs as positive numbers and inputs as negative numbers. Generally, we shall assume that the economy has a finite number of firms (the number of firms being denoted by l), but for certain purposes the assumption of an infinite number of firms will be admitted. In any case, it is clear that the input-output vector for any firm is an n-dimensional vector or point in n-dimensional euclidean space, just as are commodity bundles for consumers.

For any firm we can distinguish between *feasible* and *nonfeasible* input-output vectors, the feasibility of an input-output vector being determined by the state of technology of the economy. Thus, for example, we shall exclude input-output vectors containing only positive entries, production from nothing being beyond our present technical capacities. A considerably more restrictive assumption will be employed throughout most of the remainder of this book, the assumption that the outputs of any firm are determined solely by the inputs the firm uses and not by the input-output vectors chosen by other firms. This assumption, which will be referred to as the assumption of *independence* of input-output vectors, plays the same role in the theory of production that the assumption of selfishness plays in the theory of consumption; when independence holds, the outcome of a producer's choice is not dependent upon the choices made by other producers, just as when selfishness holds, the outcome of a consumer's choice (say the level of utility attained) is not dependent upon the choices made by other consumers. The phrase "absence of external economies (or diseconomies) in production" is equivalent to "independence of input-output vectors." Well-known examples of such external effects include smoke and smog damage inflicted upon other firms by producers in certain climate belts, water pollution, and so forth. Once again, no great claim to realism is made with respect to this assumption; it might be remarked parenthetically that most of the arguments advanced by

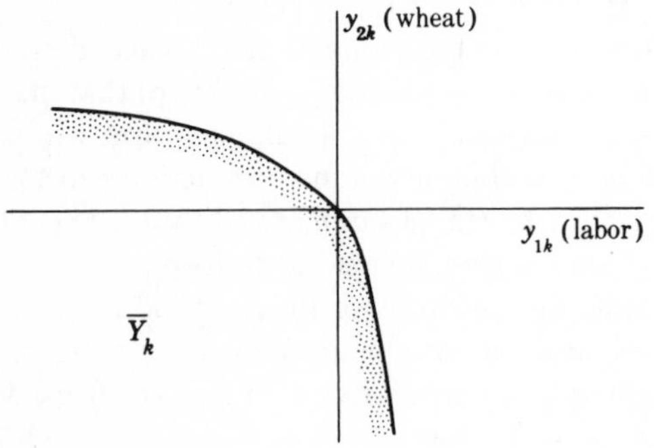

FIGURE 1-12

economists for government interference in the market mechanism are based on the existence of external diseconomies in production or consumption.

For any firm, say the kth, we can list the feasible input-output vectors as determined by the technology of the economy; under the assumption of independence of input-output vectors this set of vectors can be described independently of the input-output vectors chosen by other producers in the economy. We shall refer to the set of such vectors for the kth firm as the firm's *production set*, to be denoted by $\bar{Y}_k$. Such a set may be depicted graphically as in Fig. 1-12.

While Fig. 1-12 is not intended as a definitive graphical representation of a production set, there are certain characteristics of $\bar{Y}_k$ as pictured that might be noted, since these characteristics will appear in our discussion of axiom systems sufficient to guarantee existence of equilibrium in Chap. 3. Among these characteristics are the following:

1. The origin [the vector (0,0)] is an element of $\bar{Y}_k$.
2. No points in the positive quadrant belong to $\bar{Y}_k$ except the origin.
3. The negative quadrant is contained in $\bar{Y}_k$.
4. The set $\bar{Y}_k$ is convex.

The inclusion of the origin in the production set for the kth firm means that one possible input-output vector available to the producer is the input-output vector where nothing is produced and no inputs are used, i.e., the producer has the opportunity to withdraw from production if he so desires. As mentioned earlier, characteristic 2 simply states that it is not technically feasible to produce something from nothing. Characteristic 3 is sometimes referred to as the *free-disposal* assumption; intuitively, this characteristic of production sets is equivalent to saying that the firm can "throw away" commodities without using up inputs in the disposal process. For example, note that the negative of the vertical axis is in the set $\bar{Y}_k$, so that arbitrary large amounts of wheat can be disposed of (negative amounts "produced") using zero units of labor. Characteristic 4 is closely related to the well-known concepts of constant and decreasing returns to scale. In a manner similar to that employed in discussing convexity of consumer preferences, the concept of convexity of production sets can be formulated in terms of the following definitions:

Given any input-output vector, if $\mathbf{y}^k \in \bar{Y}_k$ implies $t\mathbf{y}^k \in \bar{Y}_k$ for any $t > 1$, *nondecreasing returns to scale* are said to occur.

If $\mathbf{y}^k \in \bar{Y}_k$ implies $t\mathbf{y}^k \in \bar{Y}_k$ for any $0 < t < 1$, then *nonincreasing returns to scale* are said to occur.

If $\mathbf{y}^k \in \bar{Y}_k$ implies $t\mathbf{y}^k \in \bar{Y}_k$ for any $t > 0$, then *constant returns to scale* are said to occur.

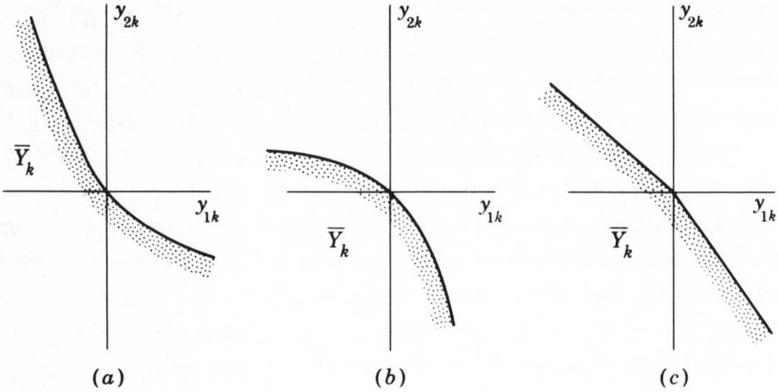

FIGURE 1-13

In two dimensions, these concepts may be represented as shown in Fig. 1-13.

Figure 1-13*a* depicts the case of nondecreasing returns to scale. Given any point in $\bar{Y}_k$, all points on the ray through the given point and farther out along the ray than the given point are also in $\bar{Y}_k$. Figure 1-13*b* depicts the case of nonincreasing returns to scale. Given any point in $\bar{Y}_k$, all points on the ray through the given point and lying between the origin and that point are also in $\bar{Y}_k$. Figure 1-13*c* depicts the case of constant returns to scale. Given any point in $\bar{Y}_k$, all points on the ray through the given point are also in $\bar{Y}_k$.

It will be noted that production sets such as that pictured in Fig. 1-13*a* are *not* convex. The sets depicted in Fig. 1-13*b* and *c* are convex, the difference being that in Fig. 1-13*b* convexity is *strict* (no straight line segments on the boundary of the set). (It should be noted that the assumption of nonincreasing returns to scale does *not* necessarily rule out straight line segments; on the other hand, the assumption of constant returns to scale does rule out a curved boundary such as that pictured in Fig. 1-13*b*. Similarly the assumption of nondecreasing returns to scale does not rule out the possibility of constant returns, i.e., a convex set such as that pictured in Fig. 1-13*c*. In fact, the joint assumptions of nondecreasing returns to scale and nonincreasing returns to scale are equivalent to the assumption of constant returns to scale, as can easily be verified from the definitions given. By *increasing returns to scale* will be meant nondecreasing returns coupled with the absence of constant returns, and by *decreasing returns to scale* will be meant nonincreasing returns coupled with the absence of constant returns.[1])

The production set shown in Fig. 1-12 is "strictly" convex, but we shall not require such a restrictive assumption in our work with existence

[1] For a discussion of these concepts see Debreu, *op. cit.*

of equilibrium of a competitive economy. However, as is well-known, increasing returns to scale (as pictured in Fig. 1-13*a*) is incompatible with competitive equilibrium, and we shall require in our work with competitive systems the (weaker) assumption that production sets be convex.[1]

The rule that producers are assumed to follow in a price system in choosing among feasible input-output vectors is to choose that vector that gives the highest value of profits. Let p_i denote the price of the ith good or service in the economy, where $i = 1, 2, \ldots, n$. Clearly, for any input-output vector $\mathbf{y}^k$, the profits associated with that vector are given by

$$\sum_{i=1}^{n} p_i y_{ik}$$

Remember our convention that the sign of inputs is negative and the sign of outputs is positive.[2] The rule of profit maximization then states:

Given the production set $\bar{Y}_k$, the producer managing the kth firm chooses that input-output vector, say $\mathbf{y}^{k*}$, where $\mathbf{y}^{k*} \in \bar{Y}_k$, such that

$$\sum_{i=1}^{n} p_i y_{ik}^* \geq \sum_{i=1}^{n} p_i y_{ik} \qquad \text{for all } \mathbf{y}^k \in \bar{Y}_k, \text{ if such a vector } \mathbf{y}^{k*} \text{ exists}$$

In a price system, of course, the prices of goods and services depend upon the choices of input-output vectors by firms. Under the atomistic assumptions of competitive theory, however, each firm is assumed to treat prices of inputs and outputs as parameters; that is, it is assumed that the prices of inputs and outputs are independent of the particular input-output vector chosen by the firm. Given this assumption, *isoprofit curves* (sets of points all yielding the same amount of profits to the firm) are hyperplanes (straight lines in two dimensions, planes in three dimensions).[3] Figure 1-14 illustrates this in two dimensions.[4]

In Fig. 1-14, the isoprofit line through the origin is a set of points

[1] Strictly speaking, convexity need only be assumed with respect to aggregate production sets. See Sec. 2-1 and Chap. 3 in connection with this point.

[2] It will be noted that in the production sets pictured in Figs. 1-12 and 1-13, the possibility of producing labor from wheat is admitted (the production set contains points in the fourth quadrant). The question of which goods will be inputs and which outputs clearly depends upon the relative profitability of processes, so that a steel manufacturer, using coke in his production process, might shift to producing coke using steel implements, for a sufficiently different set of prices. Labor in the figures is used in place of physical inputs that could be outputs of a "reversed" production process.

[3] By a hyperplane H is meant the following: H is a set of points such that each point $\mathbf{z} \in H$ satisfies $\sum_{i=1}^{n} a_i z_i = b$, where z_i is the ith component of $\mathbf{z}$, and a_i and b are fixed constant, $i = 1, 2, \ldots, n$.

[4] The symbol Π is used to denote profits, so that in Fig. 1-14, Π_i denotes an isoprofit line with profits equal to Π_i, for $i = 1, 2, 3, 4, 5$, where $\Pi_5 > \Pi_4 > \cdots > \Pi_1$.

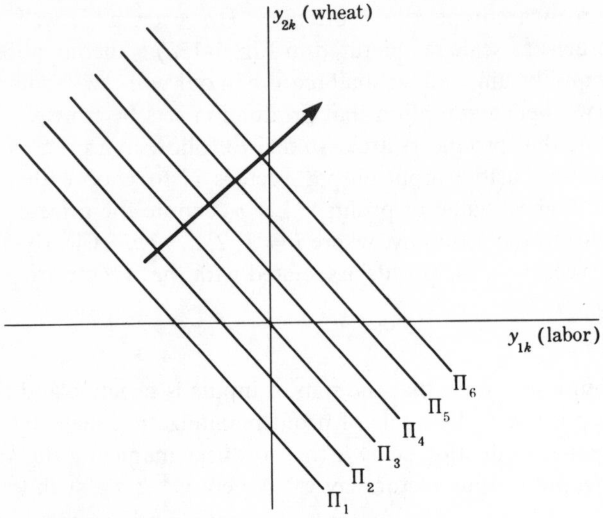

(Arrow indicates direction of increasing profits)

FIGURE 1-14

all of which have zero profits associated with them. (To verify this, note that the origin is on the line and that zero profits are clearly associated with no outputs and no inputs.) Isoprofit lines crossing the first quadrant have positive profits associated with them, while isoprofit lines crossing the third quadrant have negative profits associated with them. It is easy to verify that the slope of the isoprofit line is the negative of the ratio of the price of labor to the price of wheat. In Fig. 1-15, isoprofit lines as drawn in Fig. 1-14 are superimposed on production sets of the type shown in Fig. 1-13.

Figure 1-15*a* shows the profit-choice problem of a firm operating under increasing returns to scale, Fig. 1-15*b* for a firm operating under decreasing returns to scale, and Fig. 1-15*c* for a firm operating under constant returns to scale. It is easy to see from Fig. 1-15*a* why increasing returns to scale is incompatible with competitive conditions: given fixed prices for inputs and outputs, the profit-maximizing output level is unbounded, so that the firm will grow to such a size that it can no longer ignore the effects of its actions on the prices of inputs and outputs; in short, increasing returns leads to monopoly. Under decreasing returns to scale, as depicted in Fig. 1-15*b*, profits will be a maximum at the tangency point between the boundary of the production set and the isoprofit line touching the set at that point.[1] In Fig. 1-15*c*, the isoprofit lines as

[1] Since production sets characterized by decreasing returns to scale may have straight line segments along the boundary, the profit-maximizing point need not be a tangency point. Such sets are illustrated in Chap. 2.

drawn indicate that a maximum of profits occurs at the origin, since any other attainable input-output vector has negative profits associated with it. For a flatter set of isoprofit lines (higher price of wheat relative to labor), say a set with slope equal to the slope of the boundary of the production set in the second quadrant, every input-output vector along that boundary is equally desirable (all yielding zero profits). If the slope is even flatter than this, the optimal output level becomes unbounded with unlimited amounts of profits made by the firm. Thus for competitive conditions to prevail with constant returns to scale, the slope of the isoprofit lines must be at least as steep as the slope of the boundary of the production set, which implies that output for the firm is either zero or indeterminate, and in either case, profits for the firm are zero. With decreasing returns to scale, positive profits can be associated with a competitive environment. Negative profits are excluded because the "no inputs, no outputs" alternative (the origin) is in the production set of each firm.

It is clear from the above discussion that no profit-maximizing firm will operate at any point not on the boundary of its production set.

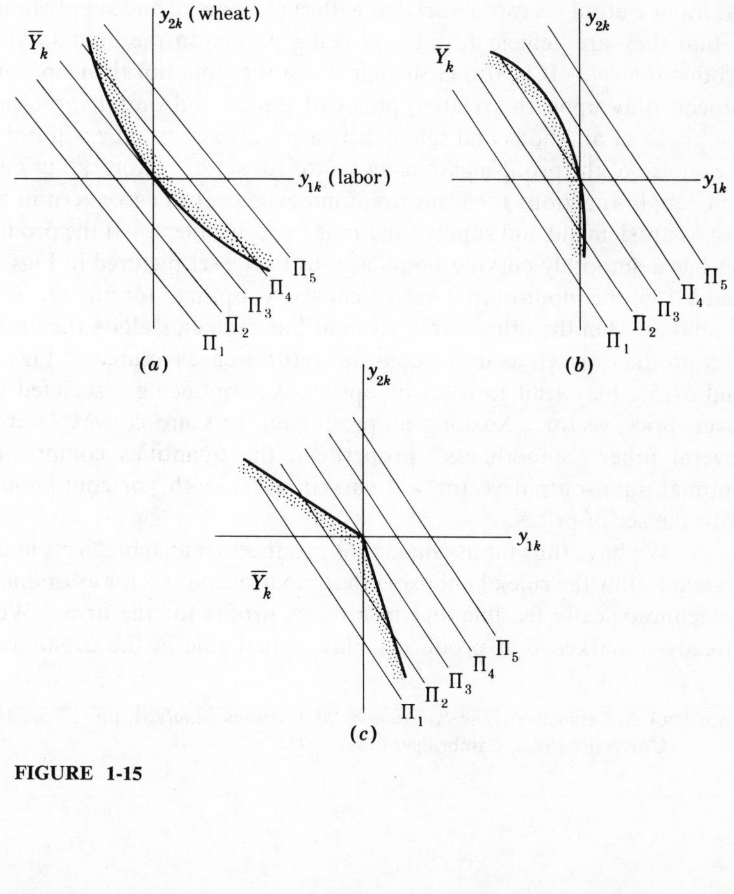

FIGURE 1-15

Interior points of the set are "inefficient" in the sense that by using the same amounts of inputs, larger amounts of outputs can be attained by moving to the boundary. The boundary of the production set is thus the set of "efficient" input-output vectors for the firm. In the neoclassical literature, this set of points is referred to as the *production function* of the firm, stated in implicit form. As Samuelson has pointed out, the very concept of a production function already presupposes that maximizing activities have taken place in the firm in the sense of eliminating inefficient input-output vectors from consideration.[1]

Given any set of prices of inputs and outputs, the rule of profit maximization leads to the choice of certain input-output vectors by firms as *optimal* (or possibly sets of such input-output vectors if production sets have boundaries with straight line segments). But this is simply a statement of the amounts of various goods and services that will be demanded by firms as inputs or supplied as outputs, at the given prices. Thus, as prices are permitted to vary, an inspection of the input-output vectors chosen as optimal (profit-maximizing) by the firm will allow us to construct the firm's demand and supply functions (or correspondences) for inputs and outputs. As has been noted earlier, one characteristic of the input-output vectors associated with such demand and supply functions is that they are "efficient," always being points on the boundary of the production set. It is also clear that, since the slopes of the isoprofit lines depend only upon the relative prices of inputs and outputs, multiplying the prices of all goods and services by a positive constant t will not affect the choice of the profit-maximizing vector (or set of vectors); thus demand and supply functions for firms are homogeneous of degree zero in prices, just as are demand and supply functions for consumers. If the production set has a smoothly curving boundary, as in the set pictured in Figs. 1-13*b* and 1-15*b*, the input-output vector chosen as optimal for any set of prices is unique. On the other hand, straight line segments along the boundary of a production set, as in the constant returns case pictured in Figs. 1-13*c* and 1-15*c*, may lead to a set of optimal vectors being associated with a given price vector. So long as production sets are convex (and enjoy several other "smoothness" properties), the quantities comprising the optimal input-output vector will vary in a "smooth" or continuous way with the set of prices.

We have thus far assumed that producers managing firms in a price system follow the rule of choosing that input-output vector as optimal that is technologically feasible and maximizes profits for the firm. We have already remarked that producers play a dual role in the economy, also

[1] See Paul A. Samuelson, *The Foundations of Economic Analysis*, pp. 57–58, Harvard University Press, Cambridge, Mass., 1955.

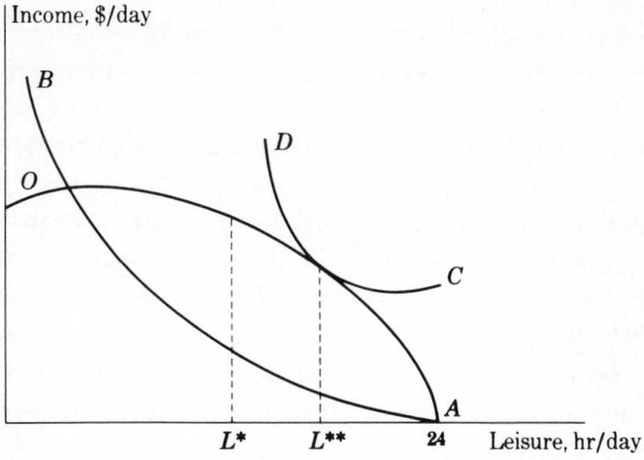

FIGURE 1-16

appearing as consumers. As a consumer, it is assumed that an individual chooses among commodity bundles according to his preference ranking among such bundles; however, as a producer, the rule of profit maximization determines his choices. Is this inconsistent? Scitovsky has pointed out that these two sets of assumptions concerning behavior patterns are, in general, inconsistent if it is assumed, as in the classical theory of the entrepreneur, that profits earned by the firm are paid to the producer.[1] The argument can be seen from Fig. 1-16, where leisure and real income for the producer are plotted on the two axes.

The curve labeled OA is the opportunity curve of the entrepreneur or producer, reflecting earnings above costs by the firm (excluding compensation to the producer). When the producer works no hours (24 hr per day of leisure), earnings above costs are zero, and as the number of hours worked increases, earnings above costs increase at a decreasing rate as diminishing returns set in. The indifference curve labeled AB gives the combinations of leisure and real income that are indifferent from the producer's point of view to no income and 24 hr of leisure per day. If we consider any point on the curve AB, the income coordinate is the "normal profits" associated with the producer working 24 hr minus the leisure coordinate, since if the producer receives any less income, no producer managing services will be supplied. Profits for the firm are defined as the difference between earnings and total costs (including normal profits), which attain a maximum at the point L^*. However, it is clear that a utility-maximizing producer will choose that point, labeled L^{**}, at which the opportunity curve is tangent to the indifference curve CD. Thus profit maximization and utility maximization are inconsistent,

[1] See T. Scitovsky, *Welfare and Competition*, pp. 142–147, Richard D. Irwin, Inc., Homewood, Ill.. 1951.

unless it is assumed that indifference curves between income and leisure are parallel with respect to the leisure axis. (If the qualification holds, it is easy to show that the points L^* and L^{**} must coincide.)

An alternative to this treatment of the role of the producer is to view the producer as an employee of the firm who performs the duties of calculating the relative profitability of various alternative input-output vectors and of assigning tasks on the basis of the highest profit alternative. Like any other employee, he is paid a wage equal to the marginal-value product of his work, which in turn will be not more than the costs associated with replacing him by a mechanical calculator. The stockholders of the firm impose the rule of maximizing profits, because their interest in the operation of the firm is strictly monetary; if the producer does not follow the profit-maximization rule, the stockholders presumably will replace the manager with someone else. The choice of that input-output vector as optimal which maximizes profits is thus imposed by consumers (as stockholders), who are acting rationally as long as their utility functions are assumed to depend only upon the quantities of goods and services they themselves obtain. Because the producer's incentive is not the profits earned by the firm as a source of income to him, there is no inconsistency in postulating that producers (at the behest of stockholders) follow the rule of profit maximization as their way of earning a living as employees, while following the rule of maximizing utility as consumers. Of course, in a simplified model such as we are working with, there is no place for such important producer tasks as expanding the set of technologically feasible input-output vectors, differentiating the product through advertising, packaging, etc., tasks that do have "quasi rents" associated with them. Since, with minor exceptions, this book restricts itself to the discussion of the static competitive economy, the idealized conception of a producer as a noninnovating employee of the firm appears to be adequate for our needs.

TWO

THE SETTING: SUPPLY AND DEMAND

2-1 SET SUMMATION AND AGGREGATES

In Chap. 1 we discussed some of the characteristics of individual consumption and production sets and the way in which choices from these sets are made by consumers and producers following the rules of utility and profit maximization. Under the assumptions of selfishness of consumer preferences and independence of input-output vectors in production, the aggregated (net) amounts of commodities demanded and supplied for any vector of prices can be determined by a simple summation of the amounts demanded and supplied by individual consumers and producers. Thus, given the price vector $\mathbf{p}$, where $\mathbf{p} = (p_1, p_2, \ldots, p_n)$, we can write $x_{ij}(\mathbf{p})$ as the amount of the ith commodity consumed (or supplied as an input in production) by the jth individual at the set of prices given by $\mathbf{p}$, and $y_{ik}(\mathbf{p})$ as the amount of the ith commodity produced (or used up as an input in production) by the kth firm at the set of prices given by $\mathbf{p}$. Then the aggregate (net) consumption of commodity i by consumers is given by $x_i(\mathbf{p}) = \sum_{j=1}^{m} x_{ij}(\mathbf{p})$, and the aggregate (net) production of commodity i by producers is given by $y_i(\mathbf{p}) = \sum_{k=1}^{l} y_{ik}(\mathbf{p})$ for $i = 1, 2, \ldots, n$. We then define $\mathbf{x}(\mathbf{p})$ and $\mathbf{y}(\mathbf{p})$ by $\mathbf{x}(\mathbf{p}) = (x_1(\mathbf{p}), x_2(\mathbf{p}), \ldots, x_n(\mathbf{p}))$ and $\mathbf{y}(\mathbf{p}) = (y_1(\mathbf{p}), y_2(\mathbf{p}), \ldots, y_n(\mathbf{p}))$.

A point such as $\mathbf{x}(\mathbf{p})$ is said to lie in the *aggregate consumption set* for the economy, and $\mathbf{y}(\mathbf{p})$ in the *aggregate production set* for the economy, two concepts that will be useful in our discussion of existence of competitive equilibrium in Chap. 3. Before defining these concepts, we shall review some elementary notions from the calculus of sets.

Let S be a set, and let s denote an element of S. S is said to be a *point set* if every element of S can be represented as a point in some space. We shall assume that S is a set in euclidean n-space, such that each element of S is a vector. We define a *subset* of S as a set all of whose elements belong to the set S; thus the set A is a subset of S, written $A \subset S$, if $s \in A \Rightarrow s \in S$. (For example, a two-dimensional production set is a subset of the set consisting of all the points in euclidean two-dimensional space.) For any two subsets of S, A and B, we define the following symbols:

$A \cup B$ (read "the union of A and B") is the set of all points that are in A or B or both.

$A \cap B$ (read "the intersection of A and B") is the set of all points that are in both A and B.

$S \sim A$ (read "the complement of A in S") is the set of all points in S that are not in A.

$A + B$ (read "the sum of A and B") is the set of all points such that each point is the sum of a point in A and a point in B.

$A \times B$ (read "the cartesian product of A and B") is the set of all ordered pairs such that the first of the pair is a point in A and the second is a point in B.

We might write these definitions more concisely as follows:

$$A \cup B = \{s \mid s \in A \text{ or } s \in B\}$$

$$A \cap B = \{s \mid s \in A \text{ and } s \in B\}$$

$$S \sim A = \{s \in S \mid s \notin A\}$$ (where the symbol $\notin$ is read "does not belong to")

$$A + B = \{s = y + z \mid y \in A, z \in B\}$$

$$A \times B = \{(y,z) \mid y \in A, z \in B\}$$

In Fig. 2-1, $A \cup B$ consists of the region with horizontal stripes, vertical stripes, and the crosshatched area. $A \cap B$ is simply the

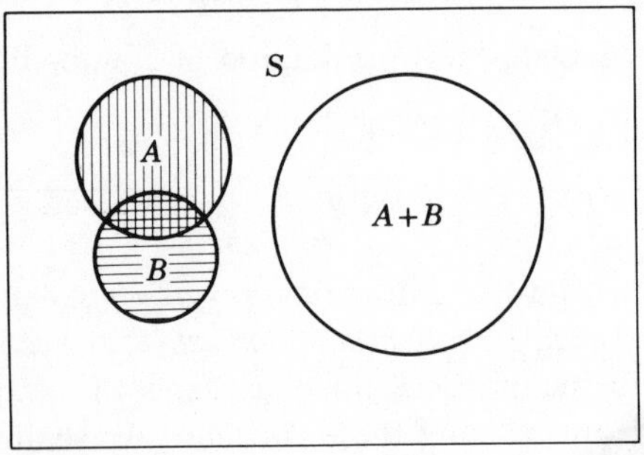

FIGURE 2-1

crosshatched area. $S \sim A$ is all of S except A. $A + B$ is the region so labeled.[1] ($A \times B$ is hard to illustrate in Fig. 2-1 for, if A, B are two-dimensional, four dimensions would be required to draw $A \times B$.)

Let us illustrate these concepts again by choosing S to be the set consisting of 0 and the first nine positive integers. Let A be the set consisting of the numbers 0, 1, 2, and B be the set consisting of the numbers 0, 3. That is, $S = \{0,1,2,3,4,5,6,7,8,9\}$, $A = \{0,1,2\}$, and $B = \{0,3\}$. It follows that:

1. $A \cup B = \{0,1,2,3\}$
2. $A \cap B = \{0\}$
3. $S \sim A = \{3,4,5,6,7,8,9\}$
4. $A + B = \{0,1,2,3,4,5\}$
5. $A \times B = \{(0,0), (0,3), (1,0), (1,3), (2,0), (2,3)\}$

If we denote the set $A \cap B$ by C and the set $S \sim A$ by D, then the set $C \cap D$ does not contain any elements. A set that has no elements is called the *empty set* and is denoted by $\varnothing$.

Since we are particularly interested in convex sets, the following three theorems are of importance to us:

I. The intersection of any number of convex sets is a convex set.
II. The sum of any number of convex sets is a convex set.
III. The cartesian product of any number of convex sets is a convex set.

The proofs of these theorems are simple for the case of two convex sets, as are the extensions to an arbitrary finite number of sets.[2]

Let A and B be two convex sets. Then if x', $x'' \in A$, $tx' + (1 - t)x'' \in A$ for $0 \leq t \leq 1$, and similarly for B. Assume y', $y'' \in A \cap B$. But if y', $y'' \in A \cap B$, y', $y'' \in A$ and y', $y'' \in B$. Since A and

[1] Some mathematics books, to the possible confusion of economists, use $A + B$ as a synonym for $A \cup B$. When this occurs, we hope that the context will be sufficiently revealing to preclude confusion.

[2] Let A_i $(i = 1, 2, \ldots, n)$ be n sets. The intersection of the n sets, denoted by $\bigcap_{i=1}^{n} A_i$, is the set of elements all of which belong to each of the n sets. Similarly, $\sum_{i=1}^{n} A_i$ is the set of all points such that each point is the sum of a point in A_1 plus a point in A_2, etc., up to A_n, that is, $\sum_{i=1}^{n} A_i = \left\{z = \sum_{i=1}^{n} y_i, \text{ where } y_i \in A_i, \text{ for } i = 1, 2, \ldots, n\right\}$. $\bigtimes_{i=1}^{n} A_i$ is the set of all ordered n-tuples such that the first of the n-tuples is an element of A_1, the second is an element of A_2, etc., the nth being an element of A_n, that is, $\bigtimes_{i=1}^{n} A_i = \{(y_1, y_2, \ldots, y_n), y_i \in A_i\}$.

B are convex, we must have $ty' + (1 - t)y'' \in A$ and $ty' + (1 - t)y'' \in B$ for all $0 \leq t \leq 1$. Thus $A \cap B$ is convex.

For Theorem II, we must show that if $C = A + B$, A and B being convex sets, C is also convex. Let $z', z'' \in C$. Then $z' = x' + y'$, where $x' \in A$ and $y' \in B$. Similarly $z'' = x'' + y''$, where $x'' \in A$ and $y'' \in B$. But $tz' + (1 - t)z'' = t(x' + y') + (1 - t)(x'' + y'') = \{tx' + (1 - t)x''\} + \{ty' + (1 - t)y''\}$, which is clearly an element of C, since the first term $tx' + (1 - t)x'' \in A$, and the second, $ty' + (1 - t)y'' \in B$.

For Theorem III, we must show A, B convex implies $A \times B$ convex. Let $(x',y'), (x'',y'') \in A \times B$. Then $t(x',y') + (1 - t)(x'',y'') = (tx' + (1 - t)x'', ty' + (1 - t)y'')$. By convexity of A, B, the first of this ordered pair is an element of A and the second is an element of B. Thus $A \times B$ is convex.

We are now in a position to define aggregate consumption and production sets. The *aggregate consumption set*, denoted by $\bar{X}$, is defined by $\bar{X} = \sum_{j=1}^{m} \bar{X}_j$, and the *aggregate production set*, denoted by $\bar{Y}$, is defined by $\bar{Y} = \sum_{k=1}^{l} \bar{Y}_k$.

As was noted earlier, if $\mathbf{x} \in \bar{X}$, then $\mathbf{x} = (x_1, x_2, \ldots, x_n)$, where $x_i = \sum_{j=1}^{m} x_{ij}$, that is, each point in the aggregate consumption set is a vector, the ith coordinate of the vector being the aggregate (net) consumption of the ith good or service by consumers. Similarly, if $\mathbf{y} \in \bar{Y}$, then $\mathbf{y} = (y_1, y_2, \ldots, y_n)$, where $y_i = \sum_{k=1}^{l} y_{ik}$, that is, each point in the aggregate production set is a vector, the ith coordinate of which is the aggregate (net) production of the ith good or service by firms. By Theorem II, the assumption that each of the individual consumption and production sets is convex is sufficient to guarantee that the aggregate consumption and production sets are convex. A significantly weaker assumption is that the aggregate consumption (or production) set is convex; as we shall see in the next chapter, in the axiom systems sufficient to establish existence of a competitive equilibrium, it is sometimes assumed only that the aggregate production set is convex, but the (stronger) assumption that individual consumption sets are convex is required in these proofs.

One other interesting characteristic of sets formed by set summation occurs in connection with maximization. Although any conscious maximizing behavior that one postulates in economics must be at the level of the individual economic agents, nevertheless one can sometimes represent aggregate behavior in terms of "maximizing" behavior also. This proposition becomes clear in terms of profits. For a given set of prices, if each producer is maximizing profits on his production set, then it must follow that the sum of the profits obtained by all producers must be at least as large as the sum of profits from any other set of points chosen by individual producers, the points lying in the production sets of the producers. This follows immediately from the assumption of independence with respect to production. In effect this proposition states, in the context of profit functions, that if a function is defined as the sum of a number of other functions (aggregate profit equals the sum of the individual profits), each with specified sets over which the individual functions are defined, then the aggregate function will be maximized if and only if the component functions are individually maximized.

It might be useful to state formally and prove this proposition:

Let $A_1, A_2, \ldots, A_n$ be sets and $f_1, f_2, \ldots, f_n$ real-valued functions, with f_i defined on A_i. Define $A = A_1 + A_2 + \cdots + A_n$ and $f(A) = \sum_{i=i}^{n} f_i(A_i)$. Then f attains its maximum over A at a point $\hat{a} = \hat{a}_1 + \hat{a}_2 + \cdots + \hat{a}_n$, if and only if f_i attains its maximum over A_i at $\hat{a}_i$.

PROOF: $f_i(\hat{a}_i) \geqq f_i(a_i)$ for all $a_i \in A_i$ clearly implies

$$f(\hat{a}) = \sum_{i=i}^{n} f_i(\hat{a}_i) \geqq \sum_{i=i}^{n} f_i(a_i) = f(a)$$

Conversely, suppose

$$f(\hat{a}) = \sum_{i=i}^{n} f_i(\hat{a}_i) \geqq \sum_{i=i}^{n} f_i(a_i) = f(a) \qquad \text{for all } a \in A$$

while $f_k(\hat{a}_k) < f_k(\tilde{a}_k)$ for some $\tilde{a}_k \in A_k$.

Then $f_1(\hat{a}_1) + \cdots + f_{k-1}(\hat{a}_{k-1}) + f_k(\tilde{a}_k) + f_{k+1}(\hat{a}_{k+1}) + \cdots + f_n(\hat{a}_n) > f(\hat{a})$. Denoting the point $\hat{a}_1 + \cdots + \hat{a}_{k-1} + \tilde{a}_k + \hat{a}_{k+1} + \cdots + \hat{a}_n$ by $\tilde{a}$, we have $f(\tilde{a}) > f(\hat{a})$, a contradiction. Therefore $f_i(\hat{a}_i) \geqq f_i(a_i)$ for all $i = 1, 2, \ldots, n$.

2-2 MAXIMIZATION AND SOME MATHEMATICAL CONCEPTS

It has been necessary, in our discussions of utility and profit maximization, to qualify our statements concerning maximizing conduct with the phrase "if such a (maximizing) element exists in the set." Here we intend to summarize without proof the most important theorem (for our purposes) relating to the existence of elements that maximize real-valued functions defined over sets, with several examples that illustrate the need for the conditions imposed in stating the theorem. The theorem is the following:

Let f be a continuous real-valued function defined over a closed and bounded set in euclidean n-dimensional space. Then f takes on its minimum and maximum values at some points in the set.

In order to facilitate understanding of this basic theorem in maximization, it seems advisable to recall some of the mathematical notions involved in the theorem. We might begin by reviewing the notion of a function. Most generally a function (or mapping, transformation, etc.) is a rule for associating elements in one set with those of another. A function f is said to have domain S and range T if f is a rule for associating with each element of S one element of T. f is sometimes said to "map S into T." The set of points which S is mapped into by f is called the *image* of f. Whenever the term "function" is used in these pages, it will mean that each element in the domain has associated with it, via the function, one and only one element in the range. Thus both the utility function of the consumer and the profit function of the firm have a subset of real numbers as the range and some subset of euclidean n-dimensional space as the domain of the functions. When the range of the function f is the set of real numbers (or some subset of the set of real numbers), f is said to be a real-valued function. Certain of the functions we shall deal with are not real-valued; for example, demand functions have as their domain and range subsets of euclidean n-dimensional space, the domain of the demand function for a consumer being the set of price vectors and the range the set of commodity bundles, both n-dimensional vectors.

For any set, a distinction may be drawn between algebraic and topological properties of the set. By algebraic properties are meant properties of the set relating to operations involving elements of the set, such as addition, subtraction, and scalar multiplication. The concepts of continuity, closedness, and boundedness of sets are topological in nature, being related to the notion of open sets defined with respect to the set under study.

In euclidean n-dimensional space, we may define the distance of one point from another by the square root of the sum of squared differences between corresponding elements of the two points. That is, the distance between two points $\mathbf{x}$ and $\mathbf{y}$, denoted by $d(\mathbf{x},\mathbf{y})$, where $\mathbf{x} = (x_1, x_2, \ldots x_n)$ and $\mathbf{y} = (y_1, y_2, \ldots, y_n)$, is given by the following formula:

$$d(\mathbf{x},\mathbf{y}) = \sqrt{(x_1 - y_1)^2 + \cdots + (x_n - y_n)^2}$$

In two-dimensional space, the concept of distance of $\mathbf{x}$ from $\mathbf{y}$ is illustrated in Fig. 2-2.

Using this concept of distance, we might consider the set of all points whose distance from a given point is less than some arbitrary distance, say r, where r is any positive number. In the case of two dimensions, it is clear that the set of points so defined would constitute all points inside a circle, excluding the boundary, with r as the radius and the given point as the center. In general, we refer to such a set of points as an

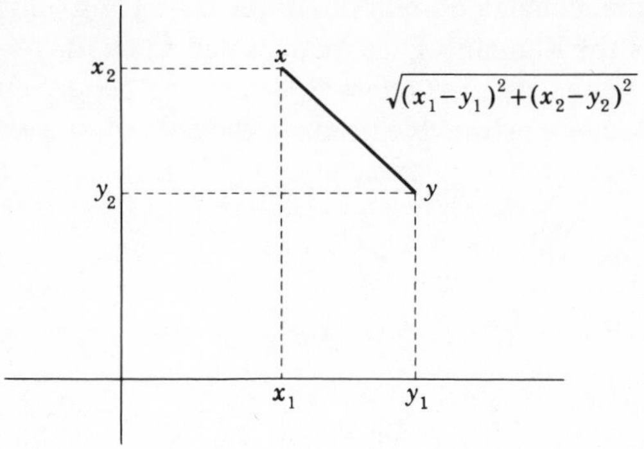

FIGURE 2-2

"open sphere of radius r" about the given point. In euclidean n-dimensional space, such open spheres are defined as the open sets associated with the space, thus defining a topology on the space.[1]

A set of points is said to be *closed* if it is the complement of an open set, i.e., if the set of points not belonging to the set is an open sphere or a union (or finite intersection) of open spheres. Very roughly, in euclidean space a set is closed if it contains its boundary; more precisely, it is closed if it contains its limit points. Sets may be either closed, open, neither, or both.[2]

A set of points is said to be *bounded* if the distance between any two points in the set is finite. Finally, a function f from a set S to a set T (with domain S and range T) is said to be *continuous* if, given any open sphere V about a point in the range of the function ($f(x_0) \in V$ for some $x_0 \in S$), there exists an open sphere U about $x_0 \in S$ such that the image of all points in U is contained in V. In particular, if f is a real-valued function, this means that given $\epsilon > 0$, there exists $\delta > 0$ such that $d(x,x_0) < \delta$ implies $|f(x) - f(x_0)| < \epsilon$, the usual textbook definition of continuity of a real-valued function.

It is easy to show that if any one of the conditions, continuity of the function or closedness or boundedness of the domain of the function, is violated, the function no longer necessarily attains its maximum (or

[1] For an arbitrary set S, a topology is said to be defined with respect to S if open sets in S are defined with the characteristics that (1) the empty set and the set S are both open; (2) any union of open sets is open; and (3) every finite intersection of open sets is open. Clearly these characteristics hold with respect to open spheres defined as the open sets of euclidean n-dimensional space.

[2] The set S and the empty set are defined to be both open and closed. A half-open, half-closed interval on the real line, such as $0 < x \leq 1$, is neither open nor closed.

minimum) value in the defined domain. In the following illustrative cases, we shall take as the domain of our real-valued function f a subset of the real line. (In such a case, f is referred to as a real-valued function of a real variable.) To demonstrate the need for the continuity condition, consider the function

$$f(x) = \begin{cases} \dfrac{1}{|x|} & \text{if } -1 \leq x \leq 1, x \neq 0 \\ 1 & \text{if } x = 0 \end{cases}$$

Clearly the domain of the function $[-1,1]$ is a closed and bounded set of euclidean space. However, the function defined is obviously not continuous at $x = 0$. This function does not have a maximum in $[-1,1]$, as is clear from the graph of the function in Fig. 2-3.

Next we consider the function $f(x) = x$ defined for all $x \geq 0$. The function is obviously continuous, and the set of points defined by $x \geq 0$ is closed. However, the function has no maximum on the set of points designated, because the set $x \geq 0$ is not bounded.

If we consider the same function $f(x) = x$ defined on the open interval $(0,1)$, that is, $0 < x < 1$, a maximum of the function does not exist with respect to this domain because, although the domain is bounded and the function is continuous, the domain of the function is not closed. This is clear because all numbers less than 1 and greater than 0 constitute the range of this function and there is no largest number in the range. If the interval were changed so as to include the end point 1, then the maximum would exist and be equal to 1. In the case of the interval not including 1, the value 1 is said to be the *least upper bound* of the range of the function. This means that every element of the range of the function is no greater than 1 (1 is an upper bound) and every upper bound is at least as large as 1 (1 is a least upper bound). The least upper bound of a set of numbers is often called the *supremum* or *sup* of the set of numbers.

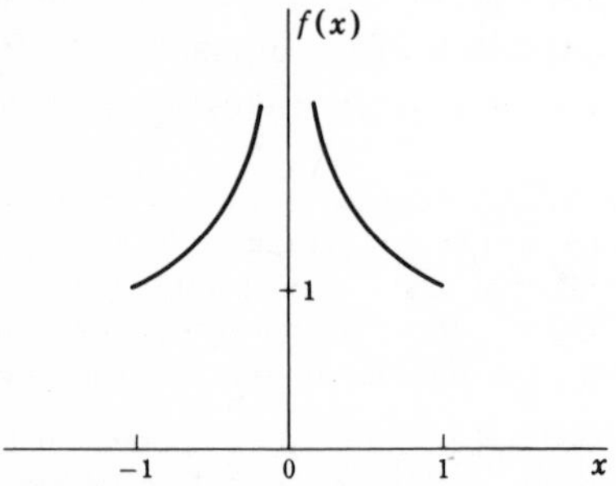

FIGURE 2-3

Analogously, there is defined the *greatest lower bound* of a set of numbers. The greatest lower bound is often called the *infimum* or *inf*.

A final word about this discussion: as the example in the preceding paragraph illustrates [half-open, half-closed interval (0,1)], the assumptions of the theorem stated earlier are sufficient but are not necessary for existence of a maximum. Similar illustrations can be constructed in which discontinuous functions defined on open, unbounded sets have both maximum and minimum values. However, just because the conditions listed are sufficient, it should not be surprising to find out that the economic axiom systems dealing with sets such as consumption and production sets (and preference sets) will employ assumptions such as the assumption of closedness. To go somewhat ahead of our discussion, it can be stated here that in order to establish the existence of competitive equilibrium, all of the above-mentioned sets will be assumed closed. Boundedness turns out to be an assumption that is not needed with respect to the individual (and aggregate) sets, since a somewhat weaker assumption will lead to precisely the same conclusion.

It might also be noted that all of the discussion of this section has dealt with functions, that is, single-valued relations between domain and range. As has been continually emphasized, in much of the economics of general equilibrium theory, set-valued functions will be used arising from straight line segments along indifference curves, constant returns to scale in production, and other sources. An extended discussion of the complications introduced by such set-valued functions (or correspondences) is given in Chap. 3; however, economists who are used to dealing with this phenomenon as it appears in perfectly elastic demand curves and perfectly elastic supply curves should not be overly perturbed by this.

We conclude this section with a very brief discussion of convexity definitions for real-valued functions. A real-valued function f defined on a convex subset S of euclidean space is said to be *concave* if, for all $0 \leq \alpha \leq 1$ and all $\mathbf{x}, \mathbf{x}' \in S$, $f(\alpha\mathbf{x} + (1 - \alpha)\mathbf{x}') \geqq \alpha f(\mathbf{x}) + (1 - \alpha)f(\mathbf{x}')$. A real-valued function g defined on S is said to be *convex* if $-g$ is concave. If we take S to be an interval on the real line, the heuristically pleasing qualities of the terms concave and convex become apparent.

In dealing with utility functions of consumers and the associated indifference maps, it is often assumed that the utility function is quasiconcave. A function f defined on S is said to be *quasiconcave* if for all $\mathbf{x}, \mathbf{x}' \in S$ and all $0 \leqq \alpha \leqq 1$, $f(\mathbf{x}) \leqq f(\mathbf{x}') \Rightarrow f(\alpha\mathbf{x} + (1 - \alpha)\mathbf{x}') \geqq f(\mathbf{x})$. Quasi concavity is a logically weaker assumption than concavity, since obviously any concave function is also quasiconcave, while a quasiconcave function need not be concave. To verify the last statement, we need only consider the function $f(\mathbf{x}) = x_1x_2$ defined on the positive quadrant and check this function against the definition to see that it is in fact quasiconcave. To see that x_1x_2 is not a concave function it suffices to note that the definition of concavity breaks down for $\mathbf{x} = (3,4)$ $\mathbf{x}' = (1,2)$ and $\alpha = \frac{1}{2}$.

2-3 SUPPLY AND DEMAND FUNCTIONS AND CORRESPONDENCES

The basic tool of microeconomics is supply and demand analysis, and the same is true of general equilibrium theory. Because of the central importance of this tool in the chapters that follow, we shall briefly summarize what is meant by a supply function or demand function and illustrate how these are derived from the principles of utility and profit maximization, using the concepts of consumption and production sets. For simplicity, we shall use the term *supply function* when dealing with producers, and the term *demand function* when dealing with consumers, even though there is little formal difference between these two notions. In addition, the derivation of supply and demand correspondences is illustrated.

By a supply function for a producer is meant a rule that tells us, given the prices of all commodities, the number of units of each commodity that the producer will supply to the market and the number of units of each commodity that will be used up by him as an input in production. In terms of the phraseology used earlier, a supply function for a producer has as its domain the set of price vectors (points in n-dimensional euclidean space) and as its range the set of input-output vectors (again points in n-dimensional euclidean space). Alternatively, we can say that the supply function maps price vectors into input-output vectors. Similarly, by a demand function for a consumer is meant a rule that specifies, given the prices of all commodities, the number of units of each commodity that the consumer will consume and the number of units of each commodity that will be supplied as inputs for production. A consumer's demand function maps price vectors into commodity bundles (again, points in n-dimensional space). The abstract notion of a demand or supply function has a simple interpretation in terms of graphical depiction, as is illustrated in Fig. 2-4 for the case of the supply function of a producer.

In Fig. 2-4 it is assumed that the price of labor is \$1 per hr, and the price of wheat is \$3 per bu and \$2 per bu. [The vector $\mathbf{p}^0 = (1,3)$, while the vector $\mathbf{p}^1 = (1,2)$.] The profit-maximizing input-output vectors associated with the price vectors $\mathbf{p}^0$ and $\mathbf{p}^1$, labeled $\mathbf{y}^0$ and $\mathbf{y}^1$, are given by $\mathbf{y}^0 = (-5,2.67)$ and $\mathbf{y}^1 = (-2,1.5)$, where the first component of the vectors refers to labor and the second to wheat. It will also be noted that the amount of profits earned at the maximizing points (measured in terms of bushels of wheat) is given by the intersection of the isoprofit lines with the wheat axis. Figure 2-4*b* is a freehand sketch of the *supply curve*

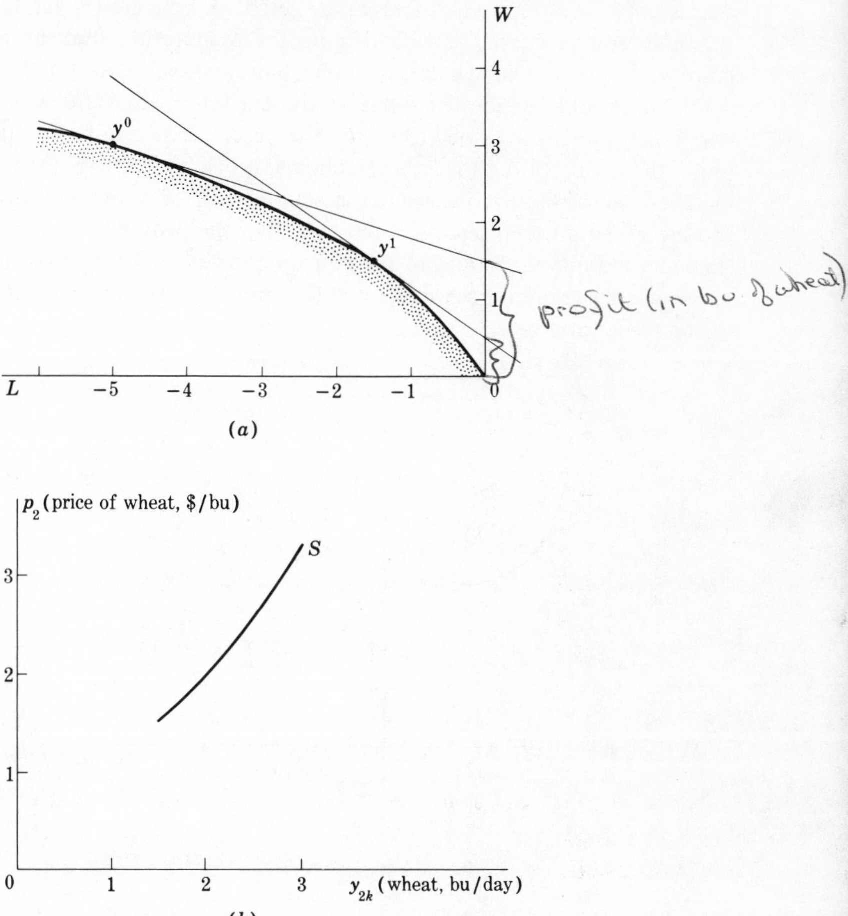

FIGURE 2-4

of wheat for the firm, given the assumption that the price of labor is $1 per hr. Similarly, Fig. 2-5 illustrates the derivation of a demand function of a consumer, including the plotting of a *demand curve* for wheat.

In Fig. 2-5 it is assumed that the consumer has initial holdings of 1.2 bu of wheat; thus the budget line for the consumer, labeled $B(\mathbf{p})$, has x_{2j} intercept 1.2. We assume that the price of labor is fixed at $1 per hr and the price of wheat is allowed to vary from $1 per bu to 50 cents per bu. [The price vectors $\mathbf{p}^0$ and $\mathbf{p}^1$ are then given by $\mathbf{p}^0 = (1,1)$ and $\mathbf{p}^1 = (1,0.5)$.] The utility-maximizing commodity bundles associated with the price vectors $\mathbf{p}^0$ and $\mathbf{p}^1$ are labeled $\mathbf{x}^0$ and $\mathbf{x}^1$, where $\mathbf{x}^0 = (-3.5,4.7)$

and $\mathbf{x}^1 = (-2.5, 6.2)$. The freehand sketch in Fig. 2-5*b* gives the consumer's demand curve for wheat under the assumption that the price of labor is $1 per hr and the consumer has initial wheat stocks of 1.2 bu.

It should be pointed out that the existence of profit- and utility-maximizing vectors associated with the price vectors pictured depends upon the assumption that the boundaries of the appropriate sets are included in those sets, i.e., that the sets are closed. In the case of the producer's supply function, it is required that the production set be closed (include its boundary), and in the consumer's case, it is required that the appropriate preference sets be closed (the indifference curves must belong to the preference sets).

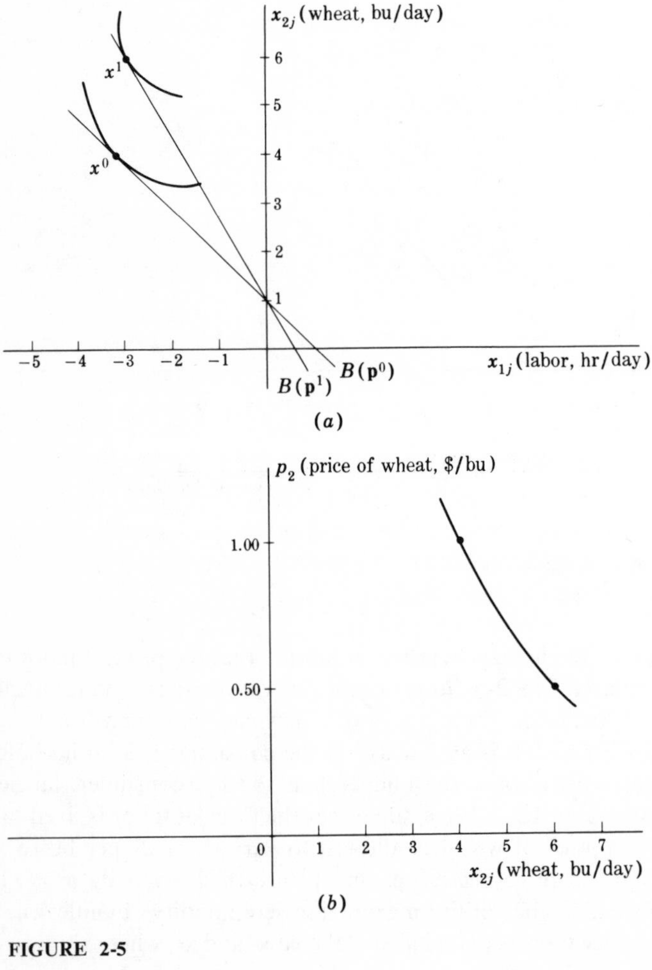

FIGURE 2-5

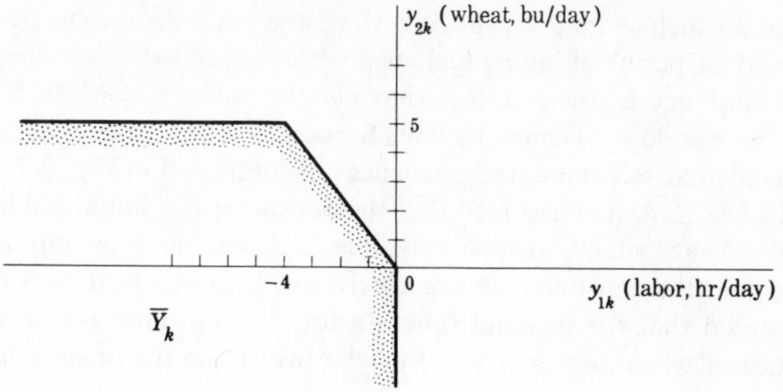

(a)

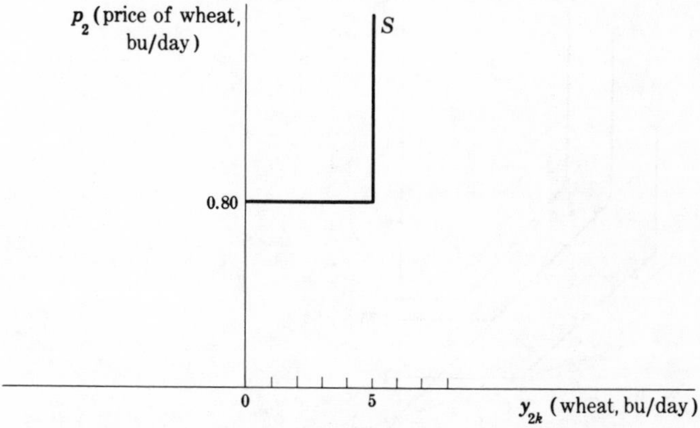

(b)

FIGURE 2-6

The more complicated case of demand and supply correspondences may also be depicted graphically, as shown in Fig. 2-6 for the case of a producer's supply correspondence.

The production set shown in Fig. 2-6*a* has a boundary composed of straight line segments. The existence of a boundary made up of straight line segments leads to a supply function for the producer that is a correspondence (set-valued function) rather than the usual single-valued function. Assuming that the price of labor is $1 per hr, it is clear that as long as the price of wheat is less than 80 cents per bu, every input-output vector on the straight line segment of the boundary extending from the origin to the point (−4,5) is equally desirable, each point giving zero profits. Further, the "kink" at the point (−4,5) leads to the same point (−4,5) being chosen as optimal for any price of wheat above 80 cents per bu. The set-valued characteristic of the supply relation is shown most clearly in a diagram such as that of Fig. 2-6*b*, since at a price of 80 cents per bu of wheat (and \$1 per hr of labor) there is a whole set of values of wheat that might be supplied by the producer, namely any amount of wheat between 0 and 5 bu per day. Demand curves for consumers with perfectly elastic segments also arise from correspondences, as indicated in Fig. 2-7.

In Fig. 2-7*a* it is assumed that the consumer has initial holdings of $\frac{1}{2}$ bu of wheat, which, incidentally, lies outside his consumption set, meaning that the consumer cannot survive on $\frac{1}{2}$ bu of wheat per day. It will be noted that the demand function for the consumer is not defined for a price of wheat higher than \$3 per bu (assuming the price of labor is

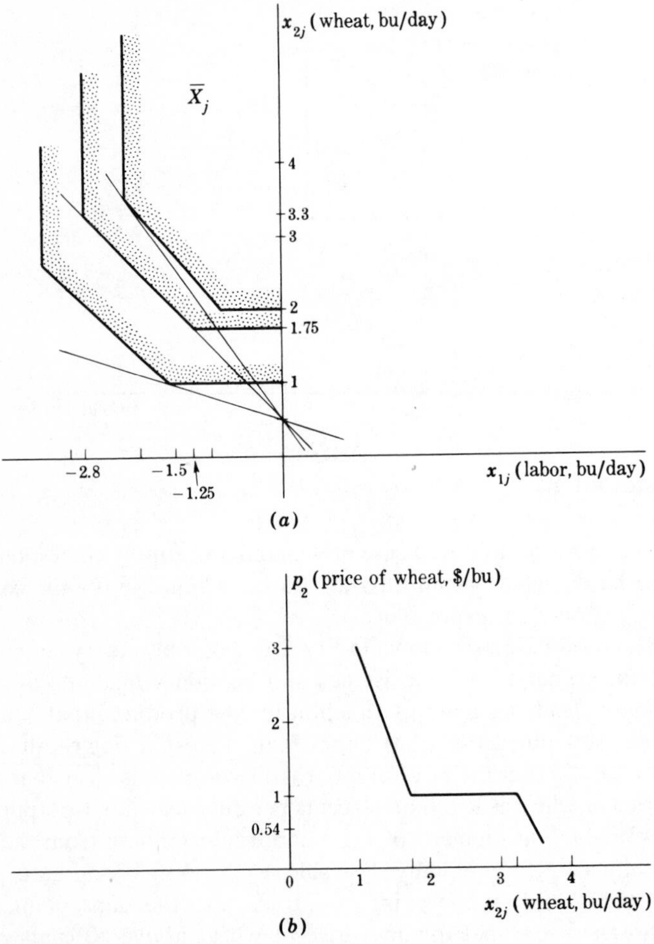

FIGURE 2-7

\$1 per hr), since for such a high price of wheat, the consumer does not survive. The problem of ensuring the existence of demand functions defined over all sets of price vectors will be investigated in Chap. 3. At a price of wheat of \$3 per bu, the budget line touches the lower boundary of the consumption set at the commodity bundle (−1.5,1). As the price of wheat falls, the utility-maximizing commodity bundles lie in the interior of $\bar{X}_j$, and when the price falls to \$1, all commodity bundles lying on the line segment having (−1.25,1.75) and (−2.8,3.3) as end points are utility-maximizing bundles. The graph of the demand curve for wheat by the consumer is shown in Fig. 2-7*b*, again illustrating the set-valued nature of the demand relation, any amount of wheat between 1.75 and 3.3 bu per day being demanded at a price of \$1 per bu of wheat.

Clearly, since aggregate amounts demanded and supplied are obtained by simple summation of individual consumer and producer demand and supply functions, the existence of set-valued functions at the individual level leads to the existence of set-valued functions at the aggregate level. Unless we are willing to rule out the case of perfect substitutes from the point of view of a consumer (straight line segments along indifference curves) and constant returns to scale in production (straight line segments along the boundary of production sets), we must accept the fact that demand and supply correspondences, and not simply single-valued functions, must be taken into account in our analysis.

2-4 CHARACTERISTICS OF DEMAND AND SUPPLY FUNCTIONS IN A NEOCLASSICAL ENVIRONMENT[1]

The neoclassical analysis (analysis of the Hicks-Samuelson type) of individual economic agent behavior and of markets does not utilize the notions of consumption sets and production sets, but rather begins with utility functions defined over commodities and production functions defined over inputs. Under appropriate assumptions on these functions, individual and aggregate demand and supply functions of the "usual" variety are derived.

[1] For a detailed treatment of the subject matter outlined in this section the reader is referred to Paul A. Samuelson, *The Foundations of Economic Analysis*, Harvard University Press, Cambridge, Mass., 1955, and J. R. Hicks, *Value and Capital*, 2d ed.; Oxford University Press, London, 1946. Also J. M. Henderson and R. E. Quandt, *Microeconomic Theory*, McGraw-Hill Book Company, New York, 1958. For a discussion of maximization or minimization of functions, in addition to Appendix A of Samuelson, the reader is referred to Harris Hancock, *Theory of Maxima and Minima*, Dover Publications, Inc., New York, 1960. For the implicit function theorem almost any advanced calculus book should suffice.

One might wonder why economists have bothered to set up an environment different from the neoclassical one. The answer, in large part, is a highly pragmatic one: that environment or framework is chosen that will be more helpful in solving the problem at hand. For example, the set-theoretic approach seems more fruitful than the neoclassical approach for the existence-of-equilibrium problem, while the reverse is true for analysis of the stability of equilibrium.

We have no intention of creating the impression that, in going from one environment to the other in our discussion, we are vacillating between two unrelated sets of concepts. Rather, we take the point of view that, with suitable assumptions, one might construct consumption and production sets having those properties required to give rise to the types of utility and production functions assumed in the neoclassical framework.

We shall devote the remainder of this chapter to a brief review of some of the highlights of supply and demand analysis in the Hicks-Samuelson setting.

The individual consumer is assumed to have a utility function that is twice differentiable, which he maximizes over the commodity bundles that his budget constraint permits him to attain. Formally, if the jth consumer has utility function u^j and income I, and if the prices of the commodities are denoted by $p_1, p_2, \ldots, p_n$, then the problem of the jth consumer is to choose quantities of the commodities $\bar{x}_1, \bar{x}_2, \ldots, \bar{x}_n$ such that $u^j(\bar{x}_1, \bar{x}_2, \ldots, \bar{x}_n) \geq u^j(x_1, x_2, \ldots, x_n)$ for all $x_1, x_2, \ldots, x_n$ satisfying $p_1x_1 + p_2x_2 + \cdots + p_nx_n \leq I$. It is further assumed that the consumer's indifference curves are strictly convex to the origin (the utility function is strictly quasiconcave), that they do not intersect any axis, and that the consumer has no bliss point. It follows that the consumer will spend his entire income and that his utility-maximizing commodity bundle will contain positive amounts of all commodities.

Given this setting of the consumer's decision problem, it might be worthwhile at this point to recall certain results concerning conditions for the existence of maxima and minima for real-valued functions of several real variables having continuous partial derivatives of second order. We recall that for a twice-differentiable real-valued function of several variables, $f(z_1, z_2, \ldots, z_n)$, a necessary condition for f to have a local maximum or minimum at $(\bar{z}_1, \bar{z}_2, \ldots, \bar{z}_n)$ is that the partial derivatives $f_i = \partial f/\partial z_i$ evaluated at this maximizing or minimizing point be zero. If in addition, denoting the second-order partial derivatives $\partial^2 f/(\partial z_i\, \partial z_j)$ by f_{ij},

$$f_{11} < 0 \qquad \begin{vmatrix} f_{11} & f_{12} \\ f_{21} & f_{22} \end{vmatrix} > 0, \ldots, (-1)^n \begin{vmatrix} f_{11} & f_{12} & \cdots & f_{1n} \\ f_{21} & f_{22} & \cdots & f_{2n} \\ \cdots & \cdots & \cdots & \cdots \\ f_{n1} & f_{n2} & \cdots & f_{nn} \end{vmatrix} > 0$$

we have sufficient conditions for the unconstrained function f to have a (local) maximum at $(\bar{z}_1, \bar{z}_2, \ldots, \bar{z}_n)$. Similarly, if in addition to the above necessary first-order conditions we have

$$f_{11} > 0 \qquad \begin{vmatrix} f_{11} & f_{12} \\ f_{21} & f_{22} \end{vmatrix} > 0, \ldots, \begin{vmatrix} f_{11} & f_{12} & \cdots & f_{1n} \\ f_{21} & f_{22} & \cdots & f_{2n} \\ f_{n1} & f_{n2} & \cdots & f_{nn} \end{vmatrix} > 0$$

we have sufficient conditions for a minimum at $(\bar{z}_1, \bar{z}_2, \ldots, \bar{z}_n)$. It is to be understood that all the second partials as well as the first partials in these conditions are evaluated at $(\bar{z}_1, \bar{z}_2, \ldots, \bar{z}_n)$.

We note that the first- and second-order conditions stated are sufficient conditions.[1] However, in our discussion we shall restrict ourselves to considering *regular* maxima and minima, that is, maxima and minima that do satisfy the second- as well as the first-order conditions. We impose this restriction in order to be in a position to treat the stated conditions as necessary as well as sufficient.

More relevant to the problem at hand are the conditions for a regular constrained maximum or minimum. Suppose that the function $f(z_1, z_2, \ldots, z_n)$ is to be maximized subject to the constraint $g(z_1, z_2, \ldots, z_n) = 0$. If f and g have continuous partial derivatives of first and second order, then necessary and sufficient conditions for the constrained maximum or minimum may be stated in terms of the Lagrangian $L = f(z_1, z_2, \ldots, z_n) + \lambda g(z_1, z_2, \ldots, z_n)$. Necessary conditions for a constrained maximum or minimum at the point $(z_1, z_2, \ldots, z_n)$ are that

$$L_i = 0 \qquad i = 1, 2, \ldots, n$$
$$L_\lambda = 0$$

where $L_i = \partial L/\partial z_i$ and $L_\lambda = \partial L/\partial \lambda$, all partials being evaluated at $(\bar{z}_1, \bar{z}_2, \ldots, \bar{z}_n)$.

The determinantal conditions

$$\begin{vmatrix} L_{11} & L_{12} & g_1 \\ L_{21} & L_{22} & g_2 \\ g_1 & g_2 & 0 \end{vmatrix} > 0$$

$$\begin{vmatrix} L_{11} & L_{12} & L_{13} & g_1 \\ L_{21} & L_{22} & L_{23} & g_2 \\ L_{31} & L_{32} & L_{33} & g_3 \\ g_1 & g_2 & g_3 & 0 \end{vmatrix} < 0, \ldots, (-1)^n \begin{vmatrix} L_{11} & L_{12} & \cdots & L_{1n} & g_1 \\ L_{21} & L_{22} & \cdots & L_{2n} & g_2 \\ \cdots & \cdots & \cdots & \cdots & \cdots \\ L_{n1} & L_{n2} & \cdots & L_{nn} & g_n \\ g_1 & g_2 & \cdots & g_n & 0 \end{vmatrix} > 0$$

[1] Consider, for example, the behavior of the function $f(z) = z^2$ in a neighborhood of $z = 0$.

when joined to the first-order conditions, comprise necessary and sufficient conditions for a regular constrained maximum. The negativity of all the determinants, when joined to the first-order conditions, comprise necessary and sufficient conditions for a regular constrained minimum.

Applying the first-order conditions for a constrained maximum to the problem of utility maximization for the consumer (suppressing the j superscript), we have

$$\begin{aligned} &u_i(x_1, x_2, \ldots, x_n) + \lambda p_i = 0 \qquad i = 1, 2, \ldots, n \\ &p_1 x_1 + p_2 x_2 + \cdots + p_n x_n - I = 0 \end{aligned} \tag{1}$$

The goal of the study of consumer behavior is knowledge of the demand functions of the consumer. What we are after are functions in which quantities demanded are explicitly expressed as functions of prices and income. Equations (1) obviously have the situation "turned around" from this desired state of affairs. There is a theorem in calculus that enables us to rectify this. This theorem is called the *implicit function theorem* and asserts the following:

Let $f_k(z_1, z_2, \ldots, z_m, y_1, y_2, \ldots, y_r) = 0$ $(k = 1, 2, \ldots, m)$ be a system of simultaneous equations such that each f_k has continuous first partial derivatives in all the variables. Let $(\bar{z}_1, \bar{z}_2, \ldots, \bar{z}_m, \bar{y}_1, \bar{y}_2, \ldots, \bar{y}_r)$ satisfy the above equations. Then if the determinant

$$\begin{vmatrix} f_{11} & f_{12} & \cdots & f_{1m} \\ f_{21} & f_{22} & \cdots & f_{2m} \\ \cdots & \cdots & \cdots & \cdots \\ f_{m1} & f_{m2} & \cdots & f_{mm} \end{vmatrix} \qquad \text{where } f_{kj} = \frac{\partial f_k}{\partial z_j}$$

is not zero at $(\bar{z}_1, \bar{z}_2, \ldots, \bar{z}_m, \bar{y}_1, \bar{y}_2, \ldots, \bar{y}_r)$, there exist unique functions g_k having continuous first partial derivatives such that $z_k = g_k(y_1, y_2, \ldots, y_r)$ for all $y = (y_1, y_2, \ldots y_r)$ near $\bar{y} = (\bar{y}_1, \bar{y}_2, \ldots, \bar{y}_r)$.

Assuming that the consumer is in a position of utility maximization, we may now apply the implicit function theorem to Eqs. (1). The theorem applied to Eqs. (1) asserts that if

$$\begin{vmatrix} u_{11} & u_{12} & \cdots & u_{1n} & p_1 \\ u_{21} & u_{22} & \cdots & u_{2n} & p_2 \\ \cdots & \cdots & \cdots & \cdots & \cdots \\ u_{n1} & u_{n2} & \cdots & u_{nn} & p_n \\ p_1 & p_2 & & p_n & 0 \end{vmatrix} \neq 0$$

then in a sufficiently small neighborhood of the utility-maximizing point there exists a unique solution

$$\begin{aligned} x_i &= h_i(p_1, p_2, \ldots, p_n, I) \qquad i = 1, 2, \ldots, n \\ \lambda &= h_0(p_1, p_2, \ldots, p_n, I) \end{aligned}$$

The nonzero value of the above determinant is guaranteed by the last of the second-order conditions for a constrained regular maximum, so that we do, in fact, have the h_i functions, which are the demand functions of the consumer. Furthermore, the implicit function theorem asserts the continuity of the demand functions and the existence of continuous first partial derivatives. Also, eliminating λ from the first n equations of (1) shows that the implicitly defined quantities are unaltered if prices and income are multiplied by the same positive constant. Consequently the demand functions obtained are seen to be homogeneous of degree zero in income and prices.

However, in the quest for demand functions, the knowledge of their existence is comforting only up to a point. The step from knowledge of the existence of a demand function to finding the function might be not feasible. Moreover, derivation of particular demand functions for the consumer would depend upon imputing a particular utility function to the consumer. Consequently, one attempts to ascertain properties of demand functions without requiring knowledge of the exact form of these functions.

To be specific, we are interested in the reaction of the utility-maximizing consumer to changes in prices. That is to say, we shall see how the consumer alters the composition of his optimum commodity bundle as a consequence of price changes. If, for example, we are able to say something about the partial derivative $\partial x_i/\partial p_j$ (the rate of change of the amount of the ith commodity in the consumer's optimum commodity bundle with respect to the jth price), then to that extent we have garnered some information about the demand function of the consumer for the ith commodity. We follow the usual Hicks-Samuelson procedure in investigating the properties of $\partial x_i/\partial p_j$.

The approach is to consider the $n + 1$ equations (equilibrium conditions) that comprise the first-order conditions for the consumer's constrained maximization and to permit all the variables to vary, insisting only that the consumer still be in a position of maximizing his utility function subject to the budget constraint (the equilibrium conditions still hold).

Operationally this means that the total differentials of each of the $n + 1$ equations must equal zero. Denoting $\partial u/(\partial x_i\, \partial x_j)$ by u_{ij}, we have

$$\begin{aligned}
&u_{11}\,dx_1 + u_{12}\,dx_2 + \cdots + u_{1i}\,dx_i + \cdots + u_{1n}\,dx_n + p_1\,d\lambda = -\lambda\,dp_1\\
&u_{21}\,dx_1 + u_{22}\,dx_2 + \cdots + u_{2i}\,dx_i + \cdots + u_{2n}\,dx_n + p_2\,d\lambda = -\lambda\,dp_2\\
&u_{j1}\,dx_1 + u_{j2}\,dx_2 + \cdots + u_{ji}\,dx_i + \cdots + u_{jn}\,dx_n + p_j\,d\lambda = -\lambda\,dp_j\\
&\cdots\cdots\cdots\cdots\cdots\cdots\cdots\cdots\cdots\cdots\cdots\cdots\\
&u_{n1}\,dx_1 + u_{n2}\,dx_2 + \cdots + u_{ni}\,dx_i + \cdots + u_{nn}\,dx_n + p_n\,d\lambda = -\lambda\,dp_n\\
&p_1\,dx_1 + p_2\,dx_2 + \cdots + p_i\,dx_i + \cdots + p_n\,dx_n + 0\,d\lambda = dI\\
&\qquad\qquad\qquad\qquad - (x_1\,dp_1 + x_2\,dp_2 + \cdots + x_n\,dp_n)
\end{aligned}$$

Using Cramer's rule to solve for dx_i, and denoting the cofactor of the

i, j element in the matrix of coefficients of the above equations by D_{ij}, we have, where D stands for the determinant formed from the matrix of coefficients,

$$dx_i = \frac{\begin{array}{r}-\lambda\, dp_1 D_{1i} - \lambda\, dp_2 D_{2i} - \cdots - \lambda\, dp_j D_{ji} - \cdots - \lambda\, dp_n D_{ni} \\ + (dI - x_1\, dp_1 - \cdots - x_n\, dp_n) D_{n+1,i}\end{array}}{D}$$

Taking the partial derivative $\partial x_i / \partial p_j$, we have

$$\frac{\partial x_i}{\partial p_j} = \frac{-\lambda D_{ji} - x_j D_{n+1,i}}{D}$$

Similarly,

$$\frac{\partial x_i}{\partial I} = \frac{D_{n+1,i}}{D}$$

It follows that

$$\frac{-x_j D_{n+1,i}}{D} = -x_j \frac{\partial x_i}{\partial I} \qquad \text{and} \qquad \frac{-\lambda D_{ji}}{D} = \frac{\partial x_i}{\partial p_j}$$

utility being constant. Therefore

$$\frac{\partial x_i}{\partial p_j} = \left(\frac{\partial x_i}{\partial p_j}\right)_{u=u_0} - x_j \frac{\partial x_i}{\partial I}$$

This equation is called Slutsky's equation, and $S_{ij} \equiv (\partial x_i / \partial p_j)_{u=u_0}$ is called the substitution or Slutsky term. We have thus reached the familiar proposition that the effect of a change in the price of a commodity on the quantity of the commodity purchased by the consumer may be expressed as the sum of two distinct effects: the *substitution effect* and the *income effect*.

A case of particular interest, especially from the point of view of Marshallian partial equilibrium analysis, is that in which we study the effect of a change in the price of a commodity on the quantity of the commodity consumed. Setting $i = j$ in the formula for $\partial x_i / \partial p_j$, we have

$$\frac{\partial x_i}{\partial p_i} = \frac{-\lambda D_{ii}}{D} - \frac{x_i D_{n+1,i}}{D}$$

From the second-order conditions for a regular constrained maximum, we have that the substitution term has to be negative (because D_{ii} is a principal minor of order one less than D and we are free to number the commodities any way we please). Consequently, a necessary, but not sufficient, condition for the *law of demand* to be violated (for Giffen's paradox to occur) is that the commodity have a negative income effect (be an inferior good).

If we consider the effect of a change in the price of some commodity on the quantity demanded of some other commodity, then our theory provides no information as to the sign of the substitution term. In fact, the sign of the substitution term is one way to define what is meant by substitutability and complementarity between commodities.[1] It follows from the assumption of continuous second-order partial derivatives of the utility function that the matrix from which D was formed is symmetric. Consequently $D_{ij} = D_{ji}$, which immediately yields $S_{ij} = S_{ji}$.

Another approach that may be taken in deriving consumer demand functions is that of revealed preference.[2] Let $\mathbf{x}^a$, an n-dimensional vector, denote the quantities of the n commodities in the economy purchased by the individual when the prevailing prices are given by the n-dimensional vector $\mathbf{p}^a$. We define $\mathbf{x}^b$ and $\mathbf{p}^b$ in completely analogous fashion. If, using the vector-product notation discussed in Sec. 1-2, $\mathbf{p}^a \cdot \mathbf{x}^b \leq \mathbf{p}^a \cdot \mathbf{x}^a$ for $\mathbf{x}^b \neq \mathbf{x}^a$, then commodity bundle $\mathbf{x}^a$ is said to be *revealed preferred* to $\mathbf{x}^b$. In other words, since the consumer could have purchased $\mathbf{x}^b$ and did not, he must prefer $\mathbf{x}^a$ to $\mathbf{x}^b$. The *weak axiom of revealed preference* asserts that not both $\mathbf{x}^a$ revealed preferred to $\mathbf{x}^b$ and $\mathbf{x}^b$ revealed preferred to $\mathbf{x}^a$ can hold, or $\mathbf{p}^a \cdot \mathbf{x}^b \leq \mathbf{p}^a \cdot \mathbf{x}^a$ implies $\mathbf{p}^b \cdot \mathbf{x}^b < \mathbf{p}^b \cdot \mathbf{x}^a$, for $\mathbf{x}^b \neq \mathbf{x}^a$. Samuelson has shown that the single-valuedness and homogeneity properties of demand functions, as well as Slutsky's equation, may be derived from the weak axiom.[3]

At this point we might ask the question whether or not the preference pattern established by behavior in accordance with the weak axiom of revealed preference is consistent with the notion of utility, in that it is possible to construct a utility function out of the information provided by the behavior of the consumer. This problem is referred to in the literature as the "integrability" problem, since mathematically the problem is that of asking whether a certain differential equation is integrable. It turns out that the weak axiom is not adequate to guarantee the existence of a utility function for the consumer, if there are more than two commodities.

[1] If the substitution term is positive, the commodities are said to be substitutes. If the substitution term is negative, the commodities are said to be complements. Sometimes the income term is not excluded in discussing substitutability and complementarity. In this case, so as to avoid confusion, we shall follow the convention of speaking of *gross* substitutes or complements.

[2] This approach was introduced by Samuelson, apparently to replace the utility concept, in Note on the Pure Theory of Consumer's Behavior, *Economica*, pp. 61–71, 1938. See also Chap. 5.

[3] See pp. 107–116 of the *Foundations*.

Houthakker has formulated a revealed preference axiom involving more than two commodity bundles and two price vectors.[1] This is referred to as the *strong axiom of revealed preference* and asserts: If $\mathbf{x}^a, \mathbf{x}^b, \ldots, \mathbf{x}^r$ are commodity bundles, at least two of which are distinct, and if $\mathbf{p}^a, \mathbf{p}^b, \ldots, \mathbf{p}^r$ are the associated price vectors, then the chain $\mathbf{p}^a \cdot \mathbf{x}^b \leq \mathbf{p}^a \cdot \mathbf{x}^a, \mathbf{p}^b \cdot \mathbf{x}^c \leq \mathbf{p}^b \cdot \mathbf{x}^b, \ldots, \mathbf{p}^{r-1} \cdot \mathbf{x}^{r-1} \leq \mathbf{p}^r \cdot \mathbf{x}^r$ implies $\mathbf{p}^r \cdot \mathbf{x}^r < \mathbf{p}^r \cdot \mathbf{x}^a$, for all positive integers r. Houthakker has shown that this axiom is equivalent to the existence of a utility function for the consumer. Uzawa has discussed the logical relationship between the strong and weak axioms of revealed preference and, in particular, has shown that, under appropriate restrictions, the two forms of the axiom are logically equivalent.[2]

The supply function of the individual producer is obtained in the Hicks-Samuelson setting in a manner formally very similar to that used in obtaining the demand functions of the consumer. First, the *cost function* is derived by finding the lowest-cost way of producing every output. This is approached through minimization of expenditures subject to an output constraint. Formally, if the production function of the firm is given by $x = F(v_1, v_2, \ldots, v_s)$, and the prices of the inputs are denoted by $p_1, p_2, \ldots, p_s$, then the cost function is obtained by minimizing $\sum_{k=1}^{s} p_k v_k$ subject to $x = F(v_1, v_2, \ldots, v_s)$. Since with each possible output there is, in this manner, associated a (minimum for that output) cost, we have defined a function $C(x)$ mapping output into cost. $C(x)$ is of course the cost function of the firm. If the price of the commodity being produced is denoted by p, then profits are maximized—assuming that the second-order conditions for an unconstrained maximum are satisfied—at the output such that $C'(x) = p$.

Market demand and supply functions may be obtained by the usual simple aggregating procedure from individual demand and supply functions. At each set of prices the quantity of the commodity demanded by all consumers is equal to the sum of the quantities demanded by the consumers individually at that set of prices. Similarly, at each price set, the quantity supplied by the aggregate of firms producing the commodity (the industry) is equal to the sum of the quantities supplied by the individual firms at the given prices. Certain properties of market demand and supply functions follow directly from characteristics of individual

[1] H. S. Houthakker, Revealed Preference and the Utility Function, *Economica*, vol. 17, pp. 159–175, 1950. See also in the same volume Paul A. Samuelson, The Problem of Integrability in Utility Theory, pp. 355–386.

[2] Hirofumi Uzawa, Preference and Rational Choice in the Theory of Consumption, *Proceedings of a Symposium on Mathematical Methods in the Social Sciences*, Stanford University Press, Palo Alto, Calif., 1960.

demand and supply functions. For example, single-valuedness and homogeneity properties of "aggregate" functions are obvious if the individual functions have these properties. Also, clearly, if the *law of demand* (absence of Giffen's paradox) holds for each individual demand function, the usual Marshallian market demand curves will be downward sloping.

In bringing this section and this chapter to a close, we might point out that validity of the law of demand for each consumer, while sufficient, is not necessary for the law of demand to hold for the market demand function. To see this one need only consider a case in which the individual income effects "net out" to zero, leaving a market demand curve made up entirely of individual substitution terms.

THREE

COMPETITIVE EQUILIBRIUM: EXISTENCE AND UNIQUENESS

3-1 DEFINITION OF COMPETITIVE EQUILIBRIUM

The basic concept in the economic study of a commodity is the concept of a market. Essentially, a market consists of a market demand function and a market supply function, where the market demand function is defined by aggregating the quantities demanded by the individual economic agents and the market supply function is defined by aggregating .the quantities supplied by the individual economic agents. Since for each individual economic agent the demand function for a commodity and the supply function for a commodity are functions having the price of the commodity as an independent variable, it is clear that the market demand and supply functions also have price as an independent variable.

We say that a positive equilibrium price exists in a market if there is a positive price such that the market quantity demanded and the market quantity supplied are equal at that price. Since both the market demand function and the market supply function map prices into quantities, we might define a new function by subtracting the quantity supplied on the market from the quantity demanded on the market at each price. This new function is called the *excess demand function* and also maps prices into quantities. Using the notion of excess demand function, we could rephrase the definition of a positive equilibrium price for a commodity as a positive price such that the excess demand function evaluated at this price is zero.

Graphically, a market is represented by the usual demand and supply curves drawn in the plane (euclidean two-space) with the axes representing prices and quantities. Figure 3-1*a* depicts the market for a commodity in terms of the supply and demand curves. As drawn, the

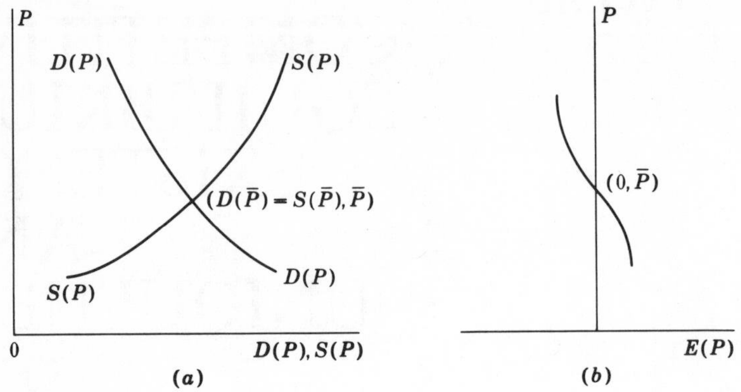

FIGURE 3-1

market is seen to have one and only one equilibrium price. Figure 3-1*b* depicts the same market situation in terms of the excess demand curve.[1]

If $D(P)$ is the function whose graph is the demand curve of Fig. 3-1*a*, and $S(P)$ is the function whose graph is the supply curve of Fig. 3-1*a*, then the equilibrium price $\bar{P}$ is seen to have the property that $D(\bar{P}) = S(\bar{P})$. Furthermore, $E(P)$, the excess demand function graphed in Fig. 3-1*b*, is defined by $E(P) = D(P) - S(P)$. In terms of $E(P)$ we see that the equilibrium price $\bar{P}$ is defined by $E(\bar{P}) = 0$.

Requiring that an equilibrium price in a market be positive is overly restrictive in that this requirement rules out the possibility of equilibrium being defined in the case of an abundant good. Rather than defining an equilibrium price as a positive price that clears the market, we might define an equilibrium price as a nonnegative price such that at this price the quantity demanded is no greater than the quantity supplied. For a single market, then, we say that $\bar{P} \geqq 0$ is an equilibrium price if $D(\bar{P}) \leqq S(\bar{P})$ and $D(\bar{P}) < S(\bar{P})$ implies $\bar{P} = 0$.

In terms of this less restrictive definition of a market equilibrium, it is easy to see that the supply and demand curves shown in Fig. 3-2*a*, with the corresponding excess demand curve shown in Fig. 3-2*b*, exhibit a unique equilibrium price of zero, while the supply and demand curves shown in Fig. 3-2*c*, with the corresponding excess demand curve shown in Fig. 3-2*d*, exhibit no equilibrium price at all.

[1] We do not mean to suggest that knowledge of the excess demand function is equivalent to knowledge of the market demand and supply functions. Perusal of Fig. 3-1 with respect to investigating the effect of a tax on the commodity depicted or of a change in income or tastes of individuals will quickly show that they are not equivalent. This is to be expected on logical grounds, since the excess demand function is an aggregate of the demand and supply function, the identity of the demand and supply functions being lost in the aggregation process.

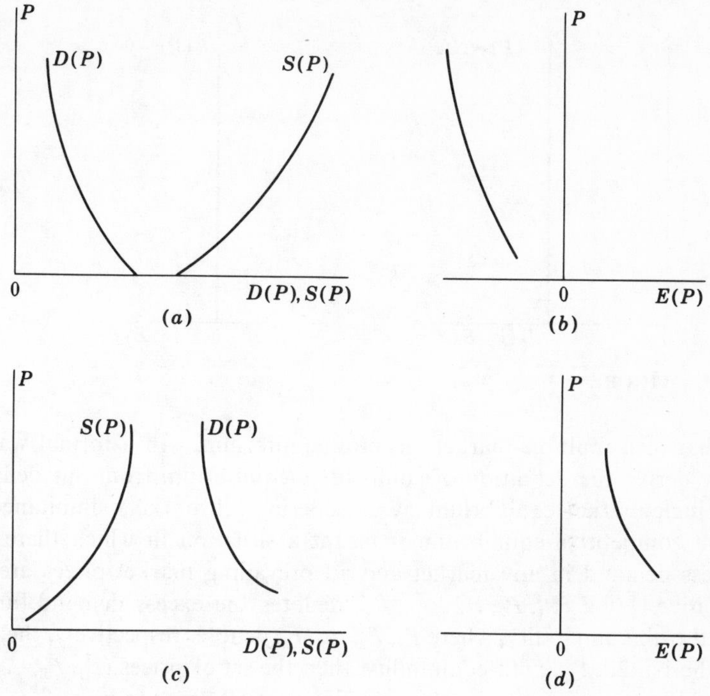

FIGURE 3-2

We now consider the rather odd case in which the market demand function and the market supply function are perfectly inelastic and coincident. It is clear that both the demand function and the supply function defined are functions rather than correspondences, because each maps a price into a single quantity value.[1] The interesting thing about this oddity from the point of view of existence of equilibrium in a market is that, since the quantity demanded is equal to the quantity supplied at each nonnegative price, every nonnegative price is an equilibrium price. In terms of the excess demand function corresponding to these demand and supply curves, we see that the excess demand function maps every price into the number zero. The demand and supply curves for this case and the corresponding excess demand curve are shown in Fig. 3-3.

The notion of equilibrium that we have been discussing is that of a single-market, partial equilibrium. The notion of competitive equilibrium

[1] The fact that each price is mapped into the same quantity by these functions means that each is a special kind of function having a single point as its range. Such a function is called a constant function. In this case, since both the supply and the demand function have the same domain and the same range consisting of a single point, the two functions are mathematically identical.

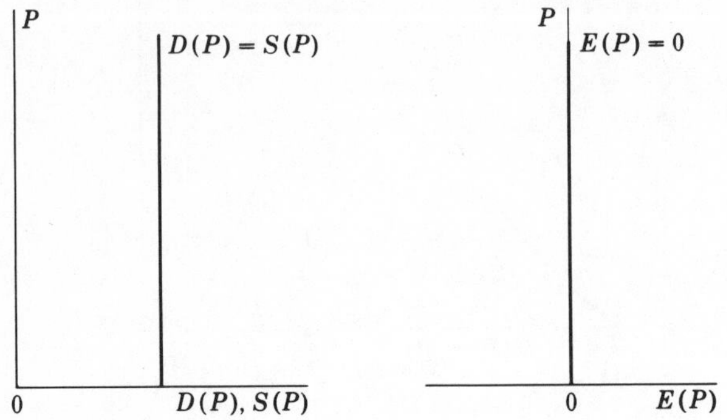

FIGURE 3-3

is that of a multiple-market, general equilibrium. In a formal way, we may derive the definition of competitive equilibrium from our definition of single-market equilibrium by considering all markets simultaneously. By a competitive equilibrium is meant a situation in which there is no excess demand in any market and all prevailing market prices are non-negative. If $E_i(P_1, P_2, P_3, \ldots, P_n)$ denotes the excess demand function for the ith commodity, where $P_1, P_2, \ldots P_n$ denote, respectively, the prices of the 1st, 2d, . . . , nth commodity, then the set of prices $(\bar{P}_1, \bar{P}_2, \ldots, \bar{P}_n)$ is said to be an equilibrium set of prices not all equal to zero if

$$E_i(\bar{P}_1, \bar{P}_2, \ldots, \bar{P}_n) \leqq 0 \qquad \text{for } \bar{P}_i \geqq 0;\ i = 1, 2, \ldots, n;\ \bar{P}_i > 0 \text{ for some } i \tag{1}$$

$$E_i(\bar{P}_1, \bar{P}_2, \ldots, \bar{P}_n) < 0 \qquad \text{implies } \bar{P}_i = 0 \tag{2}$$

Abbreviating this definition by using vector notation, we say a price vector $\bar{\mathbf{P}} = (\bar{P}_1, \bar{P}_2, \ldots, \bar{P}_n)$ is an equilibrium price vector if

$$E(\bar{\mathbf{P}}) \leqq \mathbf{0}_n \qquad \text{for } \bar{\mathbf{P}} \geq \mathbf{0}_n\dagger \tag{1'}$$

$$E_i(\bar{\mathbf{P}}) < 0 \text{ implies } \bar{P}_i = 0 \qquad \text{where } E(\bar{\mathbf{P}}) = (E_1(\bar{\mathbf{P}}), E_2(\bar{\mathbf{P}}), \ldots, E_n(\bar{\mathbf{P}})) \tag{2'}$$

3-2 THE PROBLEM OF LOGICAL CONSISTENCY

In our discussion of the single market, in addition to the "normal" supply and demand diagram, in which the supply and demand curves intersected in a unique point, we also found it easy to draw the curves such that they

† We use the symbol $\mathbf{0}_n$ to denote the zero vector (or origin) in n-space. Thus $\mathbf{0}_n$ may be thought of as an n-tuple having zero for each of its components. It is common usage to denote the fact that a given vector $\mathbf{x}$ has no negative components and at least one positive component simply by $\mathbf{x} \geq 0$. However, for the sake of consistency with the ordering on vectors established in Chap. 1, we use the notation of Eq. (1′).

intersected in an infinity of points or in no points at all. These three diagrams correspond to situations in which there is a unique market equilibrium price, there are an infinite number of equilibrium prices in the market, and there is no equilibrium price in the market. Furthermore, there is no apparent reason why the "normal" situation of a unique equilibrium price should be considered *prima facie* any more normal or realistic than a situation of multiple equilibrium prices or a situation of no equilibrium at all.

Quite to the contrary, if one dwells on the derivation of market demand and supply functions from individual maximizing behavior, it seems clear that there need not be a single price at which each consumer is maximizing utility, each producer is maximizing profits, and the market is cleared. To expect that there will be a unique price having these properties is to expect a great deal indeed.

If it could be demonstrated that the set of equilibrium prices in a market was not empty (i.e., that there was at least one equilibrium price), then it could be said that the existence of an equilibrium price had been demonstrated. To say that the equilibrium price is unique, it would further have to be demonstrated that there is exactly one equilibrium price in the market. Uniqueness clearly goes beyond existence in strength of assertion.

For the partial equilibrium case of a single market, once we have derived the market excess demand function from the maximizing behavior of the individual economic agents, the set of equilibrium prices for the market could be viewed as the set of solutions to the equation $E(P) = 0$. Once we go over to the general equilibrium case of multiple markets, the situation becomes much more complex. Maximizing behavior on the part of the individual economic agents gives rise to an excess demand function in each of the n markets. The set of equilibrium price vectors could be viewed as the set of solutions to the n simultaneous equations $E_i(P_1, P_2, \ldots, P_n) = 0$ $(i = 1, 2, \ldots, n.)$† That there is a nonempty set of solutions to these equations is far from obvious. The mere fact that there are as many unknowns as there are equations is not very reassuring, as is easily seen by considering the equations $x_1 + x_2 = 0$ and $x_1 + x_2 = 1$.

It should be clear that the "existence" of competitive equilibrium being discussed is the logical existence. In speaking of demonstrating the existence of competitive equilibrium, we are not speaking of an empirical test of the applicability of the model of perfect competition to reality. We are not here concerned with whether all industries are made up of

† For simplicity of exposition we have ignored, both here and in the case of the single market above, the possibility of there being negative excess demand in a market with an equilibrium price of zero for that commodity.

"atomistic" firms who treat prices as data rather than as policy variables. For important as these matters may be, our concern with the existence of competitive equilibrium is rather more basic. Given the competitive model, we are concerned with the logical consistency within the model of the notion of competitive equilibrium. There would, after all, be very little merit in worrying about the empirical validity of the notion of competitive equilibrium if the notion, by its very definition, carried within itself contradictions or inconsistencies so as to render the class of objects which it is supposed to identify empty on purely logical grounds.

Illustrations of equilibrium in terms of market supply and demand curves or excess demand curves do not exhibit the underlying maximizing behavior on the part of individual economic agents. To point out the relationship of individual maximizing behavior to competitive equilibrium for a simple two-commodity, two-person case, we use the familiar Edgeworth box diagram. The Edgeworth box is a model of pure trade or exchange, that is, a model in which economic activity consists entirely of trading and consuming, to the exclusion of production.

We assume that Mr. A has an endowment of X_{1A}^0 units of commodity 1 and X_{2A}^0 units of commodity 2. Similarly, we assume that Mr. B has an endowment of X_{1B}^0 units of commodity 1 and X_{2B}^0 units of commodity 2. Since this is a model with no production, clearly all trade is subject to the constraint that the total amounts of the two commodities be constant. More specifically, given Mr. A's endowment (X_{1A}^0, X_{2A}^0) and Mr. B's endowment of (X_{1B}^0, X_{2B}^0), the total amount of commodity 1 in the economy before and after trade is given by $X_1^0 = X_{1A}^0 + X_{1B}^0$, and the total amount of commodity 2 in the economy before and after trade is given by $X_2^0 = X_{2A}^0 + X_{2B}^0$.

It follows that the only possible states of the economy are those represented by a set of points contained in a rectangle having dimensions X_1^0 by X_2^0. In Fig. 3-4 we have drawn a rectangle having horizontal dimension X_1^0 and vertical dimension X_2^0. The quantities X_{1A} are measured from left to right along the horizontal axis, and the quantities X_{1B} are measured from right to left along the horizontal axis. Similarly, the quantities X_{2A} are measured from bottom to top along the vertical axis, and the quantities X_{2B} are measured from top to bottom along the vertical axis. Given the dimensions X_1^0 and X_2^0 of the box, it is apparent that for any state of the economy represented by a point in the box, $X_{1A} + X_{1B} = X_1^0$ and $X_{2A} + X_{2B} = X_2^0$. For the point (X_1^0, X_2^0) in Fig. 3-4 we see that Mr. A's holdings are X_{1A}^0 units of commodity 1 and X_{2A}^0 units of commodity 2, while Mr. B's holdings are X_{1B}^0 units of commodity 1 and X_{2B}^0 units of commodity 2.

In Fig. 3-5 we have sketched elements of the indifference map of Mr. A and Mr. B. Starting at the lower lefthand corner (labeled A), the

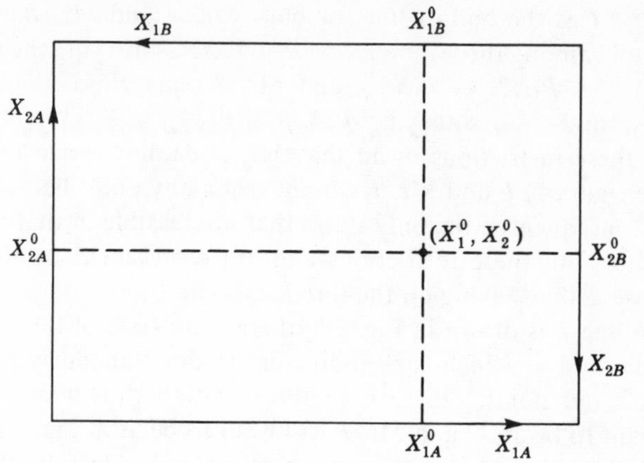

FIGURE 3-4

direction of increasing preference for Mr. *A* is upward and to the right. Similarly, starting at the upper righthand corner (labeled *B*), the direction of increasing preference for Mr. *B* is downward and to the left. Assuming that the price of commodity 1 is P_1 and the price of commodity 2 is P_2, we may represent the set of possible trades as a straight line whose slope is the negative of the ratio of P_1 to P_2. If the state of the economy before trade is represented by the point (X_1^0, X_2^0), then the set of all states of the economy attainable through trade for a given price ratio P_1/P_2 is uniquely represented by the straight line through (X_1^0, X_2^0), having slope $-P_1/P_2$.

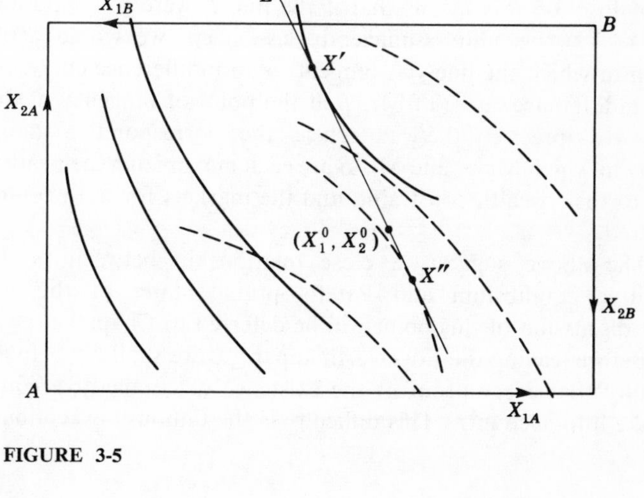

FIGURE 3-5

The line L is the budget line for both Mr. A and Mr. B. Mr. A may choose only among those amounts X_{1A} and X_{2A} satisfying the relation $P_1X_{1A} + P_2X_{2A} \leq P_1X_{1A}^0 + P_2X_{2A}^0$, and Mr. B may choose only those amounts X_{1B} and X_{2B} satisfying $P_1X_{1B} + P_2X_{2B} \leq P_1X_{1B}^0 + P_2X_{2B}^0$. Graphically, these restrictions mean that Mr. A cannot reach any point above (to the right of) L and Mr. B cannot reach any point below (to the left of) L. Consequently, the only states that are feasible in that they are consistent with both these restrictions and are represented by the same point are those actually lying on the line L.

As the line L is drawn in Fig. 3-5, there is no state of the economy that is feasible and at which each individual is simultaneously choosing his most preferred point. In fact, in the situation drawn in Fig. 3-5, Mr. A will want to be at X' and Mr. B will want to be at X'', giving rise to a total demand for commodity 2 in excess of X_2^0 and a demand for commodity 1 less than X_1^0.

We now consider the set of points corresponding to states of the economy having a particular property. To be exact, we are interested in the set of points in our Edgeworth diagram corresponding to those states of the economy such that it would be impossible to alter the holdings of Mr. A and Mr. B so as to make at least one of them better off without, in doing so, making the other worse off. A state of the economy having this property is called a Pareto optimum. The concept of Pareto optimality is discussed in greater detail in Chap. 4, but for the simple case depicted in Fig. 3-5, it is easy to see that the set of Pareto optima is represented by the set of tangencies of the indifference curves of Mr. A and Mr. B.

Furthermore, examination of Fig. 3-5 reveals that if P_1 were to fall sufficiently, we would come up with an equilibrium price vector. In terms of Fig. 3-5 this means that if the line L were to rotate about the point (X_1^0,X_2^0), becoming sufficiently less steep, we would arrive at a situation in which the line was tangent to an indifference curve of Mr. A and an indifference curve of Mr. B at the point of tangency of these two curves. It is precisely these tangencies that correspond to states of the economy in which Mr. A and Mr. B are each maximizing their satisfactions subject to their wealth constraint, and the markets for both commodities are cleared.

The above suggests a close relationship between positions of competitive equilibrium and Pareto-optimal states of the economy. Further discussion of this point will be deferred to Chap. 4.

Before leaving the Edgeworth apparatus we shall use it to illustrate a difficulty that every proof of the existence of competitive equilibrium must take into account. This difficulty is the famous "exceptional case"

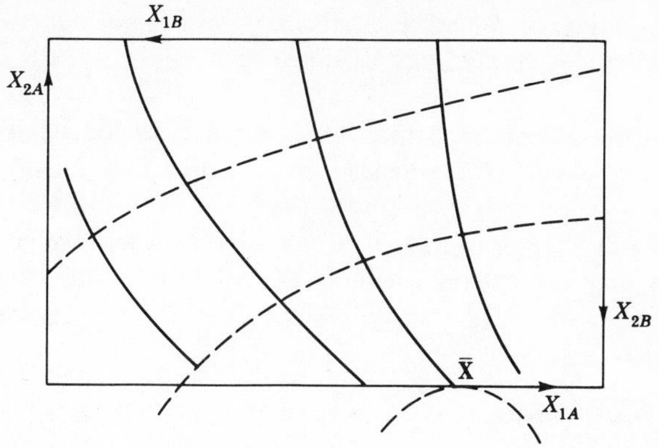

FIGURE 3-6

of the literature. We use the illustration due to Arrow[1] to discuss this difficulty.

Let the indifference map for Mr. *A* and Mr. *B* be as in Fig. 3-6. Consider the state of the economy represented by the point $\bar{\mathbf{X}}$. It is clear from the diagram that this state is a Pareto optimum. It is also clear that Mr. *B* will be maximizing his satisfaction, given the state $\bar{\mathbf{X}}$, only if the price of commodity 1 is zero.[2] However, if the price of commodity 1 is zero, Mr *A* will not be satisfied with the amount of commodity 1 that he has in state of the economy $\bar{\mathbf{X}}$. Maximizing behavior on the part of Mr. *A* would require that he want more of commodity 1 than $\bar{X}_{1A}$. We are forced to conclude that there is no price vector that would serve as an equilibrium price vector for the state of the economy denoted by $\bar{\mathbf{X}}$, even though $\bar{\mathbf{X}}$ represents a Pareto optimum. corner maximum

From Fig. 3-6 it appears that the anomalous character of the point $\bar{\mathbf{X}}$ may be summarized in terms of any of the following observations:

1. There is no possible state of the economy such that Mr. *A*'s holdings of commodity 2 would be less than they are in the state $\bar{\mathbf{X}}$. Consequently, for some set of nonnegative prices, namely any set such that $P_1 = 0$, the point $\bar{\mathbf{X}}$ has the property that the value of Mr. *A*'s holdings in the state $\bar{\mathbf{X}}$ is the minimum value over the entire set of possible consumptions of Mr. *A*, for that set of prices.

[1] Kenneth J. Arrow, An Extension of the Basic Theorems of Classical Welfare Economics, in J. Neyman (ed.), *Proceedings of the Second Berkeley Symposium on Mathematical Statistics and Probability*, pp. 507–532, University of California Press, Berkeley, 1951.

[2] $P_1 = 0$ means that the price line is a horizontal line.

2. The marginal utility of commodity 1 for Mr. *B* is not positive in state $\bar{\mathbf{X}}$.
3. Mr. *A* has nothing desired by Mr. *B* in state $\bar{\mathbf{X}}$.

It therefore appears that the "exceptional case" depicted in two dimensions in Fig. 3-6 could be ruled out by assuming that (1), (2), and (3) do not hold.

Later in this chapter more will be said about the specific manner in which the various proofs of the existence of competitive equilibrium take care of the "exceptional case."

3-3 FIXED-POINT THEOREMS AND RELATED MATHEMATICAL TOOLS

Since the discussion of the existence of competitive equilibrium in the previous section was carried on largely in graphic form, the dimensionality of the problem was sharply restricted. There was really no way to represent in diagrams the fact that there are many commodities, many producers, and many customers simultaneously involved in the general equilibrium situation that is our concern. It follows that use of diagrams such as those of Sec. 3-2, while hopefully of some heuristic value, are inadequate for a discussion of the existence question in all its multidimensionality.

Since the existence of competitive equilibrium is a deep question, it is not surprising that the mathematical tools used to answer this question are powerful tools. Among the main studies of competitive equilibrium that have been made since the time of Walras, the kind of mathematical device used, with one notable exception, has been a member of the class of theorems called *fixed-point* theorems. The reason for the name "fixed-point" becomes obvious upon statement of any of this class of theorems.

Possibly the most widely applied of the fixed-point theorems is the Brouwer theorem. The Brouwer fixed-point theorem asserts that any continuous mapping of a closed and bounded convex set in euclidean space into itself maps at least one point into itself.[1] As an example we consider any continuous mapping of the closed unit interval on the real line into itself.

Since the closed unit interval (which is denoted by [0,1]) is a closed and bounded set in euclidean one-space, Brouwer's theorem asserts that any continuous function $f:[0,1] \rightarrow [0,1]$ leaves at least one point unchanged. The geometric interpretation of this is that any continuous curve originating on the line $x = 0$ and terminating on the line $x = 1$ and confined to

[1] That is, if f is a continuous function from a closed bounded convex set of euclidean space C into itself, then there exists $\hat{x} \in C$, such that $f(\hat{x}) = \hat{x}$.

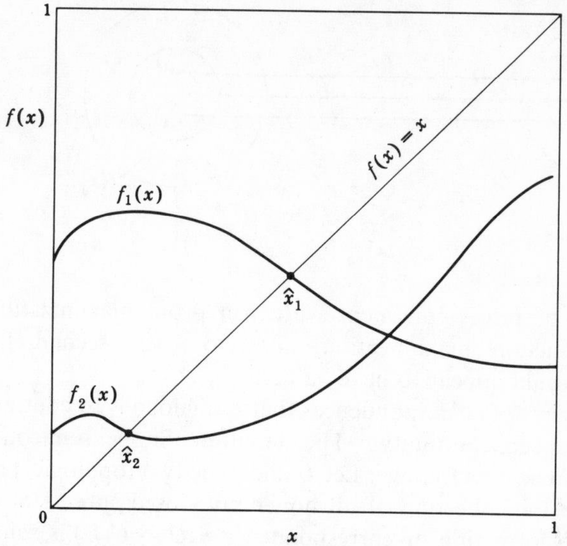

FIGURE 3-7

the unit square must intersect the diagonal at least once. Figure 3-7 shows examples of continuous mappings from [0,1] into [0,1]. f_1 and f_2 are each seen to have exactly one fixed point. These are labeled $\hat{x}_1$ and $\hat{x}_2$, respectively. This is clear because the diagonal is the graph of the equation $f(x) = x$; thus a fixed point of a function may be identified graphically as the intersection of the graph of the function with the diagonal.[1]

The Brouwer theorem has been generalized in two directions. The underlying space in which the set constituting the domain and the range of the function is imbedded has been generalized away from euclidean space. Also, the mapping in the theorem has been generalized from a continuous function to an upper semicontinuous correspondence. Since for proving the existence of competitive equilibrium it is perfectly adequate to think of the commodity space as being contained in euclidean space, the first of these lines of generalization will be of little interest to us. However, it will be recalled from Chap. 1 that if we permit regions of constant returns for producers, and do not insist on strictly convex preferences for consumers, we can expect more than one state of the economy

[1] That the Brouwer theorem says nothing about uniqueness of a fixed point immediately follows from the realization that the function $f(x) = x$ is also a continuous function on [0,1]. For the function $f(x) = x$, every point in the interval [0,1] is a fixed point.

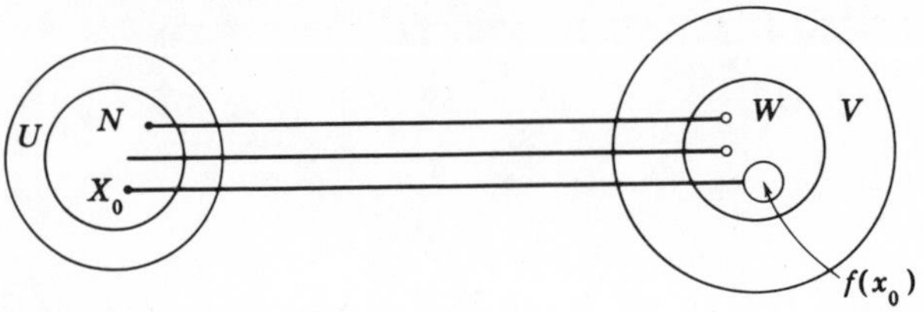

FIGURE 3-8

for a given set of prices consistent with firm profit maximization and consumer satisfaction maximization. Therefore the second line of generalization would appear to have value for us.

The property of correspondences that is analogous to continuity of functions is upper semicontinuity. The definition of upper semicontinuity of a correspondence is as follows: Let U and V be two topological spaces, and let $C(V)$ be the collection of all nonempty closed subsets of V. A point-to-set transformation or correspondence $f: U \to C(V)$ is said to be *upper semicontinuous* if for any $x_0 \in U$ and any open set $W \subset V$ such that $f(x_0) \subset W$, there exists a neighborhood N of x_0 such that $x \in N$ implies $f(x) \subset W$. Figure 3-8 illustrates the notion of an upper semicontinuous correspondence.

In Fig. 3-8 f maps the point x_0 into the closed set $f(x_0)$, which is a subset of the open set W of the space V. The correspondence f is seen to be upper semicontinuous because all points of the neighborhood N of x_0 are mapped into closed sets contained in the set W. Figure 3-8 shows that the images of two points of N, in addition to x_0 itself, are contained in W.

With this discussion we are in a position to state the Kakutani fixed-point theorem, which is the main mathematical tool used by Debreu[1] in his existence proof. The Kakutani theorem may be stated as follows: Let K be a closed and bounded convex set in euclidean space, and let $C(K)$ denote the family of all nonempty closed convex subsets of K. Then if the mapping $f: K \to C(K)$ is upper semicontinuous there exists a point $\hat{x} \in K$ such that $\hat{x} \in f(\hat{x})$. The similarity between the Brouwer and Kakutani theorems is seen in that the former asserts that, under proper conditions, a function maps a point into itself, while the latter asserts that, again under proper conditions, a correspondence maps a point into a set of points containing itself.

[1] Gerard Debreu, *Theory of Value*, John Wiley & Sons, Inc., New York, 1959. Actually, the first application of the Kakutani theorem to prove the existence of equilibrium was due to Lionel McKenzie in On Equilibrium in Graham's Model of World Trade, *Econometrica*, vol. 22, pp. 147–161, 1954.

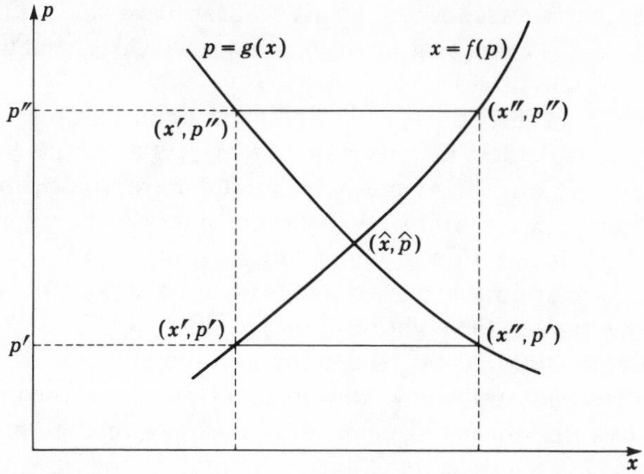

FIGURE 3-9

It might be useful at this point to illustrate the workings of a fixed-point theorem for the simple case of a single market.[1]

Consider the market depicted in Fig. 3-9, in which the "average" slopes over some interval $[x',x'']$ of the demand and supply functions are equal in absolute value. We are going to show that there is an equilibrium in this market by means of the Brouwer theorem. We concentrate on the boxlike region having vertices $[x',p']$, $[x',p'']$, $[x'',p'']$, and $[x'',p']$. The interval $[x',x'']$ is evidently a closed and bounded convex set in euclidean one-space. Similarly, the interval $[p',p'']$ is a closed and bounded convex set in euclidean one-space. It follows that the boxlike region, being the cartesian product of $[x',x'']$ and $[p',p'']$, is a convex, closed, and bounded set in euclidean two-space.[2]

That part of the demand function lying within the box has domain $[x',x'']$ and range $[p',p'']$, and that part of the supply function lying within the box has domain $[p',p'']$ and range $[x',x'']$, so that the range of $g(x)$ is the domain of $f(p)$ and the range of $f(p)$ is the domain of $g(x)$. Denoting the interval $[p',p'']$ by P and the interval $[x',x'']$ by X, we define a mapping Φ on $X \times P$ into itself by $\Phi(x,p) = (f(p), g(x))$. As was already mentioned,

[1] If fixed-point methods work in the general equilibrium case of many commodities, many consumers, and many producers, we would expect these methods to work for the partial equilibrium case of a single market in which the behavior of the economic agents has already been summarized into market supply and demand functions. The fact of the matter is, of course, that one is not likely to resort to fixed-point theorems in studying a single, isolated market.

[2] See Sec. 2-1. The fact that the cartesian product of closed and bounded sets in euclidean space is itself closed and bounded follows from a theorem of Tychonoff.

$X \times P$ is a closed and bounded convex set of euclidean two-space. Furthermore, since $f(p)$ and $g(x)$ are continuous functions, $\Phi(x,p)$ is a continuous mapping of $X \times P$ into itself.

If follows from the Brouwer fixed-point theorem that there exists a point $(\hat{x},\hat{p}) \in X \times P$ such that $\Phi(\hat{x},\hat{p}) = (f(\hat{p}), g(\hat{x})) = (\hat{x}, \hat{p})$, so that $g(\hat{x}) = \hat{p}$ and $f(\hat{p}) = \hat{x}$. This is precisely the statement that the market has an equilibrium at $(\hat{x},\hat{p})$. In Fig. 3-10 we illustrate how the mapping Φ takes a point (x,p) of $X \times P$ into point $(f(p), g(x))$ of $X \times P$. We trace the mapping for two arbitrarily chosen points (x_0,p_0) and (x_1,p_1). We see that the mapping Φ takes the point $(\hat{x},\hat{p})$ into itself.

Since Debreu utilizes the Kakutani fixed-point theorem in his existence proof, we illustrate how this theorem might be used in the single-market case in which the demand and supply relationships are correspondences rather than functions. Naturally, the use of the Kakutani theorem in this case is strictly for illustrative purposes, just as the use of the Brouwer theorem was in the previous case.

Figure 3-11*a* shows supply and demand curves labeled $f(p)$ and $g(x)$, and Fig. 3-11*b* shows the corresponding excess demand curve. Both the supply and demand relationships are correspondences rather than functions, because $g(\bar{x})$ and $f(\bar{p})$ are sets of more than one point. As before, we call the set $[x',x'']$ in euclidean one-space X and the set $[p',p'']$ in euclidean one-space P. The cartesian product $X \times P$ is a closed and bounded convex set in euclidean two-space. Again as before, we define the mapping Φ by $\Phi(x,p) = (f(p), g(x))$. Φ maps every point of $X \times P$ into a closed convex (nonempty) set of $X \times P$, (x,p) being mapped by Φ into

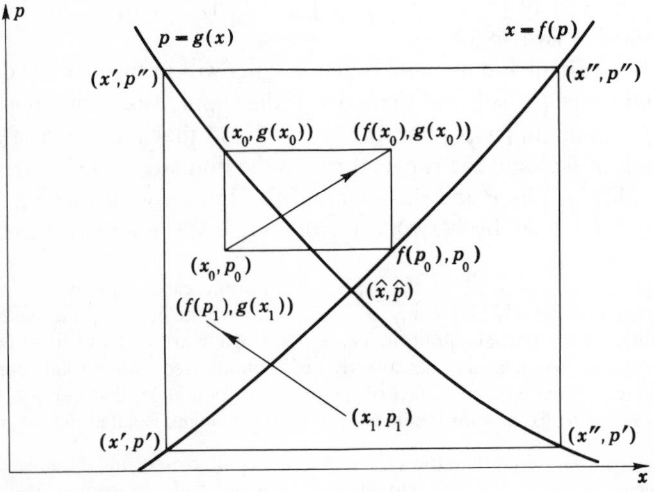

FIGURE 3-10

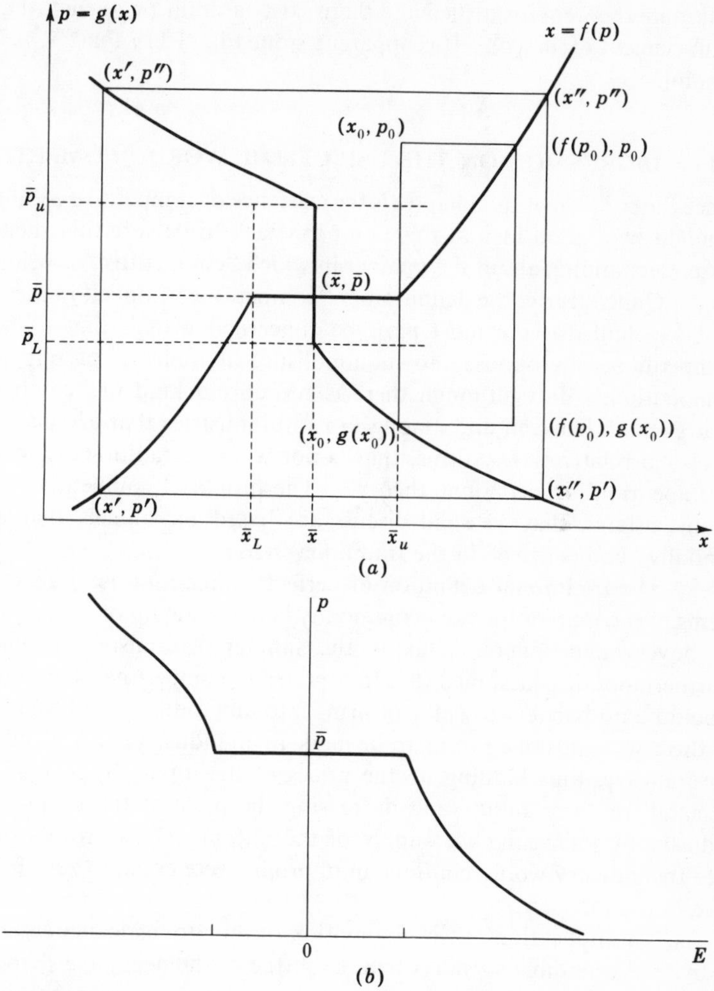

FIGURE 3-11

the closed convex subset comprising the rectangle having vertices $(\bar{x}_L,\bar{p}_L)$, $(\bar{x}_L,\bar{p}_U)$, $(\bar{x}_U,\bar{p}_U)$, and $(\bar{x}_U,\bar{p}_L)$.† It is easy to see that Φ satisfies the definition of upper semicontinuity. Consequently the hypothesis of the

† Any point of the form $(\bar{x},p)$ $p \neq \bar{p}$ is mapped into a closed interval of the form $(x, [p_1,p_2])$, while any point of the form $(x,\bar{p})$ $x \neq \bar{x}$ is mapped into the closed interval of the form $([x_1,x_2], p)$. Any point of the form (x,p), $x \neq \bar{x}$, $p \neq \bar{p}$, is mapped into a point which is a convex set and which may be assumed to be a closed set in euclidean space.

Kakutani theorem is satisfied and there exists a point (x,p) such that (x,p) is an element of $\Phi(x,p)$. It is apparent from Fig. 3-11*a* that $(\bar{x},\bar{p})$ is such a point.

3-4 A DIGRESSION ON THE USE OF THE WORD "COMPETITIVE"

Since the concern of this chapter is the existence of competitive equilibrium, it might be a good idea at this point to check to be sure that there is no misunderstanding about the manner in which "competitive" is being used.

Quite clearly, the definition of "competition" implicit in the models that we shall, for the most part, be concerned with is that of "perfect competition," as opposed to monopolistic, duopolistic, or oligopolistic competition.[1] For although there is certainly a kind of "competition" that goes on between and among firms in industries that are made up of two or a relatively few firms, that is not what is traditionally meant by "competition" in economic theory.[2] The proofs of competitive equilibrium existence that we shall discuss are based on models that are essentially "competitive" in the traditional sense.

The traditional definition of perfect competition is often stated in terms of the market for each commodity being made up of a large number of buyers and sellers. This is the familar "atomistic" assumption. Furthermore, it is assumed that in a perfectly competitive economy there would be no barriers to entry of firms into any industry and that as long as there were positive profits to be made in an industry, firms would enter the industry, thus bidding up the prices of the inputs by increasing the demand for these inputs and decreasing the price of the output by the industry by increasing the supply of the output. This process of entry into the industry would continue until profits were equal to zero for every firm in the industry.

An implication of the assumption of the atomistic character of the individual economic agents is that, by virtue of the negligible share of the market that an individual economic agent represents, an economic agent has negligible effect on prices. This, of course, is the familar parametric view of prices postulated for economic agents in the competitive model.

[1] An example of a noncompetitive model used very much in the spirit of this chapter is given in Takashi Negishi, Monopolistic Competition and General Equilibrium, *Review of Economic Studies*, vol. 28, pp. 196–201, 1962.

[2] One kind of competition that is available in a situation such as this is the manipulation of prices to increase share of the market. As is noted below, a situation in which price is a decision variable is inconsistent with the definition of a competitive economy in the usual sense.

Often this assumption is stated in terms of economic agents behaving "as if" they have no control over prices. The use of the phrase "as if" suggests that producers and consumers might behave as though they had no control over prices, when in fact they really do. To the extent that such is the case, the parametric price notion is logically completely separable from the atomistic assumption; a complete monopoly could, after all, behave "as if" it had no control of the price of its output. However, in the presence of complete information it is difficult to see why a monopoly would behave in this way in maximizing profits. On the other hand, free entry into the industry would suffice to force firms to behave atomistically, regardless of their numbers.

In addition to being essentially perfectly competitive, the models in the context of which we shall discuss the existence of competitive equilibrium have no explicit time structure. We might impose a time structure on the model by dating the commodities, so that a loaf of bread at one time is considered a different commodity from a loaf of bread at some other time. In this interpretation, consumers choose a plan of consumption over their lifetime under conditions of complete information concerning the future. Although admittedly the assuming away of uncertainty concerning the future is disturbing, there are difficulties with this interpretation even in the certainty case. For, as Koopmans has pointed out,[1] there is no explanation in the models of how firms come to be, the birth of a firm being, after all, an economic decision. At any rate, the device of treating a loaf of bread this year as a completely different commodity from a loaf of bread next year introduces time in only the most formal way, shedding little light on the relationship between a loaf of bread this year and a loaf of bread next year in terms of either production or valuation.

Perhaps a more appealing interpretation of the models we shall discuss would be that of stationary-state models. Tastes of consumers, technology, population, and, in general, the basic underlying nature of the economy are assumed to be constant. Under these assumptions each consumer is thought of as choosing a level of consumption and each producer is thought of as choosing a level of production, which levels will remain constant over time. The particular difficulty of entry of firms might be somewhat further alleviated by carrying on the analysis in terms of the aggregate production set without being specific about the number of individual producers.

[1] T. C. Koopmans, Allocations of Resources and the Price System, *Three Essays on the State of Economic Science*, pp. 64ff, McGraw-Hill Book Company, New York, 1957.

3-5 A RESTATEMENT OF THE PROBLEM OF THE EXISTENCE OF COMPETITIVE EQUILIBRIUM

In this section we shall reformulate the existence problem in all its multidimensional complexity and shall see that, under appropriate restrictions on the production and consumption sets, the existence of competitive equilibrium can be established. The formulation used will be essentially that of Debreu.[1]

The fundamental notions of this formulation of the existence problem are the notions of consumption and production sets that were discussed in Chap. 1. We recall that each consumption set and each production set is thought of as a set in euclidean space. More particularly, if there are n commodities in the economy and there are l firms and m consumers, then there is associated with each consumer a consumption set $\bar{X}_j$ $(j = 1, 2, \ldots, m)$ and with each producer a production set $\bar{Y}_k$ $(k = 1, 2, \ldots, l)$, where the $\bar{X}_j$ and $\bar{Y}_k$ are taken to be sets in euclidean n-space.

It is assumed that there is a quantity of resources available in the economy. We denote this resource bundle by $\mathbf{r}$. $\mathbf{r}$ is also represented as a point in euclidean n-space, $\mathbf{r} = (r_1, r_2, \ldots, r_n)$, where r_i denotes the quantity of the ith commodity in the resource bundle. A state of the economy $(\mathbf{x},\mathbf{y})$ is said to be an *attainable* state if $\mathbf{x}^j \in \bar{X}_j$ $(j = 1, 2, \ldots, n)$, $\mathbf{y}^k \in \bar{Y}_k$ $(k = 1, 2, \ldots, l)$, and $\sum_{j=1}^{m} \mathbf{x}^j - \sum_{k=1}^{l} \mathbf{y}^k = \mathbf{r}$. Attainability is thus seen to be defined in terms of (1) each economic agent choosing a consumption or production from his consumption set or production set and (2) the resulting aggregate excess demand (including the resource endowment) being equal to the origin, i.e., all markets are cleared.

If we specify that each consumer is to choose a consumption that is at least as preferred as any other consumption he might choose and that each producer is to choose a production yielding at least as much profit as any other production he might choose, how can we guarantee that all markets will be cleared? Looking at this situation slightly differently, does there exist an attainable state such that, in this state, each consumer chooses a bundle at least as preferred as any other he can choose and each producer chooses an input-output vector yielding as much profit as any other he can choose?

The specification of the phrase "can choose" needs clarification. For in the case of the consumer, unless we admit bliss points, there is no point that is at least as preferred as any other, and for the case of the producer, profits must be defined in terms of some prices. It is at this

[1] Debreu, *op. cit.*

point that the "competitive" aspect of competitive equilibrium comes into focus. There are actually two distinguishable characteristics of a competitive economy that are involved. One is the parametric view of prices in the model. By this, as was pointed out in the previous section, is meant that all economic agents take the prevailing market prices as data, thinking only of quantities, and not prices, as policy or decision variables. The second has to do with the ownership of resources and the manner in which production is organized.[1] The resources of the economy are assumed to be distributed among the consumers, with $\mathbf{r}^j$ denoting the holdings of the jth consumer, so that $\mathbf{r}^j = (r_{1j}, r_{2j}, \ldots, r_{nj})$ and $\sum_{j=1}^{m} \mathbf{r}^j = \mathbf{r}$. Also, the consumers are assumed to be stockholders in the firms, the profits of the firms being distributed among the consumers. Each consumer is assumed to have a "stock portfolio" $\mathbf{s}^j$, where $\mathbf{s}^j = (s_{j1}, s_{j2}, \ldots, s_{jl})$ and $\sum_{j=1}^{m} s_{jk} = 1$, for $k = 1, 2, \ldots, l$. s_{jk} is interpreted as the share of the profits of the kth firm accruing to the jth consumer.

If, as we shall see, prices can be represented as points in the nonnegative orthant of euclidean n-space, then for the kth firm to maximize profits means that the kth firm, given a price vector $\mathbf{p}$, selects an input-output vector $\hat{\mathbf{y}}^k \in \bar{Y}_k$ having the property that the vector product $\mathbf{p} \cdot \hat{\mathbf{y}}^k \geq \mathbf{p} \cdot \mathbf{y}^k$ for all $\mathbf{y}^k \in \bar{Y}_k$. Similarly, the jth consumer chooses a consumption vector $\hat{\mathbf{x}}^j$ having the property that $\hat{\mathbf{x}}^j \, \mathrm{R}_j \, \mathbf{x}^j$ for all $\mathbf{x}^j \in \bar{X}_j$ that satisfy his budget constraint. The budget constraint of the jth consumer is straightforward in that the total wealth of the jth consumer is given by $\mathbf{w}^j = \mathbf{p} \cdot \mathbf{r}^j + \sum_{k=1}^{l} s_{jk} \, \mathbf{p} \cdot \hat{\mathbf{y}}^k$. This says that the wealth of the jth consumer is equal to the value of the resources he owns plus the profits distributed to him from the producers. The budget constraint of the jth consumer may then be written $\mathbf{p} \cdot \mathbf{x}^j \leq \mathbf{p} \cdot \mathbf{r}^j + \sum_{k=1}^{l} s_{jk}\mathbf{p} \cdot \hat{\mathbf{y}}^k$.

A competitive equilibrium may now be defined as an $(m + l + 1)$-tuple $((\bar{\mathbf{x}}^j),(\bar{\mathbf{y}}^k),\bar{\mathbf{p}})$ of points in euclidean n-space.[2] To constitute an

[1] Debreu, in *Theory of Value*, makes this distinction clear by calling an economy characterized by the ownership of firms and resources by consumers a "private ownership economy." One might easily envisage a situation, after all, in which all resources are owned by the state but there is a highly decentralized plan so that individual economic agents are permitted or commanded to maximize, given government-determined prices. The parametric price aspect is often justified by the atomistic assumption that individual economic agents are too small to have any control over prices, or by assuming free entry.

[2] To spell it out, $((\bar{\mathbf{x}}^j), (\bar{\mathbf{y}}^k), \bar{\mathbf{p}}) = (\bar{\mathbf{x}}^1, \bar{\mathbf{x}}^2, \ldots, \bar{\mathbf{x}}^m; \bar{\mathbf{y}}^1, \bar{\mathbf{y}}^2, \ldots, \bar{\mathbf{y}}^l; \bar{p}_1, \bar{p}_2, \ldots, \bar{p}_n)$.

equilibrium, such an $(m + l + 1)$-tuple must have the following three properties, where $\bar{\mathbf{x}}^j \in \bar{X}_j$, $\bar{\mathbf{y}}^k \in \bar{Y}_k$; $j = 1, \ldots, m$; $k = 1, \ldots, l$:

$$\bar{\mathbf{x}}^j \; \mathrm{R}_j \; \mathbf{x}^j \qquad \text{for all } \mathbf{x}^j \in \bar{X}_j \text{ such that } \bar{\mathbf{p}} \cdot \mathbf{x}^j \leq \bar{\mathbf{p}} \cdot \mathbf{r}^j + \sum_{k=1}^{l} s_{jk} \bar{\mathbf{p}} \cdot \bar{\mathbf{y}}^k; \quad j = 1, \ldots, m \tag{3}$$

$$\bar{\mathbf{p}} \cdot \bar{\mathbf{y}}^k \geq \bar{\mathbf{p}} \cdot \mathbf{y}^k \qquad \text{for every } \mathbf{y}^k \in \bar{Y}_k;\ k = 1, \ldots, l \tag{4}$$

$$\sum_{j=1}^{m} \bar{\mathbf{x}}^j - \sum_{k=1}^{l} \bar{\mathbf{y}}^k = \mathbf{r} \tag{5}$$

Examination of properties (3) to (5) verifies that this definition is a precise statement of what we want equilibrium to mean, namely, an attainable state of the economy in which each consumer maximizes utility and each producer chooses a profit-maximizing input-output vector.

Before proceeding, we might note that the definition of equilibrium stated here is, because of (5), the more restrictive of the two mentioned above. The proof that Debreu actually gives is for the more general case of

$$\sum_{j=1}^{m} \bar{\mathbf{x}}^j - \sum_{k=1}^{l} \bar{\mathbf{y}}^k \leqq \mathbf{r} \tag{5'}$$

To prove the existence proposition we must find conditions on the production sets, consumption sets, and the ordering relation that guarantee the logical existence of a state of the economy and a price vector satisfying (3), (4), and (5) or (5′).

In Debreu's formulation of the existence problem, strict convexity of preferences or strictly decreasing returns are not assumed. As we saw in Sec. 1-6, it follows that there will be a multiplicity of points in $\bar{X}_j$, in general, from which the jth consumer may arbitrarily choose in maximizing utility with respect to a given price vector. Similarly, there will be a multiplicity of points in $\bar{Y}_k$, in general, from which the kth producer may choose in maximizing his profits with respect to a given price vector. Consequently, in general, we would expect there to be a multiplicity of aggregate demand points and aggregate supply points that would be consistent with individual agent maximizing behavior. Defining the excess demand relationship as a correspondence between prices and excess demand vectors as coming about through individual maximization, it follows that the excess demand relation is a correspondence from the set of price vectors to the set $X - Y - \mathbf{r}$, where X is the aggregate consumption set, Y is the aggregate production set, and $\mathbf{r}$ is the one-point set in euclidean n-space that represents the resource endowment. We denote the set $X - Y - \mathbf{r}$ by Z. Then for a given price vector there is an associated subset of Z generated by individual consumer and individual producer maximizing behavior.

The question of the existence of a competitive equilibrium may, then, be phrased in terms of whether or not there is an attainable state of the economy consistent with individual maximizing behavior for some price vector. Or, equivalently, whether there is a set of prices such that the subset of Z generated by individual economic agent maximization at this set of prices contains the origin. The latter formulation embodies the notion of exact clearance of all markets. If we want to use the less restrictive notion, permitting the possibility of negative excess demand in some markets, then the existence problem amounts to asking for a set of prices such that the subset of Z generated by individual maximizing behavior will have a nonempty intersection with the negative orthant of euclidean n-space, the price being zero for any commodity for which the excess demand is negative.

A natural question to raise concerns the set of prices we must consider in searching for an equilibrium price vector. As we shall see shortly, it turns out that we may restrict our search for an equilibrium price vector to a particular subset of euclidean n-space.

In proceeding to this result we first show that the homogeneity properties of demand and supply functions, well known from the more traditional calculus treatment of microeconomics, carry over to our correspondences.

Let us suppose that the set of input-output vectors comprising profit-maximizing points for the kth producer relative to the price vector $\mathbf{p}$ is denoted by $S_k(\mathbf{p})$. Then any point, say $\hat{\mathbf{y}}^k(\mathbf{p}) \in S_k(\mathbf{p}) \subset \bar{Y}_k$, has the property that $\mathbf{p} \cdot \hat{\mathbf{y}}^k(\mathbf{p}) \geq \mathbf{p} \cdot \mathbf{y}^k$ for all $\mathbf{y}^k \in \bar{Y}_k$. If all prices are multiplied by a positive constant, then the value of profits is multiplied by this constant, as is readily seen by factoring out the constant in the profit expression, that is, $(t\mathbf{p}) \cdot \mathbf{y}^k = t(\mathbf{p} \cdot \mathbf{y}^k)$. Therefore the set of profit maximizers is invariant with respect to multiplication of the price vector by a positive constant. Formally, $S_k(\mathbf{p}) = S_k(t\mathbf{p})$ for arbitrary positive t $(k = 1, \ldots, l)$.

Suppose that the set of consumptions comprising most preferred points for the jth consumer relative to the price vector $\mathbf{p}$ is denoted by $D_j(\mathbf{p})$. Then any point, say $\hat{\mathbf{x}}^j(\mathbf{p}) \in D_j(\mathbf{p}) \subset \bar{X}_j$, has the property that $\hat{\mathbf{x}}^j(\mathbf{p})\ \mathrm{R}_j\ \mathbf{x}^j$ for all $\mathbf{x}^j \in \bar{X}_j$ such that $\mathbf{p} \cdot \mathbf{x}^j \leq \mathbf{p} \cdot \mathbf{r}^j + \sum_{k=1}^{l} s_{jk}\mathbf{p} \cdot \hat{\mathbf{y}}^k$. Now if all prices are multiplied by an arbitrary positive constant, factoring out this constant from both sides of the budget constraint expression gives us precisely the original budget constraint. Therefore, the set of most preferred consumptions must be the same for both price vectors. Formally, for arbitrary $t > 0$, $D_j(\mathbf{p}) = D_j(t\mathbf{p})$ for $j = 1, \ldots, m$.

Thus the demand correspondences of the individual consumers and the supply correspondences of the individual producers are seen to be homogeneous of degree zero in prices.[1] It follows that the aggregate demand and supply correspondences are homogeneous of degree zero and therefore that, for any positive real number t,

$$E(t\mathbf{p}) = E(\mathbf{p}) \qquad \text{where } E(\mathbf{p}) = \sum_{j=1}^{m} D_j(\mathbf{p}) - \sum_{k=1}^{l} S_k(\mathbf{p}) \tag{6}$$

If we add the individual consumers' budget constraints together we get

$$\mathbf{p} \cdot \sum_{j=1}^{m} \mathbf{x}^j \leq \mathbf{p} \cdot \mathbf{r} + \sum_{j=1}^{m} \sum_{k=1}^{l} s_{jk} \mathbf{p} \cdot \hat{\mathbf{y}}^k$$

which, using the fact that $\sum_{j=1}^{m} s_{jk} = 1$ for $k = 1, \ldots, l$, yields $\mathbf{p} \cdot \sum_{j=1}^{m} \mathbf{x}^j \leq \mathbf{p} \cdot \mathbf{r} + \mathbf{p} \cdot \hat{\mathbf{y}}^k$. Adding this expression across all firms and bringing all terms over to the left-hand side of the inequality sign, we get $\mathbf{p} \cdot \mathbf{z} \leq 0$, where $\mathbf{z}$ is, as above, the aggregate excess demand vector. It is possible to give a geometric interpretation to the scalar product of two vectors, as we saw in Sec. 1-2. Consequently, the set of excess demand points satisfying $\mathbf{p} \cdot \mathbf{z} \leq 0$ is the set of points lying in or below the hyperplane having the equation $\mathbf{p} \cdot \mathbf{z} = 0$ or, equivalently, the set of vectors forming a right or obtuse angle with the vector $\mathbf{p}$. Figure 3-12 illustrates in two dimensions the set of points satisfying $\mathbf{p} \cdot \mathbf{z} \leq 0$ for the particular $\mathbf{p}$ shown.

If we assume that producers may dispose of commodities at no cost, then under the assumptions made above, $S_k(\mathbf{p})$ is nonempty if and only if $\mathbf{p} \geqq \mathbf{0}_n$. Free disposal means that all points of the negative orthant are in the production set of the kth producer, and if any price were permitted to be negative, the kth producer's profits could be made arbitrarily large.[2] Furthermore, the jth consumer, if confronted by a set of prices each of which was zero, would be able to choose a most preferred point only if there were a point in his consumption set that was at least as preferred as any other point in $\bar{X}_j$ with no budget constraint. But this would mean that the jth consumer had a bliss point. It follows that if there exists a

[1] Homogeneity of degree zero of functions came up in Chap. 2 in connection with demand and supply functions. In general, a function or correspondence $f(x_1, x_2, \ldots, x_n)$ is said to be homogeneous of degree h in $x_1, x_2, \ldots, x_n$ if for $t > 0, f(tx_1, tx_2, \ldots, tx_n) = t^h f(x_1, x_2, \ldots, x_n)$.

[2] The converse, namely that $\mathbf{p} \geqq \mathbf{0}_n$ implies that each producer has a profit-maximizing production relative to $\mathbf{p}$, is established rigorously by associating with each individual production set a closed and bounded convex set, which we know has a maximizing value for a continuous function. Similarly, Debreu establishes that each consumer has a nonempty "most preferred" set if $\mathbf{p} \geq \mathbf{0}_n$ by associating an appropriate closed and bounded convex set with each individual consumption set.

"most preferred" bundle for each individual relative to a given price vector, and if at least one consumer fails to have a bliss point, the equilibrium price vector cannot be the zero vector. Combining the nonnegativity constraint imposed by assuming free disposal on any candidate for the role of equilibrium price vector, with the nonzero constraint imposed by assuming that at least one consumer fails to have a point of bliss, we have that $\mathbf{p} \geq \mathbf{0}_n$, meaning that no commodity has a negative price and at least one commodity is not a free good.

In the search for an equilibrium price vector we may then restrict ourselves to points in the positive orthant of euclidean n-space, excluding the origin. Therefore, the only price vectors that need be considered in our search for an equilibrium price vector are those having the property that $\sum_{i=1}^{n} p_i > 0$, where $\mathbf{p} = (p_1, \ldots, p_n)$. By the homogeneity of degree zero of the aggregate excess demand correspondence [Eq. (6)], letting $t = 1 \Big/ \sum_{i=1}^{n} p_i$, we have

$$E\left(\frac{1}{\sum_{i=1}^{n} p_i}\mathbf{p}\right) = E(\mathbf{p}) \qquad \text{for all } \mathbf{p} \geq \mathbf{0}_n$$

Consequently, in searching for a $\mathbf{p} \geq \mathbf{0}_n$ such that $E(\mathbf{p}) = \mathbf{0}_n$ [or using the less restrictive definition of equilibrium, $E(\mathbf{p}) \leq \mathbf{0}_n$], we need look no

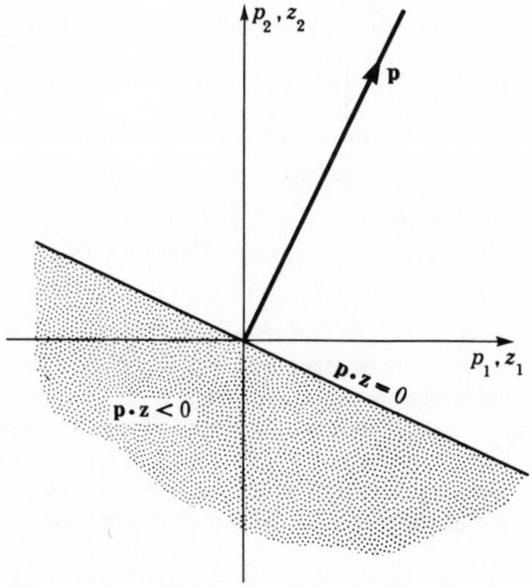

FIGURE 3-12

further than the "normalized" price vectors, that is, the intersection of all nonnegative price vectors with the set of points satisfying the equation $\sum_{i=1}^{n} p_i = 1$. This situation is drawn in Fig. 3-13 for the case $n = 2$. If the set of points $E(\mathbf{p})$ associated with the vector $\mathbf{p}$ is as depicted in Fig. 3-13*a*, then $\mathbf{p}$ is not an equilibrium price vector. In order for $\mathbf{p}$ to be an equilibrium price vector in the stricter definition of equilibrium, the set $E(\mathbf{p})$ must have the origin as an element. In order for the price vector to be an equilibrium price vector in the looser definition of equilibrium, it is necessary only that the intersection of the set $E(\mathbf{p})$ with the negative orthant (where of course the negative orthant is assumed to have the origin) be nonempty. The situation in which $\mathbf{p}$ is an equilibrium vector according to the stricter definition of equilibrium is shown in Fig. 3-13*b*. The situation in which $\mathbf{p}$ is an equilibrium price vector only according to the less strict definition is shown in Fig. 3-13*c*. In Fig. 3-13*a*, $\mathbf{p}$ is not an equilibrium price vector according to either definition.

Debreu's proof of the existence of competitive equilibrium is accomplished by means of the following theorem.[1]

THEOREM 1: Let $\tilde{Z}$ be a closed and bounded set in euclidean n-space. If $\tilde{E}(\mathbf{p})$ is an upper semicontinuous correspondence $\tilde{E}: P \to \tilde{Z}$, mapping every $\mathbf{p} \in P$ into a nonempty convex set such that $\mathbf{p} \cdot \tilde{E}(\mathbf{p}) \leq 0$, then there exists a $\hat{\mathbf{p}} \in P$ such that $\tilde{E}(\hat{\mathbf{p}})$ intersected with the negative orthant of euclidean n-space is a nonempty set.

We outline the proof of this theorem as given by Debreu. The set P of the theorem is precisely the normalized price vectors of the positive orthant discussed above. That is, $P = \left\{\mathbf{p} \geq \mathbf{0}_n \,\middle|\, \sum_{i=1}^{n} p_i = 1\right\}$. P is obviously nonempty, since any unit vector (having a 1 in some component and zeros everywhere else) is an element of P. It is furthermore clear that P is the set of all weighted averages or centers of gravity of the unit vectors.[2] Consequently, P is closed, bounded, and convex. A set Z' is selected in euclidean

[1] The strategy of the existence proof is to show that there exists some set of prices such that at this set of prices individual economic agents choosing consumption bundles and input-output vectors from their respective consumption and production sets, in accordance with their choice criteria, will give rise to a state of the economy in which markets are cleared. (Note that the less restrictive sense of market clearance is used.) The proof of existence now hinges on proving Theorem 1 and showing that the model of the economy employed satisfies the hypothesis of Theorem 1.

[2] The reader might recognize that the set P is the unit $(n - 1)$ simplex.

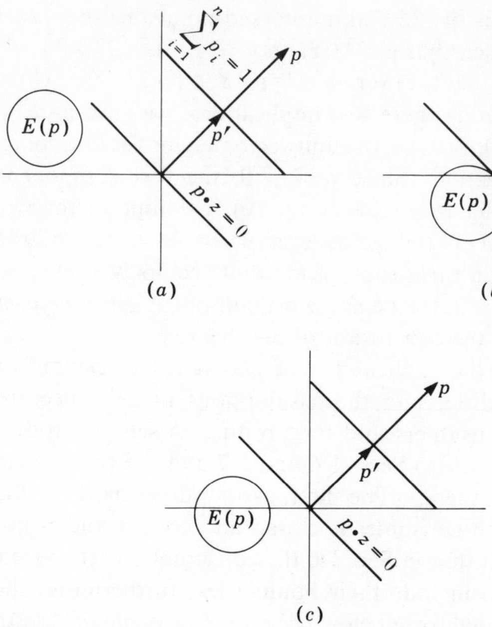

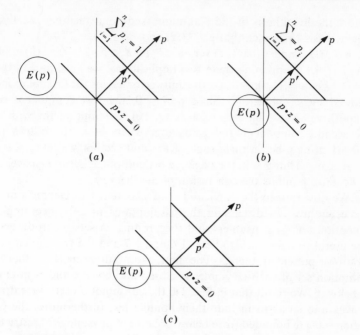

FIGURE 3-13

n-space such that Z' is closed, bounded, and convex and $Z' \supset \tilde{Z}$. By hypothesis, P nonempty implies $\tilde{Z}$; hence Z' is nonempty.

For any $\mathbf{z} \in Z'$, $\mathbf{z} \cdot \mathbf{p} = \sum_{i=1}^{n} z_i p_i$ is certainly a continuous real-valued function on P. Consequently $\mathbf{z} \cdot \mathbf{p}$ assumes its maximum value on P.† It follows that if we denote the set of values in P that maximize $\mathbf{p} \cdot \mathbf{z}$ for a particular $\mathbf{z}$ by $M(\mathbf{z})$, $M(\mathbf{z})$ is not empty. Also, $M(\mathbf{z})$ is upper semicontinuous.[1] Furthermore, if $\mathbf{z} = \mathbf{0}_n$, $M(\mathbf{z}) = P$, since $\mathbf{0}_n \cdot \mathbf{p} = 0$ for all $\mathbf{p} \in P$, while if $\mathbf{z} \neq \mathbf{0}_n$, $M(\mathbf{z})$ is made up of all points in P that are also in the hyperplane defined by $\mathbf{p} \cdot \mathbf{z} = \max \mathbf{p} \cdot \mathbf{z}$. Finally, we note that if $\mathbf{z}$ has both negative and nonnegative components, all elements of $M(\mathbf{z})$ will have zero components corresponding to the negative $\mathbf{z}$ components, and in general, $M(\mathbf{z})$ assigns positive prices to only the largest component(s) of $\mathbf{z}$.

We now define a correspondence $\Phi: P \times Z' \to P \times Z'$ by $\Phi(\mathbf{p},\mathbf{z}) = M(\mathbf{z}) \times \tilde{E}(\mathbf{p})$. $P \times Z'$, being the cartesian product of two nonempty, closed, bounded, and convex sets in euclidean $2n$-space, is also nonempty, closed, bounded, and convex. Furthermore, Φ is upper semicontinuous.

† See Sec. 2-2.

[1] This follows from the closed and bounded character of P.

Therefore the hypothesis of the Kakutani fixed-point theorem is satisfied and there exists $(\hat{\mathbf{p}},\hat{\mathbf{z}})$ such that $\hat{\mathbf{p}} \in M(\hat{\mathbf{z}})$ and $\hat{\mathbf{z}} \in \tilde{E}(\hat{\mathbf{p}})$.

$\hat{\mathbf{p}} \in M(\hat{\mathbf{z}})$ implies that for every $\mathbf{p} \in P$, $\mathbf{p} \cdot \hat{\mathbf{z}} \leq \hat{\mathbf{p}} \cdot \hat{\mathbf{z}}$. $\hat{\mathbf{z}} \in E(\hat{\mathbf{p}})$ implies that $\hat{\mathbf{p}} \cdot \hat{\mathbf{z}} \leq 0$. Combining these two implications, we have $\mathbf{p} \cdot \hat{\mathbf{z}} \leq 0$ for all $\mathbf{p} \in P$. Let $\mathbf{p} = (1, 0, \ldots, 0)$, the unit vector having the first component 1 followed by $n - 1$ zeros. Since $\mathbf{p} \cdot \hat{\mathbf{z}} \leq 0$, the first component of $\hat{\mathbf{z}}$ is nonpositive. Now let $\mathbf{p} = (0, 1, 0, \ldots, 0)$, the unit vector with a 1 in the second component and zeros everywhere else. It follows that $\hat{z}_2 \leq 0$. Letting $\mathbf{p}$ be, in turn, each of the unit vectors, we get $\hat{z}_i \leq 0$ for $i = 1, \ldots, n$. Thus $\hat{\mathbf{z}}$ is in the negative orthant of euclidean n-space, and since $\hat{\mathbf{z}} \in \tilde{E}(\mathbf{p})$, $\hat{\mathbf{p}}$ fulfills the conclusion of the theorem.

We now turn to the applicability of Theorem 1 to Debreu's model of the economy. In discussing the assumptions made concerning the consumption sets of consumers and the production sets of producers, it will be useful to refer back to Secs. 1-6 and 1-7 and the two-dimensional illustrations presented there. The first assumption made is that the consumption set of each consumer is closed and convex and is bounded from below. We recall that in Sec. 1-6 the consumption sets were drawn as convex and so as to include their boundaries; furthermore, the consumption sets are bounded from below because of physiological restriction on the consumer's inputs and outputs. The second assumption is that there is no bliss point for any consumer. This rules out the situation illustrated in Fig. 1-9 in Sec. 1-6. The third assumption is that each consumer has convex preferences, as defined in Sec. 1-6. As was pointed out in Sec. 1-6, convexity of preferences rules out thick indifference curves, but permits indifference curves to have rectilinear regions.

We now come to an assumption that did not come up in Sec. 1-6. Let us begin by stating this assumption formally: For every $\mathbf{x}'_j \in \bar{X}_j$, the sets $\{\mathbf{x}_j \in \bar{X}_j \mid \mathbf{x}_j \, \mathrm{R}_j \, \mathbf{x}'_j\}$ and $\{\mathbf{x}_j \in \bar{X}_j \mid \mathbf{x}'_j \, \mathrm{R}_j \, \mathbf{x}_j\}$ are closed in $\bar{X}_j$ $(j = 1, 2, \ldots, m)$. This assumption means that if, with respect to a given consumption bundle, there is a sequence of bundles, each of which is at least as preferred as (or not preferred to) the given bundle by the consumer, then any bundle to which the sequence converges is at least as preferred as (or not preferred to) the given bundle by the consumer. It is easy to verify that this assumption on the closedness of preference sets (sometimes called continuity of preferences) excludes R_j being the lexicographic ordering discussed in Secs. 1-4 and 1-5. A final assumption made on consumption sets is that there is a consumption bundle in each consumer's consumption set which is strictly smaller (in the vector-ordering sense) than the consumer's resource holdings. This means that each consumer is able to sell (or throw away) positive quantities of each commodity and still remain in his consumption set, and enables one to get around the "exceptional case."

As for assumptions concerning the production sets, Debreu makes four of these. The first is that the production set of each producer contains the origin. This assumption permits each producer to exercise the option of using no inputs and producing no outputs. The remaining three assumptions all have to do with the aggregate production set and are weaker than would be corresponding assumptions made about the individual production sets in that some individual production sets may fail to satisfy some of the assumptions, even though the aggregate production set does.[1] It is assumed that the aggregate production set is closed and convex. In particular, this assumption implies that the aggregate production set includes its boundaries and that there are no increasing returns to scale in the aggregate. It is also assumed that there are no two input-output vectors in the aggregate production set such that one is the negative of the other, or, in other words, there is no pair of input-output vectors for the entire economy such that the inputs of each are the outputs of the other. Still another way to phrase this assumption is to say that aggregate production is irreversible. The final assumption made about production sets is that the aggregate production set includes the negative orthant of the commodity space. This means that commodities may always be disposed of at no cost. For the two-commodity case used to illustrate production sets earlier, clearly Fig. 1-16 of Sec. 1-7, Figs. 1-21, 1-22, and 1-23 of Sec. 1-7, and Fig. 2-14 of Sec. 2-3 satisfy the Debreu assumptions.

It now appears that if we could apply Theorem 1 to our set $Z = X - Y - \mathbf{r}$, and to our excess demand correspondence $E(\mathbf{p})$, we would have achieved our goal of proving the existence of a competitive equilibrium. Our excess demand correspondence, under the assumptions made on the consumption and production set, is indeed upper semicontinuous. However, there is no reason to expect Z to be closed and bounded. Quite to the contrary, since Y was assumed to include the negative orthant of the commodity space and since X was not assumed to be bounded from above, we would expect Z to be unbounded from above. Thus, in order to render Theorem 1 applicable, some "doctoring" of the set Z must be undertaken.

A useful fact to recall at this point is that since there is a finite amount of each commodity in the resource endowment $\mathbf{r}$, even though individual production and consumption sets may be unbounded, one might expect the set of attainable states to be bounded. To repeat, since there is a fixed, finite resource endowment, even though individual production and consumption sets may be unbounded, one would expect the

[1] Debreu credits Uzawa with first noting that these assumptions made for aggregate rather than individual sets are adequate for proving the existence of equilibrium. See Debreu, *op. cit.*, p. 88.

subsets of these consumption and production sets corresponding to attainable states to be bounded.[1]

Debreu shows that the existence problem stated may be substituted for by a problem in which (1) the aggregate production set is imbedded in the smallest convex set containing it and (2) individual production and consumption sets are replaced by the intersection of these sets with closed, bounded, convex sets in which the individual attainable sets are imbedded.[2] The convexity of the individual production sets and the individual consumption sets guarantees the convexity of the set into which the price vectors of P are mapped. [E is the aggregate excess demand whose range is confined to the set Z defined by (1) and (2) above.] Z, now being the sum of closed and bounded sets, is also closed and bounded. Consequently the hypothesis of Theorem 1 holds and the existence of a competitive equilibrium is established.

In concluding our discussion of Debreu's proof, we reiterate certain features of the model that have economic significance and that might have been obscured by the intricacies of the proof. First, in searching for an equilibrium price vector, we were able to restrict ourselves to nonnegative prices, for otherwise profit functions would have been unbounded. Second, we were able to restrict this further to price vectors having at least one positive component, since if all prices were zero, the problem of choosing a most preferred consumption bundle would become meaningless for any consumer who did not have a bliss point. Because of the homogeneity properties of demand and supply correspondences, we were then able to confine our discussion to normalized prices, the sum of the components of each normalized price vector being unity.

By the definition of $M(\mathbf{z})$, we saw that for a given $\mathbf{z}$, positive prices were assigned to only the largest components of $\mathbf{z}$. This has the familiar

[1] Debreu employs the concept of the "asymptotic cone" of a set to establish boundedness of the attainable set. Recalling that a *ray* through any point $\mathbf{x}$ in euclidean space is the set of points $\lambda\mathbf{x}$ for all real numbers $\lambda \geqq 0$ (graphically, the line from the origin through $\mathbf{x}$ and continuing indefinitely beyond $\mathbf{x}$), the *asymptotic cone* of a set S is defined to be the union of the origin with the set of rays through points of S such that at most a finite length of any ray lies outside S. An immediate consequence of this definition is that a set is bounded if and only if its asymptotic cone is the origin. (Clearly no bounded set can contain all but a finite length of any ray.) The fact that the asymptotic cone of the attainable set is the origin thus establishes the boundedness of this set. (In particular, note that the assumed boundedness from below of the consumption set implies that its asymptotic cone is the nonnegative orthant, while the impossibility of free production—derived from the irreversibility and free-disposal assumptions—implies that the production set contains no points of the nonnegative orthant other than the origin.)

[2] For the details of this procedure, see Debreu, *op. cit*, pp. 84–88.

economic interpretation of having high prices on those commodities for which excess demand is great, thereby cutting down on this excess demand. Furthermore, $M(\mathbf{z})$ assigned a price of zero to any commodity for which the excess demand was negative. This, of course, has the economic interpretation that a good in excess supply is a free good. Finally, we note that not all the components of the excess demand vector can be negative. This is comforting, since if the equilibrium excess demand vector were strictly smaller than the zero vector, we could expect the equilibrium price vector to be the zero vector, which we saw was impossible as long as one consumer fails to have a bliss point. To see that not all the components of the excess demand vector can be negative, we recall from Sec. 1-6 that convexity of preferences and the absence of a bliss point imply that the consumer will choose a consumption bundle the value of which is equal to his wealth. Now if $\mathbf{z} < \mathbf{0}_n$, $\mathbf{p} \cdot \mathbf{z} < 0$ or $\mathbf{p} \cdot \hat{\mathbf{x}} < \mathbf{p} \cdot \hat{\mathbf{y}} + \mathbf{p} \cdot \mathbf{r}$, which may be written as

$$\mathbf{p} \cdot \sum_{j=1}^{m} \hat{\mathbf{x}}^j < \mathbf{p} \cdot \sum_{k=1}^{l} \sum_{j=1}^{m} s_{jk} \hat{\mathbf{y}}^k + \mathbf{p} \cdot \sum_{j=1}^{m} \mathbf{r}^j$$

Consequently,

$$\mathbf{p} \cdot \mathbf{x}^j < \mathbf{p} \cdot \sum_{k=1}^{l} s_{jk} \mathbf{y}^k + \mathbf{p} \cdot \mathbf{r}^j \qquad \text{for at least one } j$$

which, given convexity of preferences, implies that some consumer must have a bliss point, contrary to assumption. Another way to state this result is to say that the excess demand set associated with any normalized price vector cannot be in the interior of the negative orthant of the commodity space, but rather must intersect at least one axis of the negative orthant.

It might be useful at this point to illustrate the Debreu equilibrium theorem graphically. We assume that the economy is made up of one consumer, one producer, and two commodities, which we call labor and wheat. In this case there is obviously no need to distinguish between individual and aggregate sets, since they are identical. Consequently we shall refer to the consumption set or the production set without qualification.

The production set as drawn contains the origin and the negative orthant and has no points other than the origin in common with the positive orthant. The production set consists of all points to the left of the negative w axis and below the boundary made up of the three line segments. The negative w axis and the broken line boundary are also included in the production set. Therefore the production set satisfies all the assumptions made by Debreu concerning production sets. We recall that in going along the L axis we are dealing with negative numbers, inputs from the point of view of production and outputs from the point of view of the consumer. The boundary of three broken lines was constructed by drawing a line of slope -1 from the origin to the point at which the labor coordinate was 16. Between $L = -16$ and $L = -26$ a line with slope $-\frac{1}{2}$ was drawn, and from $L = -26$ on, a horizontal line was drawn.[1]

We now derive the demand and supply relationships for the situation depicted in Fig. 3-14. The set of prices P over which we define these relationships is of course $P = \{(p_w,p_L) \mid p_w \geqq 0, p_L \geqq 0, p_w + p_L = 1\}$.

The consumption set was drawn so that the amount of labor supplied by the consumer must never exceed 24 hr per day and so that he must consume at least 16 units of wheat per day in order to survive. The consumer was endowed with 20 units of wheat to begin with. His indifference sets are defined by a family of broken lines having a slope of -1 to the point at which the consumer is working 8 hr per day and a slope of -2 for hours per day between 8 and 24.† The consumption set is bounded from below by the point $L = -24$, $w = 16$; the initial endowment has more of both commodities than some point of the consumption set; and the convexity and closure of the set and of the preference ordering are apparent from the construction of the graph. It is also apparent that there is no point of bliss in the consumption set.

It is easy to see in this illustration that, although the consumption set is unbounded from above and the production set, containing the entire third quadrant, is unbounded from below, the attainable consumption and production sets are bounded. Specifically, the maximum attainable consumption of wheat is 41 bu (the resource endowment of 20 plus the 21 that could be obtained by working 24 hr). Clearly, then, the attainable consumption set is bounded. Similarly, the most negative quantity of labor that is in the attainable production set is -24 hr, and the most negative quantity of wheat that is in the attainable production set is -4 bu (the greatest, net of production, quantity of wheat that can be burned is $20 - 16$ bu). Thus the attainable production set is also bounded. We therefore may choose as a closed, bounded, convex set containing the attainable consumption set as a subset, the square having vertices (0,45), (-30,45), (-30,15), and (0,15). There is nothing very special about this

[1] Constructing the boundary in this way might be defended on the grounds that given a fixed supply of wheatland, the productivity of labor decreases (in a noncontinuous fashion) until the productivity of labor for amounts of labor greater than 26 is zero.

† This can be justified by assuming that as long as the consumer is working not more than 8 hr a day he is indifferent between one more hour of labor combined with one more unit of wheat and his present position. However, as soon as he is working more than 8 hr a day he requires two additional units of wheat for each additional hour of work to remain no worse off.

particular square; clearly it is merely one element of an infinite class having the property that the attainable consumption set lies properly inside the square. Similarly, we may choose as a closed, bounded, convex set containing the attainable production set as a subset, the square having vertices (0,25), (−35,25), (−35,−10), and (0,−10). Again the particular square chosen is evidently far from being unique in properly including the attainable production set. It is easy to see in terms of Fig. 3-14 how these squares look and to locate the intersection of the squares with the consumption and production sets, respectively.

Thus our illustration is seen to satisfy the assumptions made by Debreu in proving his existence theorem. Consequently we should be able to locate an equilibrium in terms of this diagram.

Rather than attempt to depict the demand and supply sets associated with each normalized price set on the diagram, we have listed these sets in the table on page 93. We have also listed the profits associated with each price vector, which by the Debreu assumption are distributed entirely to the consumer. We note that the demand and supply relationships we get are indeed correspondences rather than functions in the strict sense, because the mappings from prices to demand and supply quantities are not single-valued.

It is easy to see that the price vector $(\frac{1}{2},\frac{1}{2})$ is an equilibrium price vector. This is true because the point (−4,4) is in the supply set associated with the price vector $(\frac{1}{2},\frac{1}{2})$ and the point (−4,24) is in the demand set associated with the price vector $(\frac{1}{2},\frac{1}{2})$. Consequently the aggregate demand minus the aggregate supply for these points is (0,20), which is equal to the resource endowment. In terms of the Debreu model this says that the aggregate excess demand set associated with the price vector $(\frac{1}{2},\frac{1}{2})$ contains the origin. The equilibrium consumption (−4,24) is denoted by the point C on the diagram. The equilibrium production (−4,4) is denoted by the point P on the diagram. It is easy to verify from Fig. 3-14 and the table on page 93 that there is only one equilibrium price vector in the set of normalized prices, but that at this price set there are an infinite number of aggregate demands and aggregate supplies such that the difference between them is equal to the resource endowment. This last observation is made solely in the interest of completeness, since the existence of a competitive equilibrium in this illustration has been demonstrated quite independently of this observation.

3-6 SUMMARY OF THE LITERATURE

In the previous section the existence of competitive equilibrium was discussed in terms of the general equilibrium model presented by Debreu in *Theory of Value*. Historically, general equilibrium analysis in a rigorous

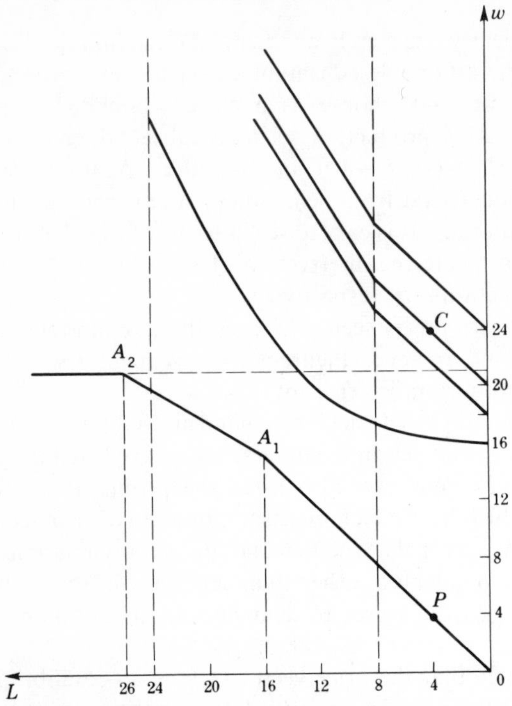

FIGURE 3-14

manner goes back to Leon Walras.[1] Walras proceeds from the point of utility maximization of individual consumers from which individual demand functions and subsequently market demand functions are derived. Somewhat less explicitly, firms are assumed to be motivated by profit maximization giving rise to supply functions. The production functions are characterized by certain constants called the *coefficients of production* which denote the amount of each of the "productive services" needed to produce one unit of each of the commodities. Walras then defines an equilibrium in this system to be quantities of "productive services," quantities of final commodities, and prices for the two kinds of goods such that the markets for all the goods are cleared and such that the value of the contributions of each of the "productive services" in terms of their market prices is equal to the market price of the final commodity produced.

The special nature of the Walrasian production equations and the equilibrium relationship between the prices is noteworthy in itself, because these features have been common in many later works in activity analysis and linear programming formulations of economic theory. In particular,

[1] Leon Walras, *Elements of Pure Economics*, translated by William Jaffe, Richard D. Irwin, Inc., Homewood, Ill., 1954.

SUMMARY OF FIGURE 3-14

$\frac{P_w}{P_L}$	*Supply set S(P)*	*Value of profit function*	*Demand set D(P)*
$0 < \frac{P_w}{P_L} < \frac{1}{2}$	$L = 0, w = 0$ Price line is steeper than steepest segment of broken line boundary	0	$L = -24,$ $w = 20 + 24 \frac{P_L}{P_w}$ Budget line is steeper than steeper segment of indifference curves
$\frac{P_w}{P_L} = \frac{1}{2}$	Same as above	0	$\{(L,w) \mid \frac{1}{3}w + \frac{2}{3}L = \frac{20}{3};$ $-24 \leq L < -8\}$ Budget line is coincident with steeper segment of highest indifference curve attainable with initial endowment if $w = 20$ and $\frac{P_w}{P_L} = \frac{1}{2}$
$\frac{1}{2} < \frac{P_w}{P_L} < 1$	Same as above	0	$L = -8,$ $w = 8 \frac{P_L}{P_w} + 20$ Budget line intersects highest indifference curve where line segments of different slopes meet
$\frac{P_w}{P_L} = 1$	$\{(L,w) \mid L,w$ in segment $0A_1\}$ Price line is coincident with line segment $0A_1$	0	$\{(L,w) \mid \frac{1}{2}L + \frac{1}{2}w = 10;$ $-8 \leq L \leq 0\}$ Budget line is coincident with portion of indifference curve having slope -1
$1 < \frac{P_w}{P_L} < 2$	$L = -16, w = 16$ All price lines defined by this inequality intersect the boundary of the production set at the point $L = -16, w = 16$	$16(P_w - P_L)$	$L = 0,$ $w = 36 - 16 \frac{P_L}{P_w}$ Budget line is flatter than flatter segment of indifference curve. w is determined by worth of capital endowment and distributed profits
$\frac{P_w}{P_L} = 2$	$\{(L,w) \mid L,w$ in line segment $A_1A_2\}$ Price line is coincident with line segment A_1A_2	$16P_L = 8P_w$	$L = 0, w = 28$
$2 < \frac{P_w}{P_L} < \infty$	$L = -26, w = 21$	$21P_w - 26P_L$	$L = 0, w = 41 - 26 \frac{P_w}{P_L}$

the kind of production equations used by Walras have also been used by Koopmans, Cassel, Leontief, von Neumann, and Wald in their studies.[1]

The salient feature of the Walrasian technology is that there is associated with each resource and each final commodity a constant, say a_{ij}, linking the ith resource and the jth final commodity such that a_{ij} units of the ith resource are needed to produce one unit of the jth commodity. Then the set of numbers a_{ij} $(i = 1, \ldots, m)$, assuming that there are m resources or "productive services," describes the production function for the jth commodity. The production function is assumed to have constant returns to scale by virtue of the fact that x_j units, $x_j \geq 0$, of the jth output are produced by using $x_j \cdot a_{ij}$ units of the ith resource. The set of numbers a_{ij} $(i = 1, \ldots, m)$ is often called the jth process or activity.

The Walrasian discussion of the existence of equilibrium is thus seen to have all the elements of the most modern treatments of the subject. Walras requires that at equilibrium each consumer is maximizing utility, each producer is maximizing profits, and all markets are cleared. Since by virtue of the constant-coefficient technology assumed by Walras there might be problems with the unboundedness of the profit function of the firm, Walras explicitly assumes that there are zero profits in all industries.

The first actual proofs of the solvability of the system of equations describing a general equilibrium were those of Abraham Wald.[2] Wald's three papers on the subject of competitive equilibrium consist of two models of production of the fixed-coefficient variety and one model of exchange or pure trade. Wald did not use any of the fixed-point theorems in proving existence. (In fact, the Kakutani theorem had not as yet been discovered at the time of Wald's work on this subject.) Instead Wald showed that his system of equations had a solution by intricate reasoning restricted to the real line.

[1] For a summary of these works, as well as references, see Robert Dorfman, Paul A. Samuelson, and Robert M. Solow, *Linear Programming and Economic Analysis*, McGraw-Hill Book Company, New York, 1958. Also, for a detailed discussion of linear economic models and the kind of mathematics needed to cope with these models, see David Gale, *The Theory of Linear Economic Models*, McGraw-Hill Book Company, New York, 1960.

[2] Abraham Wald, Über die eindeutige positive Lösbarkeit der neuen Produktionsgleichungen, *Ergebnisse eines Mathematischen Kolloquiums*, no. 6, pp. 12–20, 1933–1934.

Über die Produktionsgleichungen der ökonomischen Wertlehre, *Ergebnisse eines Mathematischen Kolloquiums*, no. 7, pp. 1–6, 1934–1935.

Über einige Gleichungssysteme der mathematischen Okonomie, *Zeitschift für Nationalokonomie*, vol. 7, pp. 637–670, 1936; English translation, On Some Systems of Equations of Mathematical Economics, *Econometrica*, vol. 19, pp. 368–403, 1951.

Another early proof of the existence of equilibrium was given by John von Neumann.[1] In this work, von Neumann established the existence of production levels and prices in an environment of uniform growth such that there are no profits in the economy and there is a uniquely determined interest rate equal to the growth rate. This paper laid the foundation for the considerable work that has recently been done on models of balanced growth of which the various "turnpike theorems" are an outstanding example.[2]

Another proof of the existence of competitive equilibrium is that due to Arrow and Debreu.[3] The model used by Arrow and Debreu is very similar to that of Debreu in *Theory of Value*. The method of proof is quite different in the two works, however. Whereas, it will be recalled, Debreu used the Kakutani fixed-point theorem, Arrow and Debreu use a generalization of the notion of a game and consequently use the notion of a Nash equilibrium in an N-person game.[4] The Arrow-Debreu result is a generalization of the Wald results, particularly in that to the extent that Wald considered production he posited a fixed-coefficient technology, while Arrow-Debreu do not. Furthermore, Wald assumed that the marginal utility function of each consumer was strictly decreasing with respect to each commodity. Arrow and Debreu do not make this assumption.

David Gale, in his paper on the existence of competitive equilibrium, also takes off from the point of individual consumption and production sets.[5] The mathematical device used by Gale is a theorem in topology that can be used to prove the Brouwer fixed-point theorem. Of the papers we discuss in this chapter, Gale's and Wald's are the only ones to concern themselves with proving uniqueness of equilibrium, as we shall see.

[1] John von Neumann, Über ein Okonomisches Gleichungssystem and eine Verallgemeinerung des Brouwerschen Fixpunktsatzes, *Ergebnisse eines Mathematischen Kolloquiums*, no. 8, pp. 73–83, 1937; English translation, A Model of General Equilibrium, *Review of Economic Studies*, vol. 13, no. 33, pp. 1–9, 1945–1946.

[2] For a discussion of some of the main "turnpike theorems," see Lionel W. McKenzie, The Turnpike Theorem of Morishima, *Review of Economic Studies*, vol. 30, pp. 169–175, 1963. Note the references on p. 176.

[3] Kenneth J. Arrow and Gerard Debreu, Existence of an Equilibrium for a Competitive Economy, *Econometrica*, vol. 22, pp. 265–290, 1954.

[4] J. F. Nash, Jr., Equilibrium States in N-person Games, *Proceedings of the National Academy of Sciences of the U.S.A.*, vol. 36, pp. 48–49, 1950.

[5] David Gale, The Law of Supply and Demand, *Mathematica Scandinavia*, vol. 3, pp. 155–169, 1955.

Lionel McKenzie has done away with the free-disposal assumption, hence with the nonnegativity of price requirement.[1] He also relaxes the irreversibility of production assumption and the assumption that each consumer has positive amounts of all goods and that these goods are of some value to all other consumers. McKenzie utilizes the notion of an *irreducible economy* to preclude the "exceptional case." An irreducible economy is one that is not capable of having all consumers partitioned into two groups such that neither is interested, in terms of individual satisfaction maximization, in trading with the other. The main mathematical result used by McKenzie is the Brouwer theorem.

Another model that might be viewed as a general equilibrium model is the Leontief model.[2] This model is also characterized by a fixed-coefficient technology. However, aside from labor, there are no resources as distinguished from goods or commodities. All the commodities present in the model serve as both inputs (intermediate commodities) and outputs (final commodities). The Leontief model was constructed as an empirically oriented model for tracing the effects on the various industries and sectors of the economy of particular changes in the economy. As such, the connection between individual consumer and producer maximizing behavior and market equilibria is not taken up in the Leontief model. Moreover, it is possible to work with the Leontief model without even explicitly talking about prices. Assuming that the Leontief model is consistent with individual maximizing behavior, it can be shown that there are prices such that all activities being used in the economy will have zero profits associated with them.[3]

The models we have discussed in connection with proofs of the existence of competitive equilibrium have been, as general equilibrium models typically are, "classical" models in the sense that money is not included as a commodity. In the language of utility functions, money is not a variable entering the consumer's utility function. A manifestation of the way money is treated in general equilibrium models is the homogeneity of degree zero in prices of the demand and supply relationships that we have noted. Homogeneity of degree zero in prices of the demand and supply relationships in the models we have considered points up the indeterminacy of the price level in these models.

[1] Lionel W. McKenzie, On the Existence of a General Equilibrium for a Competitive Market, *Econometrica*, vol. 27, pp. 54–71, 1959.

[2] Wassily W. Leontief, *The Structure of the American Economy, 1919–1939*, 2d ed., Oxford University Press, New York, 1951.

[3] See, for example, Gale, *The Theory of Linear Economic Models*, p. 302, and Dorfman, Samuelson, and Solow, *op. cit.*, p. 234.

We might at this point briefly consider the general question of the relationship of monetary theory to general equilibrium theory.[1] If money has no utility to the consumer, presumably the consumer should desire to hold no money regardless of prevailing prices. But then excess demand for money will be zero only if each consumer has zero holdings of money, for otherwise the excess demand for money would always be the negative of the amount of money initially held. In other words, since money has no utility associated with it, the consumer, in maximizing utility, should convert all his holdings of money into other commodities which do have utility associated with them. Therefore, the excess demand for money under assumptions of utility maximization should be zero only if the consumer has no holding of money at any time.

To say that the consumer has excess demand of zero, given positive initial holdings of money, is inconsistent with utility maximization if money is not a variable in the utility function. Under these circumstances the consumer would divest himself of his money holdings in favor of utility-bearing commodities.

3-7 UNIQUENESS OF COMPETITIVE EQUILIBRIUM

It might not be altogether redundant to point out that the proofs of existence discussed have, in the main, been proofs of existence and not proofs of uniqueness. In Chap. 5, uniqueness of equilibrium is discussed in connection with global stability of the competitive equilibrium. The first proof of uniqueness appears in Wald's work, utilizing the assumption that the weak axiom of revealed preference holds in the aggregate. We will return to this and other such cases in Chap. 5. Here we note some features of a proof of uniqueness due to Gale. Uniqueness of the equilibrium implies that there is only one normalized price set and only one state of the economy resulting in market clearance. There are clearly two reasons why an equilibrium may fail to be unique: (1) If we permit our demand and supply relationships to be correspondences, then even if there should be a unique normalized price vector there might be more than one associated equilibrium state of the economy. (2) If we require that all demand and supply relationships be functions rather than correspondences, there is still the possibility that there is more than one set of prices consistent with individual maximizing and market clearance. Figure 3-15 illustrates these cases for the initial endowment (X_1^0, X_2^0) in the Edgeworth box context.

It thus appears that any attempt to establish the uniqueness of

[1] For a detailed discussion of the problem of integrating general equilibrium theory and monetary theory see Don Patinkin, *Money, Interest, and Prices*, 2d ed., Harper & Row, Publishers, New York, 1965.

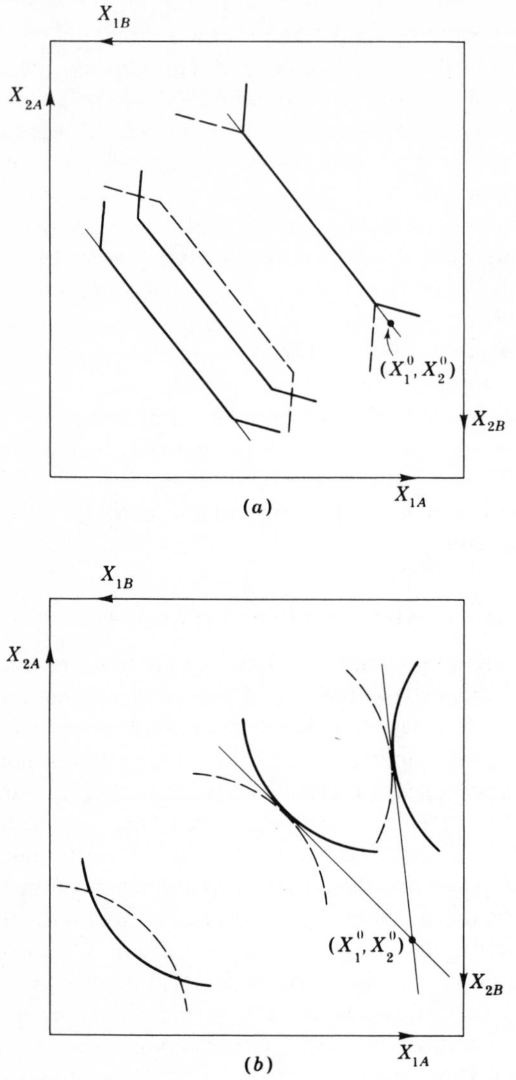

FIGURE 3-15

equilibrium will have to account both for the possibility of there being more than one state of the economy associated with an equilibrium set of prices and for the possibility of there being more than one equilibrium price vector. If we assume strictly convex consumption and production sets, or in some way guarantee that demand and supply functions are functions in the strict sense rather than correspondences, the former possibility is precluded. The latter possibility takes more doing.

This can be taken care of by assuming that as the relative price of a

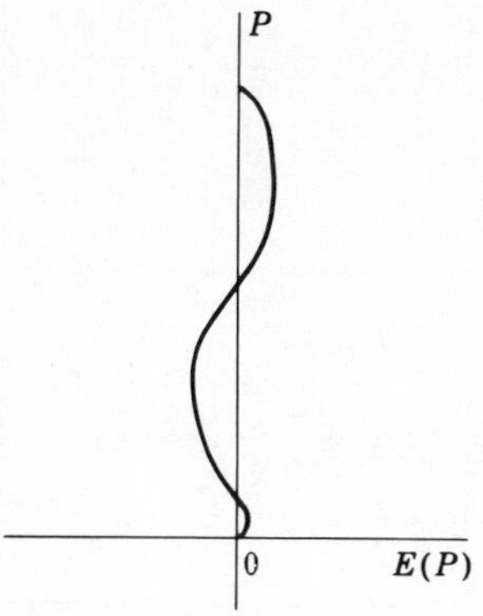

FIGURE 3-16

given commodity increases, the excess demand for it falls.[1] This in fact is the way Gale manages to get his unique equilibrium result. In particular, examination of Fig. 3-15 reveals that in going from the budget line L_1 to the budget line L_2, there was a rise in the relative price of commodity 2. Nevertheless, the aggregate demand for commodity 2 was zero at both sets of prices. The situation represented in Fig. 3-15 could be ruled out by the assumption that the excess aggregate demand for a commodity should be a monotone-decreasing function of its relative price. Figure 3-16 illustrates multiple equilibrium prices in terms of the excess demand function for some commodity. It is clear that if it were required that the excess demand function be monotone-decreasing, this situation could not occur.

3-8 COMPARISON OF ASSUMPTIONS IN PROOFS OF EXISTENCE

In this section we shall attempt to point out the similarities and dissimilarities of the assumptions used in the models of Arrow and Debreu, Gale, McKenzie, and Wald. We consider the Wald model of exchange and not the model of production. Before launching into these comparisons, we recall that essentially all that is needed to prove the existence of a utility function for a given consumer is that he have a ranking over commodity bundles and that for any point x' in his consumption set X, the sets $\{\mathbf{x} \mid \mathbf{x}\, R_j\, \mathbf{x}'\}$ and $\{\mathbf{x} \mid \mathbf{x}'\, R_j\, \mathbf{x}\}$ be closed. In the remainder of this section we shall refer to this closure property as *continuity of preferences*. It follows that assuming the existence of a utility function is not really a stronger assumption, in this sense, than the assumption of a ranking with continuity of preferences.

[1] It should be noted that this assumption is to hold whatever the values taken on by other prices, and hence is much stronger, say, than the assumption that $\partial E_i/\partial p_i < 0$. See David Gale, The Law of Supply and Demand, *Mathematica Scandinavia*, vol. 3, p. 163, 1955.

COMPARISON OF AXIOM SYSTEMS FOR EXISTENCE OF EQUILIBRIUM

	Model					
Characteristic	*Arrow and Debreu* (Econometrica, *vol. 22, 1954*)	*Debreu* (Theory of Value)	*Gale* (Mathematica Scandinavia, *vol. 3, 1955*)	*McKenzie* (Econometrica, *vol. 27, 1959*)	*Wald* (Econometrica, *vol. 19, 1951*)	*Debreu* (International Economic Review, *vol. 3, 1962*)
Individual consumption sets	Closed, convex, bounded from below	Closed, convex, bounded from below	Closed, convex, bounded, contains origin	Closed, convex, bounded from below	Positive orthant, bounded by endowment of resources	Closed, convex, not necessarily bounded from below
Bliss point	Ruled out by assuming individual utility function has no maximum on individual consumption set	Ruled out by explicit assumption	Not ruled out explicitly	Not excluded from model	Ruled out by assuming positive marginal utilities of all goods to all consumers	Consumption set may contain bliss point; however, if bliss point does exist, it must not lie in the attainable consumption set

Expression of consumer preferences	Utility function with convex preferences, that is, $u(\mathbf{x}') > u(\mathbf{x}'')$, $0 < \lambda < 1 \Rightarrow u(\lambda\mathbf{x}' + (1 - \lambda)\mathbf{x}'') > u(\mathbf{x}'')$	Convex, closed ranking	Utility function such as that of Arrow-Debreu or ranking such as that of Debreu implied by existence of supply functions	Convex, closed ranking	Strictly quasi-concave utility function	Convex, closed ranking
Exceptional case	Each consumer has holdings of each commodity greater than the amount of each commodity in some bundle in his consumption set. Subsequently weakened to: Each consumer is capable of supplying one type of productive good, say labor	Each consumer has holdings of each commodity greater than the amounts of each commodity associated with some point in his consumption set	Each agent can supply positive amounts of each good	Assumes irreducible economy, i.e., there is no way to partition consumers into two groups, such that neither is interested in trading with the other	Each individual has positive amounts of some good. Each commodity has positive marginal utility for each individual. Therefore, each individual has positive amounts of a good desired by all individuals	Assumptions are sufficient to guarantee that this does not arise

COMPARISON OF AXIOM SYSTEMS FOR EXISTENCE OF EQUILIBRIUM (*continued*)

Characteristic	*Model*				
	Arrow and Debreu	*Debreu*	*Gale*	*McKenzie*	*Debreu*
Possibility of zero production	Assumed for each production set	Assumed for each production set	Assumed for each production set	Assumed for aggregate production set. McKenzie does not make any assumptions about individual production sets	Assumed for each production set
Closure of production sets	Individual production sets are assumed closed	Aggregate production set is assumed closed	Individual production sets are assumed closed	Aggregate production set is assumed closed	Appropriately chosen set including aggregate production set is assumed closed
Convexity of production sets	Individual production sets are assumed convex	Aggregate production set is assumed convex	Individual production sets are assumed convex	Aggregate production set is assumed convex	Appropriately chosen set including aggregate production set is assumed convex
Reversibility of production	Excluded by assumption	Excluded by assumption	Boundedness assumes some irreversibility for individual production sets	Not excluded, hence possibility of negative equilibrium prices	Not ruled out
Free disposal	Implied by assuming equilibrium prices nonnegative and negative excess demands possible in equilibrium	Assumed for aggregate production set	Implied by assuming equilibrium prices nonnegative and negative excess demands possible in equilibrium	Not assumed, as such	Not assumed, as such
Free production	Explicitly ruled out	Ruled out by irreversibility and free-disposal assumptions	Not explicitly ruled out	Explicitly ruled out	Not ruled out, as such

FOUR

WELFARE ECONOMICS

4-1 INTRODUCTION

Almost without exception, the great works of economics have dealt with problems that go considerably beyond the description and analysis of the workings of the economic system; instead, economists such as Smith, Malthus, Ricardo, Marx, Walras, Marshall, and Keynes were also concerned with the critical appraisal of the operation of the economy in terms of such criteria as efficiency and equity. The distinction between the descriptive-analytical aspect of economics and the appraisal and evaluation of states of the economy or methods of organizing the economic system may be summarized in the statement that economics has a *normative* as well as a *positive* aspect—economists have been and are concerned with whether an economic system produces "good" results as well as with determining what those results are and how they are achieved. This chapter summarizes some of the important recent findings of *welfare economics* (the generic term for the normative aspect of economics), particularly with respect to equilibrium positions of a competitive economy.

The fundamental distinction between positive economics and welfare economics is that positive economics is, or pretends to be, a science. Its assumptions as well as its conclusions, at least under ideal circumstances, can be subjected to empirical and/or logical tests to determine their truth or falsity, for example, as in testing the truth of the postulate that producers are profit maximizers. The basic assumptions underlying welfare economics, on the other hand, are value judgments that any economist is free to accept or reject; there is no conceivable manner in which the truth or falsity of these axioms could be tested. Welfare economics is scientific only insofar as its conclusions are based upon the results of positive economics; thus, given value judgments sufficient to define what is meant by a "desirable" state of the economy, positive economics can be employed to determine whether such a state is possible of achievement under a certain method of organizing the economy. The conclusion of such an analysis may then be subjected to the same tests for truth or falsity as those employed in other aspects of positive economics.

A primary objective of welfare economics is to provide a guide for distinguishing between "good" ("desirable") and "bad" ("undesirable") states of the economy. Because of the diversity of opinion, even among "reasonable" men, as to the meaning of these terms, the ultimate validity of much of welfare economics must remain a matter of personal opinion. In principle, one could conceive of a whole host of theories of welfare economics, based upon differing sets of value judgments concerning the manner in which the term "desirable" state of the economy or economic system should be defined; in practice, essentially all of modern welfare economics is based upon one fundamental ethical postulate. To borrow Samuelson's phrase: In evaluating states of the economy, *individuals' preferences are to count*.[1] What this postulate amounts to is the acceptance, in some form or other, of the individualistic tradition of our society: states of the economy are to be judged "good" or "bad" according to how the members of the society judge them, not in terms of abstract standards of good and evil that are independent of the preferences of these individuals. It is within the restricted framework imposed by this fundamental ethical postulate that the remainder of the discussion of this chapter will take place.

In the next section of this chapter, the notions of social rankings and social welfare functions are introduced. A social ranking, together with its corresponding social welfare function, arises through a specialization of the fundamental ethical postulate to incorporate a particular set of value judgments about the way in which individual preferences are to be weighed in evaluating states of the economy. When combined with assumptions about the scope of the social ranking, the issue of the consistency of any set of value judgments arises. The most important result in the literature dealing with the consistency problem is Arrow's possibility theorem, which is summarized in Sec. 4-3.

A rigorous approach to the study of the welfare properties of the competitive system relative to its alternatives is just in its infancy. However, a considerable literature exists dealing with the so-called "optimality" properties of the competitive mechanism. The final sections of this chapter are concerned with the main results of this literature.

[1] Paul A. Samuelson, *The Foundations of Economic Analysis*, p. 223, Harvard University Press, Cambridge, Mass., 1955.

4-2 SOCIAL RANKINGS AND SOCIAL WELFARE FUNCTIONS

It will be recalled from Chap. 1 that the basic postulate of consumer theory states that each consumer possesses a complete, transitive, reflexive preference ranking over any set of states of the economy, and that when faced with choices from among the states comprising any such set, the consumer chooses that state, if it exists, that is highest on his preference scale. Equivalently (subject to the requirement that preference sets be closed as discussed in Chaps. 1 and 2), the consumer chooses that state, if it exists, that has the highest utility number associated with it. The postulate of well-behaved preference rankings is an assumption concerning consumer tastes and actions that is in principle verifiable and not a value judgment.[1]

In contrast, in welfare economics the problem arises of determining some generally acceptable method of constructing a ranking over any set of states of the economy in terms of what might be called the "social desirability" or "social welfare" associated with the states, using as primary data the preference rankings over the states held by the consumers in the economy. The very fact that consumer preferences are taken to be relevant to the problem of determining the social desirability of states is, as has been pointed out, a value judgment, but it is one that appears generally acceptable to economists.[2] The difficulty is, however, that in order to specify a rule for moving from individual preferences to a social preference ranking (a ranking of states in terms of social desirability), it is necessary to specialize the general ethical postulate that individuals' preferences are to count by introducing further value judgments of a more controversial nature. Any such specialization gives rise to a rule that is referred to as a *social ranking*, differences among social rankings being based on the different value judgments employed in constructing the rules.

Ideally, we would wish any social ranking to have the same general characteristics as the individual preference rankings on which the social ranking is based; i.e., given any set of states of the economy S and given any set of well-behaved individual rankings over S, then a social ranking R (to be read "is at least as socially preferred as") should satisfy the following properties.

[1] In what follows we shall use the term "well-behaved" to refer to a preference ranking that is complete, transitive, and reflexive.

[2] Fundamental to the notion that individual preferences are relevant to social desirability is the assumption that these individual preferences in turn are somehow related to the satisfaction or "happiness" of consumers, an assumption that is at least somewhat debatable. See I. M. D. Little, *A Critique of Welfare Economics*, Oxford University Press, London, 1960. See especially chap. II.

1. Completeness property: If $\mathbf{Z}', \mathbf{Z}'' \in S$, then either $\mathbf{Z}'\ \mathrm{R}\ \mathbf{Z}''$ or $\mathbf{Z}''\ \mathrm{R}\ \mathbf{Z}'$ (or both). [Given any two states of the economy (and given any set of well-behaved preference rankings by consumers over those states), the social ranking asserts either that the first is at least as socially preferred as the second, or that the second is at least as socially preferred as the first, or that both of these relations hold, in which case the two states are said to be socially indifferent.]
2. Transitivity property: If $\mathbf{Z}', \mathbf{Z}'', \mathbf{Z}''' \in S$, and if $\mathbf{Z}'\ \mathrm{R}\ \mathbf{Z}''$, $\mathbf{Z}''\ \mathrm{R}\ \mathbf{Z}'''$, then $\mathbf{Z}'\ \mathrm{R}\ \mathbf{Z}'''$. (If any state $\mathbf{Z}'$ is at least as socially preferred as a second state $\mathbf{Z}''$, and if the second state is at least as socially preferred as a third state $\mathbf{Z}'''$, then the first state must be at least as socially preferred as the third state.)
3. Reflexivity property: If $\mathbf{Z}' \in S$, then $\mathbf{Z}'\ \mathrm{R}\ \mathbf{Z}'$. (Any state of the economy is at least as socially preferred as itself.)

In a manner identical to that employed in dealing with individual preference rankings, we define strict social preference, denoted by the symbol P, by

$$\mathbf{Z}'\ \mathrm{P}\ \mathbf{Z}'' \qquad \text{if } \mathbf{Z}'\ \mathrm{R}\ \mathbf{Z}'' \text{ and not } \mathbf{Z}''\ \mathrm{R}\ \mathbf{Z}'$$

Similarly, social indifference I is defined by

$$\mathbf{Z}'\ \mathrm{I}\ \mathbf{Z}'' \qquad \text{if } \mathbf{Z}'\ \mathrm{R}\ \mathbf{Z}'' \text{ and } \mathbf{Z}''\ \mathrm{R}\ \mathbf{Z}'$$

[If R satisfies (1), (2), and (3), then P and I will both satisfy the transitivity property.]

Given any social ranking R for which properties 1, 2, and 3 hold, we can construct a social welfare function $W = W(\mathbf{Z})$ for $\mathbf{Z} \in S$, where W is an assignment of real numbers to states of the economy, in a manner that preserves the ordering of social preference determined by R, that is, W satisfies

$$W(\mathbf{Z}') \geqq W(\mathbf{Z}'') \qquad \text{if and only if } \mathbf{Z}'\ \mathrm{R}\ \mathbf{Z}''$$
$$W(\mathbf{Z}') = W(\mathbf{Z}'') \qquad \text{if and only if } \mathbf{Z}'\ \mathrm{I}\ \mathbf{Z}''$$
$$W(\mathbf{Z}') > W(\mathbf{Z}'') \qquad \text{if and only if } \mathbf{Z}'\ \mathrm{P}\ \mathbf{Z}''\dagger$$

† As in the case of utility functions for individual consumers, closure of social preference sets is needed to ensure the existence of a social welfare function associated with a social ranking R. Perhaps a more illuminating way to write W is $W = W(\mathrm{R}_1(\mathbf{Z}), \ldots, \mathrm{R}_m(\mathbf{Z}))$, since it is the ranking of states by consumers that is relevant to the determination of W. Social welfare functions satisfying this definition first appeared in the pioneering work of Bergson. See A. Bergson, A Reformulation of Certain Aspects of Welfare Economics, *Quarterly Journal of Economics*, vol. 52, pp. 310–344, 1938. For critical discussions of the concept of a social welfare function, see Samuelson, *op. cit.*, chap. VIII;

It will be noted that the social welfare function W fills the same role relative to the social ranking R that an ordinal utility function u^j does relative to an individual preference ranking R_j. In both cases, an abstract ranking relationship is replaced by an ordering over real numbers. As the analogy suggests, social welfare functions are ordinal in that any increasing transformation of a social welfare function is itself a social welfare function.

A simple example of a social ranking R (and its associated social welfare function W) satisfying the conditions given above is provided by a *dictatorial ranking*, i.e., a social ranking of states of the economy (for any set of well-behaved preferences by individuals in the economy) that is identical to that of some one individual in the economy. Since each consumer is assumed, as a matter of fact, to possess a well-behaved preference ranking, clearly a social ranking that reflects precisely the tastes of any one consumer will in turn be well-behaved and thus will be characterized by properties (1), (2), and (3) above. The social welfare function associated with this social ranking is simply the ordinal utility function of the "dictator," or any increasing transformation of his utility function. Such a ranking (or social welfare function) has little interest for us, however, involving as it does such a trivial use of the postulate that in evaluating states of the economy, "individuals' preferences are to count."

The neoclassical school of economists employed the assumption that interpersonal comparisons of utility among consumers (at least of the same social class) were possible. As has been mentioned earlier, this assumption is not, in and of itself, a value judgment; rather, it is based on the conceivably testable assumption that for each individual there exists a common measuring rod for "intensity of preference," identically calibrated as far as the units are concerned. (The "zero level" of preference need not be the same for all individuals.[1]) Given the assumption of interpersonal comparisons of utility, a whole host of social rankings and/or social welfare functions become possibilities, the rankings differing from one another according to the way in which different individuals are weighted in arriving at a total score denoting the social welfare measure

---

Jerome Rothenberg, *The Measurement of Social Welfare*, Prentice-Hall, Inc., Englewood Cliffs, N.J., 1961; and Kenneth J. Arrow, *Social Choice and Individual Values*, John Wiley & Sons, Inc., New York, 1951. Strictly speaking, in Arrow's terminology social welfare functions are defined over *social states*, in which collective commodities such as government services are included in the specification of the state. By a mild strengthening of our definition of a state of the economy, such collective commodities may be incorporated into the concept of a state of the economy.

[1] Perhaps the clearest discussion of the question of interpersonal comparisons of utility and value judgments is found in Little, *op. cit.*, chap. III.

assigned to any state. The assignment of weights to individuals in such a social ranking represents the implementation of whatever value judgments are imposed in constructing the ranking. Thus, for example, Ricardo argued for repeal of the Corn Laws essentially on the grounds that losses suffered by landlords through repeal were "less important" than the gains to laborers and capitalists, these latter constituting the "productive" members of society. Most economists today, however, are more than somewhat skeptical about the usefulness of social welfare functions based on interpersonal comparisons of utility because of the theoretical and practical difficulties associated with measurement of intensity of preference. A natural question to raise is whether there exists some other general approach to the construction of social rankings that involves less restrictive assumptions concerning the tastes of consumers. It is this problem that we next consider in the context of Arrow's possibility theorem.

4-3 THE ARROW POSSIBILITY THEOREM[1]

In specifying a rule for constructing a social ranking of states based upon individual preference rankings of states, two issues immediately arise: (1) What is to be the *scope* of the social ranking, i.e., for what class of economic environments is the rule to provide a social ranking of states? (2) What are the specific value judgments to be imposed in implementing the fundamental ethical postulate that individuals' preferences are to count in the social ranking? It has been mentioned earlier that the theorems of economics possess a substantial degree of generality, in that they hold for a rather broad class of configurations of tastes and resource endowments on the part of consumers and of production possibility sets for producers. This generality is required because of the economist's lack of precise knowledge concerning the nature of the parameters of the economic environment, coupled with the strong suspicion that these parameters are highly variable over time. On much the same grounds it may be argued that any social ranking should have a broad scope in terms of the class of economic environments to which it is applicable; if not, there is no assurance that the answers provided by the ranking rule have applicability to any particular situation the economist wishes to investigate. In particular, a rule that provides a complete, transitive, and reflexive social ranking of states for any conceivable economic environment (with individual preferences being well behaved) might be termed a *universal* social ranking rule.

The question posed in Arrow's possibility theorem is: If we exclude universal social rankings based upon interpersonal comparisons

[1] See Arrow, *op. cit.*, and Rothenberg, *op. cit.*

of utility and rankings of the dictatorial variety, is it possible to construct a universal social ranking rule that is consistent with the fundamental ethical postulate? With a proper specification of what is meant by being consistent with the fundamental ethical postulate of welfare economics, the answer to this question is that no such social ranking rule exists. That is, in a certain sense, the fundamental ethical postulate is inconsistent with the existence of universal social ranking rules. In light of this result, it will not be surprising to find that the bulk of the remainder of this chapter deals with social rankings lacking the universality characteristic or that, in most cases, the answers provided to questions by welfare economics are of a highly qualified nature.

Specifically, the conditions laid down by Arrow concerning the scope of the social ranking rule and the value judgments implementing the fundamental ethical postulate are the following:

Condition 1 (the *free triple* condition—a universality condition on the scope of the social ranking rule): Given any three states of the economy, the social ranking R must provide a complete, transitive, and reflexive ranking of the states for any set of well-behaved individual preference rankings over the states.[1]

Condition 2 (the responsiveness condition): Let $R_1, \ldots, R_m$ be the rankings of individuals $1, \ldots, m$ over two states of the economy $\mathbf{Z}'$ and $\mathbf{Z}''$. Let $R'_1, \ldots, R'_m$ be some other set of rankings over $\mathbf{Z}'$ and $\mathbf{Z}''$ such that $\mathbf{Z}'$ is ranked higher for some individuals and no lower for any individual as compared with the rankings $R_1, \ldots, R_m$. Then, if under the rankings R_j, $\mathbf{Z}' \mathrm{P} \mathbf{Z}''$, it must be the case that $\mathbf{Z}' \mathrm{P}' \mathbf{Z}''$, where the social ranking P' is associated with the individual rankings R'_j.

Condition 3 (independence of irrelevant alternatives): Let $R_1, \ldots, R_m$ and $R'_1, \ldots, R'_m$ be two sets of rankings by individuals $1, \ldots, m$ over any set of states of the economy, and let $\mathbf{Z}^*$ and $\mathbf{Z}^{*\prime}$ be the socially most preferred states, respectively, corresponding to individual rankings R_j and R'_j. Assume that for any two states $\mathbf{Z}'$, $\mathbf{Z}''$ in the set, $\mathbf{Z}' R_j \mathbf{Z}''$ if and only if $\mathbf{Z}' R'_j \mathbf{Z}''$ for every $j = 1, \ldots, m$. Then $\mathbf{Z}^* = \mathbf{Z}^{*\prime}$. [Condition 3 states that as long as the ranking of states by all individuals remains the same over any set of states, the

[1] Because of a defect in the proof of the possibility theorem as presented in the first edition of *Social Choice and Individual Values*, Arrow's condition had to be modified slightly to establish the theorem. See J. Blau, The Existence of Social Welfare Functions, *Econometrica*, vol. 25, no. 2, pp. 302–313, April, 1957. The modified condition is presented above; in the original version of this condition, Arrow required only that one set of three states exist satisfying the condition, hence the term "free triple."

most preferred state in the set (in terms of the social ranking) cannot be changed. For example, assume an individual ranks three states Z', Z'', and Z''' as Z' preferred to Z'' preferred to Z'''. Then assume that the ranking of this individual is changed to Z' preferred to Z''' preferred to Z'', every other individual retaining whatever ranking of the three states he originally held. Condition 3 asserts that if Z' were originally ranked socially preferred to Z''', it still must be the case under the new set of preference rankings, since the ranking of the states in the set consisting only of Z' and Z''' has not changed for any individual. In effect, the ranking of Z'' relative to these two states on any individual's ranking is irrelevant to the social ranking between Z' and Z'''.]

Condition 4 (the nonimposition condition): The social ranking R is not to be imposed. (A social ranking R is said to be *imposed* if, for some pair of distinct states Z' and Z'', the social ranking is $Z' \ R \ Z''$ for every set of well-behaved individual rankings $R_1, \ldots, R_m$ over the states Z' and Z''. Condition 4 excludes any social ranking that is completely insensitive to the preferences of the members of the society, since an imposed ranking provides a ranking independently of the preferences of such members. Coupled with condition 2, Arrow refers to this condition as a "citizen's sovereignty" condition.)

Condition 5 (the nondictatorship condition): The social ranking R is not to be dictatorial. (A social ranking R is said to be *dictatorial* if there exists an individual k such that for all states Z' and Z'', $Z' \ P_k \ Z''$ implies $Z' \ P \ Z''$, for any well-behaved rankings $R_1, \ldots, R_m$ of all individuals other than individual k.)

Arrow's theorem may now be stated:

ARROW POSSIBILITY THEOREM: No social ranking R exists that satisfies conditions 1 to 5.

Before outlining the proof of the Arrow theorem, it might be well to summarize the role played by each of the five conditions stated above. Condition 1 is the condition specifying the *scope* of the social ranking and involves no value judgments. The remaining conditions are Arrow's value-judgment specializations of the fundamental ethical postulate. Conditions 2, 4, and 5 are rather straightforward, but condition 3 is a little difficult to interpret. On the one hand, as the interpretation of this condition given above indicates, condition 3 states that the social ranking among states in any set depends only on the individual rankings of states *in that set;* on the other hand, it also specifies that the social rankings of states shall depend only upon the individual *rankings* of such states. A second reading of the condition indicates its place in the Arrow theorem:

Condition 3 excludes social rankings based upon interpersonal comparisons of utility because intensity of preference is not taken to be relevant to the social ranking—it is only the position in the rankings of individuals that counts in the social ranking. Thus conditions 1 to 5 exclude both universal social rankings based upon interpersonal comparisons of utility and those of a dictatorial variety.

Arrow's proof of the possibility theorem utilizes the concept of a decisive group. A group of individuals is said to constitute a *decisive group* with respect to a set of states of the economy if, when the members of the group unanimously prefer one state in the set to some other, the social ranking agrees with this ranking, regardless of the rankings with respect to these states held by the rest of the members of the community.

The steps in the proof of the possibility theorem may be outlined as follows: (1) the entire community is shown to constitute a decisive group with respect to any pair of states; (2) since a decisive group exists with respect to any pair of states, there must exist a smallest decisive group with respect to these states, i.e., a decisive group that contains no more members than any other decisive group; (3) if the smallest decisive group consists of only one individual, then that individual is shown to be a dictator; hence condition 5 is violated; (4) finally, it is shown that any decisive group consisting of two or more members contains a smaller decisive group, which establishes Arrow's theorem.

The proof of step 1 is straightforward: we wish to show that given any pair of states $\mathbf{Z}'$ and $\mathbf{Z}''$, $\mathbf{Z}' \mathrm{P}_j \mathbf{Z}''$ for every $j = 1, \ldots, m$ implies $\mathbf{Z}' \mathrm{P} \mathbf{Z}''$. By condition 4, it cannot be the case that $\mathbf{Z}'' \mathrm{R} \mathbf{Z}'$ for every set of individual rankings over these states; hence, for some sets of individual rankings, $\mathbf{Z}' \mathrm{P} \mathbf{Z}''$. Consider now changing the individual rankings so that each individual strictly prefers $\mathbf{Z}'$ to $\mathbf{Z}''$. By condition 2, this cannot change the social ranking $\mathbf{Z}' \mathrm{P} \mathbf{Z}''$, so the community constitutes a decisive group with respect to any pair of states.

We next show that if an individual is decisive with respect to some pair of states, that individual is decisive with respect to all states, i.e., the individual is a dictator. This is first established for the special case in which the set of states being ordered consists of only three states, under the special assumption that the rest of the community has identical rankings with respect to the three states; the generalization to the case in which the rest of the community's preferences are mixed and the number of states being ordered is arbitrary is then easily made.

Let three states of the economy be labeled **X**, **Y**, and **Z**. It is assumed that some individual (Mr. *A*) is decisive with respect to states **X** and **Y**, that is, Mr. *A*'s preference for **X** over **Y** determines the social ranking between **X** and **Y**. We wish to show that this implies that Mr. *A* is decisive with respect to all three states **X**, **Y**, and **Z**. We assume that Mr. *A* ranks the states $\mathbf{X} \mathrm{P}_A \mathbf{Y} \mathrm{P}_A \mathbf{Z}$ and consider in turn the six possible cases of strong rankings that could be held over the three states by the rest of the community. For convenience and to save space, the ranking symbols for Mr. *A* and for the rest of the community are compressed into the following table.

Mr. A's ranking	*Rest of community ranking*		*Proof that* **X P Y P Z**
XYZ	**XYZ**	(case 1)	Unanimity (the community is a decisive group)
XYZ	**YZX**	(case 2)	**X P Y** by hypothesis **Y P Z** by unanimity **X P Z** by transitivity of **P**
XYZ	**XZY**	(case 3)	**X P Y** by hypothesis **X P Z** by unanimity **Y P Z**(?)—Assume Mr. *A*'s ranking is changed to **YXZ**. By condition 3, this cannot change the social ranking between **Y** and **Z**. But now **Y P X** by hypothesis, **X P Z** by unanimity, and thus, by transitivity of P, **Y P Z**. Since **Y P Z** when Mr. *A*'s ranking is **YXZ**, we must have **Y P Z** when Mr. *A*'s ranking is **XYZ**.
XYZ	**ZYX**	(case 4)	**X P Y** by hypothesis **X P Z** by condition 3 and case 2 above; if the rest of the community's preferences are **YZX**, we have **X P Z**. Changing these preferences to **ZYX** does not change the ranking between **X** and **Z** on any ranking; hence the social ranking is unchanged. **Y P Z** by condition 3 and case 3 above
XYZ	**ZXY**	(case 5)	**X P Y** by hypothesis **X P Y** by condition 3 and case 2 above **Y P Z** by condition 3 and case 3 above
XYZ	**YXZ**	(case 6)	**X P Y** by hypothesis **X P Z** by unanimity **Y P Z** by unanimity

The arguments summarized in the above table are presented for the case in which the rest of the community is assumed to have a strong ranking with respect to the states **X**, **Y**, and **Z**; however, the conclusion that Mr. *A* decisive between **X** and **Y** implies Mr. *A* decisive among all three states still holds if indifference among states is admitted as a possibility for the rest of the community. Assume that Mr. *A* is decisive between **Y** and **Z** when Mr. *A* prefers **Y** to **Z** and the rest of the community prefers **Z** to **Y**. We wish to show that this decisiveness still holds when the rest of the community is indifferent between **Z** and **Y**. By condition 3, the social ranking between **Z** and **Y** depends only on the rankings of the members of the community between these two states. By condition 2, if **Y** is ranked socially preferred to **Z** under a certain set of rankings for the members of the community, **Y** must still be socially preferred to **Z** under another set of rankings under which **Y** is raised relative to **Z** on some rankings and does not fall relative to **Z** on any ranking. But this is precisely what happens when we change the rankings of the rest of the community from **Z** preferred to **Y** to **Z** indifferent to **Y**; hence the conclusion follows.

Since it has already been shown that Mr. *A* decisive between **X** and **Y** implies Mr. *A* decisive among **X, Y,** and **Z** for strong preferences on the part of the rest of the community, this conclusion holds for weak preferences as well.

If the assumption of identical preferences for all members of the community other than Mr. *A* is relaxed, the results summarized in the above table still hold. Assume Mr. *A* has the ranking **XYZ**, while various members of the community hold each of the rankings **XYZ, YZX, XZY, ZYX, ZXY,** and **YXZ**. Mr. *A* is assumed decisive between **X** and **Y**, so that the social ranking is **X** preferred to **Y**, but assume that the social ranking is **Z** preferred to **Y**. Then this ranking between **Z** and **Y** must still hold if we raise **Z** relative to **Y** on the rankings of the members of the community, by condition 2. Further, by condition 3, the social ranking between **Z** and **Y** depends only upon the individual rankings of *these* alternatives, not on their ranking relative to **X**. Hence, if we change every individual's ranking (except Mr. *A*'s) to **ZYX**, the social ranking must still be **Z** preferred to **Y**. But this contradicts case 4 of the table above, which asserts that when the rest of the community holds unanimously the preference ranking **ZYX**, the social ranking is **XYZ**. Thus Mr. *A* decisive between **X** and **Y** implies Mr. *A* decisive among **X, Y,** and **Z** even when preference rankings for the other members of the community are mixed.

The extension of the result given for the case of three states to an arbitrary number of states is made as follows: Assume Mr. *A* decisive between **X** and **Y** and assume that two other states **U** and **V** are given. If the ranking of Mr. *A* is **XYUV**, the state **U** fills the same role as **Z** above. Since the social ranking is **XYU**, Mr. *A* is decisive between **Y** and **U**, and the identical arguments used above establish that Mr. *A* is decisive between **U** and **V** (consider the ranking **YUV** for Mr. *A*, when Mr. *A* is decisive between **Y** and **U**). By essentially the same steps as those given in the table above, Mr. *A* decisive between **X** and **Y** establishes Mr. *A* decisive with respect to **X, Y,** and **U** in rankings for Mr. *A* of the form **XUY** and **UXY**; this leads to decisiveness of Mr. *A* with respect to the rankings **XUVY, UXVY, UVXY, XUVY,** and so forth. It thus may be concluded that under any set of well-behaved preference rankings for Mr. *A* and the rest of the community, if Mr. *A* is decisive with respect to any two states, Mr. *A* is decisive with respect to all states being ranked; hence Mr. *A* is a dictator.

Since the entire community constitutes a decisive group with respect to any set of alternatives, there exists a smallest decisive group associated with any set of alternatives. By the argument above, the smallest decisive group associated with any set of alternatives must include more than one individual, since if it does not, that individual will be a dictator, which violates condition 5. Hence, for the set of states **X**, **Y**, and **Z** assume that the smallest decisive group consists of two or more individuals. Let V_1 denote some member of this group and V_2 the remainder of the group. Assume that the preference ranking for V_1 is **XYZ**, while the ranking for V_2 is **YZX**. Since $V_1 \cup V_2$ is assumed decisive, the unanimous agreement of V_1 and V_2 determines the social ranking of **X**, **Y**, and **Z** for any rankings held by the rest of the community. Assume that the rest of the community unanimously ranks the states **ZXY**. Then in the social ranking, **Y** is preferred to **Z**, since V_1 and V_2 unanimously prefer **Y** to **Z**. If **X** is ranked higher than **Z**, V_1 is decisive between these two states since V_2 and the rest of the community unanimously prefer **Z** to **X**. Hence **Z** is at least as socially preferred as **X**, and, by transitivity of the social ranking, **Y** is ranked socially preferred to **X**. But this implies that V_2 is decisive between **X** and **Y**, since both V_1 and the rest of the community prefer **X** to **Y**. Therefore, V_2 is a smaller decisive group contained in the postulated smallest decisive group over the set of states **X**, **Y**, and **Z**. This contradiction establishes the Arrow possibility theorem.

Having outlined the proof of the Arrow possibility theorem, it might be well to return to the interpretation of the theorem. In essence, the possibility theorem is concerned with the logical consistency of any rule designed to provide a ranking of states of the economy with certain value judgments representing specializations of the fundamental ethical postulate of welfare economics. The theorem asserts, in effect, that if rules based upon interpersonal comparisons of utility are excluded, as are dictatorial rules, then there is no method of providing a consistent ranking of states for arbitrary well-behaved preference rankings on the part of individuals when the fundamental ethical postulate is assumed to hold. It might be noted that the theorem says nothing whatsoever about the possibility of obtaining a consistent social ranking for a *given* set of rankings on the part of individuals; such rankings can be constructed, but the theorem asserts that the rule employed in constructing the ranking will break down for some other set of rankings characterizing the members of the community—it is the impossibility of finding a rule that works in all cases, rather than the impossibility of finding a ranking for particular cases, that is relevant.

A discussion in rather complete detail of the criticisms that have been leveled at the Arrow approach is contained in the revised edition of *Social Choice and Individual Values*. We note here only certain of the objections that have centered upon condition 3, the "independence of irrelevant alternatives." It will be recalled that condition 3 asserts that if individual rankings over any set of states of the economy are altered in such a way that the same ranking of states holds for each member of the community, then the socially most preferred state in the set will remain unchanged. Is this a "reasonable" value judgment to impose? Hildreth, among others, has argued that it is not.[1] His argument is simply stated: Assume a community that consists of two individuals, Mr. *A* and Mr. *B*. Assume further that Mr. *A* ranks state **X** as "desperately" preferred to state **Y** in the sense that, as among, say, *n* states of the economy, **X** is ranked first and **Y** in the *n*th position, while Mr. *B* "barely" prefers state **Y** to state **X**, in the sense that **Y** is ranked first and **X** second in a list of the *n* states. Then, whatever the social ranking between states **X** and **Y**, by condition 3 this ranking must remain unchanged if Mr. *A*'s ranking is changed so that **X** is "barely" preferred to **Y** and Mr. *B*'s ranking is changed so that **Y** is "desperately" preferred to **X**. If **X** is ranked higher than **Y** in the social ranking, the ranking appears to be unreasonably insensitive to Mr. *B*'s preferences, while the same insensitivity with respect to Mr. *A*'s preferences is apparent if **Y** is ranked higher than **X**.

The source of difficulty, as was mentioned earlier, is that condition 3 requires that social rankings be influenced only by the *ranking* of states by individuals, not by the degree of intensity of preference among states on the part of individuals. In effect, condition 3 extends the ordinality assumption of positive economic theory to normative economics as well. The ordinality assumption has been adopted in positive economic theory because all the known characteristics of individual and aggregate demand and supply functions can be derived without being forced to resort to measures of intensity of preference; however, this does not mean that ordinality has any *a priori* claim to a preeminent position in other aspects of economic theory. In welfare economics, as Hildreth's argument indicates, ignoring intensity of preference as a relevant argument of the social welfare function leads to an implicit weighting of individuals that might well conflict with value judgments of a much more appealing character. In Chap. 1 it was noted that it is but a minor extension of the assumptions concerning the preference rankings of individual consumers to postulate not only that is a consumer able to form a well-behaved preference ranking, but also that he is capable of distinguishing among degrees of intensity of preference. One need not accept wholesale the interpersonal comparability of utility to argue that preference rankings alone are inadequate to reflect the tastes of consumers as they are to be incorporated into a social welfare function.

[1] See C. Hildreth, Alternative Conditions for Social Orderings, *Econometrica*, vol. 21, no. 1, pp. 89–90, 1953.

Whatever the appeal of this argument, in the remainder of this chapter we shall implicitly accept Arrow's position that universal social ranking rules have little if any place in welfare economics. In Secs. 4-4 and 4-5 we shall be primarily concerned with social welfare functions that "work" only for restricted sets of preference rankings for the individuals comprising the community; it is with such social welfare functions that the most important theorems of modern welfare economics are concerned.

4-4 THE PARETO RANKING

In the preceding section, it was shown that Arrow's five conditions implied that the entire community is a decisive group with respect to any set of states of the economy, i.e., if the entire community unanimously prefers some state $\mathbf{X}'$ to another state $\mathbf{X}''$, then the social ranking is $\mathbf{X}'$ socially preferred to $\mathbf{X}''$. It is difficult to conceive of any less controversial theorem following from the assumption that "individuals' preferences are to count." It is this rule, sometimes referred to as the *unanimity rule*, that forms the basis for the *Pareto ranking*.

Let the symbol R be read as "is at least as preferred as, in the Pareto sense," and P and I denote "is Pareto-superior to" and "is Pareto-indifferent to," respectively. These symbols are defined by the unanimity rule or Pareto ranking as follows:

Given a set of states of the economy S, where $\mathbf{X}', \mathbf{X}'' \in S$, then $\mathbf{X}' \mathrm{R} \mathbf{X}''$ if $\mathbf{X}' \mathrm{R}_j \mathbf{X}''$ for all $j = 1, \ldots, m$. (A state $\mathbf{X}'$ is said to be *at least as preferred as* $\mathbf{X}''$ *in the Pareto sense* if each individual in the community regards $\mathbf{X}'$ as at least as preferred as $\mathbf{X}''$.)

$\mathbf{X}' \mathrm{P} \mathbf{X}''$ if $\mathbf{X}' \mathrm{R}_j \mathbf{X}''$ for all $j = 1, \ldots, m$ and $\mathbf{X}' \mathrm{P}_k \mathbf{X}''$ for some k. (A state $\mathbf{X}'$ is said to be *Pareto-superior* to a state $\mathbf{X}'$ if every member of the community regards $\mathbf{X}'$ as at least as preferred as $\mathbf{X}''$, and for at least one individual, $\mathbf{X}'$ is regarded as strictly preferred to $\mathbf{X}''$.†)

$\mathbf{X}' \mathrm{I} \mathbf{X}''$ if $\mathbf{X}' \mathrm{I}_j \mathbf{X}''$ for all $j = 1, \ldots, m$. (A state $\mathbf{X}'$ is *Pareto-indifferent* to a state $\mathbf{X}''$ if every individual considers $\mathbf{X}'$ indifferent to $\mathbf{X}''$.)

A state $\mathbf{X}^* \in S$ is said to be a *Pareto-optimal state in* S if there does not exist a state $\mathbf{X} \in S$ such that $\mathbf{X} \mathrm{P} \mathbf{X}^*$. (A state $\mathbf{X}^* \in S$ is said to be Pareto-optimal in S if no state in S is Pareto-superior to $\mathbf{X}$.)

The Pareto ranking of states is referred to as a *partial* ranking, as contrasted with the *complete* rankings we have encountered in consumer theory, producer theory, and in the discussion of social rankings in connection with the Arrow possibility theorem. As the terms imply, a

† When a state $\mathbf{X}'$ is Pareto-superior to a state $\mathbf{X}''$, we also say that $\mathbf{X}''$ is *Pareto-inferior* to $\mathbf{X}'$.

complete ranking is one such that every element of the set under consideration can be ranked in terms of the ranking principle, while a partial ranking might specify no ranking with respect to certain elements of the set. Thus, in the Pareto ranking, if, as between two states of the economy, some individuals prefer the first to the second while others prefer the second to the first, no ranking is defined between these two states; instead the two states are said to be Pareto-noncomparable.

These concepts can be illustrated in terms of the following simple example: Assume there is \$1 available to be divided between two individuals, Mr. *A* and Mr. *B*. Further assume that both Mr. *A* and Mr. *B* are selfish in the sense defined earlier, i.e., they are each concerned solely with what they receive, not with what is received by anyone else. Both Mr. *A* and Mr. *B* are assumed to prefer more money to less. Then the feasible set of allocations of money between Mr. *A* and Mr *B* is shown in the diagram below, where it is assumed that money can be freely discarded, i.e., the total allocation can be any nonnegative amount of money up to and including \$1.

In Fig. 4-1, the set of feasible allocations *S* is the triangle, including its boundaries, with vertices at the points (0,0), (0,1), and (1,0). The set of Pareto-optimal points is clearly the boundary between (0,1) and (1,0), since no point in *S* is Pareto-superior to any point on that boundary. Consider some point in the interior of the set, say the allocation (0.25,0.50) denoted by **X**. Then, under the assumptions of selfishness and more money preferred to less, the set of points Pareto-superior to **X** is the

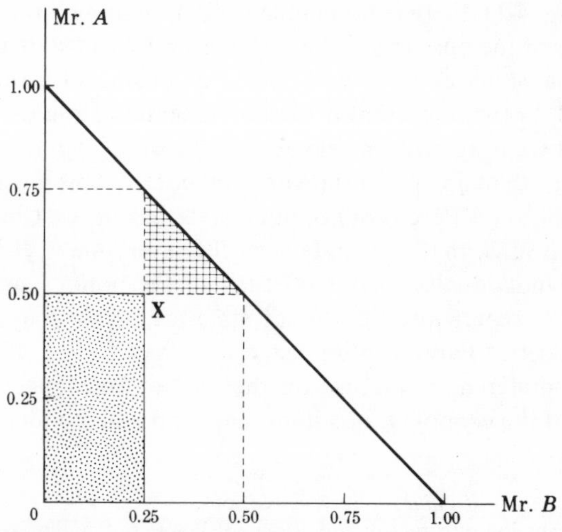

FIGURE 4-1

crosshatched region shown in Fig. 4-1, while the set of points Pareto-inferior to **X** is the shaded region of Fig. 4-1. The partial nature of the Pareto ranking is reflected in the fact that all points lying outside those two regions are noncomparable in terms of the Pareto ranking relative to the point **X**. For example, the Pareto-optimal point (1,0) is *not* Pareto-superior to **X**, and similarly for all Pareto-optimal points lying outside the boundaries (0.50,0.50) and (0.25,0.75).

In contrast to the situation depicted in Fig. 4-1, sets of states can be constructed in which no state is Pareto-optimal. For example, if the set pictured in Fig. 4-1 does not include its boundary between (0,1) and (1,0), then any point in the set has some point in the set Pareto-superior to it, as may easily be verified. Further, if the set of points under consideration is that including all points lying on or above the boundary between (0,1) and (1,0), no Pareto-optimal state exists. The similarity between the problem of ensuring the existence of a most preferred bundle for a consumer and the problem of ensuring the existence of a Pareto-optimal state is apparent. For the cases we shall consider, a sufficient condition for the existence of at least one Pareto-optimal state in a set is that the set of states being ranked be closed and bounded and that preferences of consumers be continuous, in the sense discussed in Chap. 3.[1]

It will be noted from Fig. 4-1 that the possibility exists that a set of states being ranked contains more than one Pareto-optimal state. Given two distinct Pareto-optimal states in a set *S*, say $\mathbf{X}^*$ and $\mathbf{X}^{**}$, then either $\mathbf{X}^* \,\mathrm{I}\, \mathbf{X}^{**}$ or $\mathbf{X}^*$ and $\mathbf{X}^{**}$ are Pareto-noncomparable. This follows directly from the definition of Pareto optimality. For Pareto-optimal states that are Pareto-noncomparable (e.g., as is true of all the Pareto-optimal states in Fig. 4-1), there is no manner of determining a ranking of these states in terms of the unanimity rule. However, we can state that the *set* of Pareto-optimal states constitutes a "best" set of states for the set of states being ranked, in the sense that if the fundamental axiom of welfare economics holds, there is at least one element in the set of Pareto-optimal states that is "better" than any given state not in the set. This must be the case since, by definition, a Pareto-nonoptimal state has at least one state Pareto-superior to it in *S*, that is, a state such that everyone is at least as well off and some individual(s) better off than in the nonoptimal state. For this reason, any search for the "best" state attainable may always be restricted to the set of Pareto-optimal states.

For known preference rankings on the part of consumers over a given set of states of the economy, it is in principle possible to identify the

[1] See Gerard Debreu, *Theory of Value*, John Wiley & Sons, Inc., pp. 92–93, New York, 1959, for a discussion of sufficient conditions for Pareto optimality explicitly in terms of consumption and production sets and consumer preference rankings.

set of Pareto-optimal states and to determine, for any given state, the set of states of the economy Pareto-superior to it. As has been emphasized earlier, however, precise knowledge of preference patterns of consumers is typically not available, and one might ask whether there is some method by which states of the economy can be compared in terms of the Pareto ranking in the absence of such knowledge. For the competitive case (selfish consumers, indifference curves bounding strictly convex sets, more preferred to less, parametric prices, utility maximized subject to the budget constraint), Samuelson's revealed preference approach can be utilized to provide certain comparisons of states in terms of the Pareto ranking. The following proposition holds:

Let $\mathbf{X}'$ and $\mathbf{X}''$ be two states of the economy achieved under the competitive case. Then $\mathbf{X}'$ can be judged Pareto-superior to $\mathbf{X}''$ independently of any knowledge of the specific preference patterns of consumers if and only if in $\mathbf{X}'$ each consumer has available to him that commodity bundle that was chosen as optimal by the consumer in state $\mathbf{X}''$, and some consumer has available to him a preferred bundle.

An equivalent statement of this proposition is as follows: Let $\mathbf{p}'$ and $\mathbf{p}''$ be price vectors associated with the states $\mathbf{X}'$ and $\mathbf{X}''$, where $\mathbf{p}' = (p_1', \ldots, p_n')$ and $\mathbf{p}'' = (p_1'', \ldots, p_n'')$. Assume $\mathbf{p}' \neq \mathbf{p}''$. Let $\mathbf{x}'^j = (x_{1j}', \ldots, x_{nj}')$ and $\mathbf{x}''^j = (x_{1j}'', \ldots, x_{nj}'')$ denote the commodity bundles chosen by the jth consumer in states $\mathbf{X}'$ and $\mathbf{X}''$, and let I'^j and I''^j denote the income of the jth consumer in states $\mathbf{X}'$ and $\mathbf{X}''$, where $I'^j = \mathbf{p}' \cdot \mathbf{x}'^j$, $I''^j = \mathbf{p}'' \cdot \mathbf{x}''^j$ for all $j = 1, \ldots, m$. Then the proposition asserts that $\mathbf{X}'$ may be judged Pareto-superior to $\mathbf{X}''$, independently of knowledge of the preference patterns of consumers, if and only if $\mathbf{p}' \cdot \mathbf{x}''^j \leqq I'^j$ for all $j = 1, \ldots, m$. That is, at the set of prices prevailing in state $\mathbf{X}'$ and given the income distribution in state $\mathbf{X}'$, each consumer must be able to choose, if he wishes, the commodity bundle he chose in state $\mathbf{X}''$.†

Clearly, if the condition $\mathbf{p}' \cdot \mathbf{x}''^j \leqq I'^j$ does not hold for some j, there is no way to guarantee that the consumer is as well off in $\mathbf{X}'$ as in $\mathbf{X}''$; hence the revealed preference condition is necessary for a comparison of states independently of knowledge of the preference patterns of consumers. On the other hand, if the condition is satisfied for each consumer, no consumer can be worse off in $\mathbf{X}'$ than in $\mathbf{X}''$. Under a smoothness condition on indifference curves and assuming indifference curves do not intersect the axes, $\mathbf{p}' \neq \mathbf{p}''$ implies that every consumer has available to him preferred bundles in $\mathbf{X}'$ as compared to $\mathbf{X}''$ because of strict convexity; hence $\mathbf{X}'$ is Pareto-superior to $\mathbf{X}''$. Figure 4-2 illustrates the proposition for the case of a one-consumer world.

† In order to ensure Pareto superiority of $\mathbf{X}'$ over $\mathbf{X}''$, some condition such as a one-to-one correspondence between price-income vectors and quantities demanded is required; otherwise $\mathbf{X}'$ and $\mathbf{X}''$ might be Pareto-indifferent.

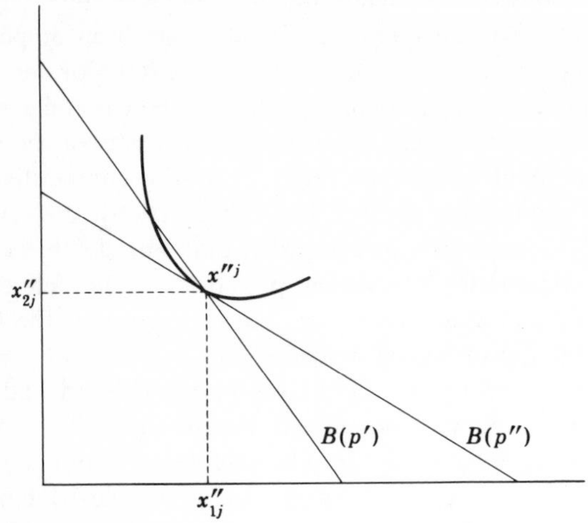

FIGURE 4-2

In Fig. 4-2, $B(\mathbf{p}'')$ is the budget constraint in state $\mathbf{X}''$ under the price vector $\mathbf{p}''$, and $\mathbf{x}''^j$ is chosen as optimal. In state $\mathbf{X}'$, $B(\mathbf{p}')$ is such that $\mathbf{x}''^j$ could be chosen; as the graph indicates, this means that bundles are available under $B(\mathbf{p}')$ that are strictly preferred to $\mathbf{x}''^j$. [The same conclusion follows, of course, if $B(\mathbf{p}')$ and $B(\mathbf{p}'')$ are interchanged.]

Even when precise knowledge concerning preference rankings of consumers is available, of course, in many cases it is not possible to rank states in terms of the Pareto ranking. Various attempts have been made to extend the scope of the Pareto ranking; we next consider briefly the most important of these efforts, the Hicks-Kaldor *compensation principle*.[1]

In essence, the compensation principle is an attempt to bypass the problems associated with distribution of income among consumers and to formulate a social ranking of states by examining the *real income* or level of output associated with states. The argument underlying the compensation principle as originally formulated is as follows: Assume two states of the economy, $\mathbf{X}'$ and $\mathbf{X}''$. If, in state $\mathbf{X}'$, the level of production is such that it is possible for those who gain in changing from $\mathbf{X}''$ to $\mathbf{X}'$ to compensate those who lose in changing from $\mathbf{X}''$ to $\mathbf{X}'$, so that everyone could potentially be at least as well off in $\mathbf{X}'$ as in $\mathbf{X}''$ and some consumers could

[1] A vast literature exists dealing with the compensation principle. Important sources include N. Kaldor, Welfare Propositions in Economics, *Economic Journal*, vol. 49, pp. 549–552, 1939; J. R. Hicks, Foundations of Welfare Economics, *Economic Journal*, vol. 49, pp. 696–712, 1939; Little, *op. cit.*, especially chap. VI; Rothenberg, *op. cit.*, especially chaps. 3 and 4; and Arrow, *op. cit.*, chap. 3.

be better off in **X**′, then **X**′ is to be judged socially preferred to state **X**″ even if no compensation is paid.

Scitovsky has pointed out a crucial objection to the compensation principle in the version outlined above.[1] The difficulty is that in this formulation of the compensation principle it might well turn out both that **X**′ is to be regarded as socially preferred to **X**″ *and* that **X**″ is to be regarded as socially preferred to **X**′, that is, the gainers can compensate the losers in moving from **X**′ to **X**″, and the gainers can compensate the losers in moving from **X**″ to **X**′. If this sounds a little paradoxical, consider the following example:

Assume two individuals, Mr. *A* and Mr. *B*, and two commodities, *a* and *b*. The distribution of output in two states of the economy **X**′ and **X**″ is shown in the table below:

	X′		X″	
	a	*b*	*a*	*b*
Mr. *A*	2	0	1	0
Mr. *B*	0	1	0	2

Assume that the preferences of Mr. *A* and Mr. *B* are given by:

Mr. *A*: 1 unit of *a* and 1 unit of *b* preferred to 2 units of *a* and 0 units of *b* preferred to 1 unit of *a* and 0 units of *b*.

Mr. *B*: 1 unit of *a* and 1 unit of *b* preferred to 0 units of *a* and 2 units of *b* preferred to 0 units of *a* and 1 unit of *b*.

Is **X**′ better than **X**″, using the compensation principle? Yes, since if in state **X**′, Mr. *A* gives one unit of *a* to Mr. *B*, then Mr. *B* is better off than in state **X**″, and Mr. *A* is no worse off than in state **X**″. Is state **X**″ better than state **X**′? Again yes, since if Mr. *B* gives one unit of *b* to Mr. *A*, then Mr. *A* is better off in **X**″ than in **X**′, while Mr. *B* is no worse off than in **X**′. Gainers can compensate losers in moving from **X**′ to **X**″ or in moving from **X**″ to **X**′. Under the compensation principle, we thus have **X**′ socially preferred to **X**″ and **X**″ socially preferred to **X**′.

This basic inconsistency can be cleared up if we require compensation to be actually paid out, but a further problem arises in this case.

[1] T. Scitovsky, A Note on Welfare Propositions in Economics, *Review of Economic Studies*, vol. 9, pp. 77–88, 1941.

Assume that in state **X**′ it is possible to compensate the losers from state **X**″ and that everyone is at least as well off (and someone better off) after compensation as in state **X**″. As Scitovsky's analysis indicates, it is not possible to state that **X**′ itself is socially preferred to **X**″, but it can be stated that **X**‴ (derived from **X**′ by actually paying compensation) is socially preferred to **X**″. When compensation is actually paid, however, this simply means that **X**‴ is Pareto-superior to **X**″, so the scope of the Pareto ranking has not been extended at all.

One further version of the compensation principle states that **X**′ is to be regarded as socially preferred to **X**″ if it is possible for the gainers to compensate the losers in moving from **X**′ to **X**″, but the gainers cannot compensate the losers in moving from **X**″ to **X**′. While this value judgment eliminates the Scitovsky paradox, it leads, as Arrow has shown, to the further paradox that a social ranking based on this criterion is not necessarily transitive.[1]

Arrow's example involves two individuals, two commodities, and three states of the economy. The holdings of each individual in each state are as follows:

Social state	*Mr. A*		*Mr. B*	
	Commodity 1	*Commodity* 2	*Commodity* 1	*Commodity* 2
X′	2.0	1.0	2.0	1.0
X″	1.7	1.3	1.8	1.1
X‴	1.0	2.0	1.0	2.0

Assume that Mr. A's preferences are such that in order of decreasing preference we have (2.1,1.0), (1.0,2.0), (2.4,0.7), (1.7,1.3), (2.0,1.0) and that the indifference curve containing (1.0,2.0) contains no bundle in which there is less than 0.9 of commodity 2. Also assume that the preferences of Mr. *B* are such that in order of decreasing preference we have (1.4,1.4), (1.0,2.0), (1.6,1.3), (1.8,1.1), (2.0,1.0) and that the indifference curve containing (1.0,2.0) contains no bundle in which there is less than 1.2 units of commodity 2.

Clearly both *A* and *B* are strictly better off in state **X**″ than they are in state **X**′. It goes without saying then that there is a way of redistributing the goods in state **X**″ so that everybody will be at least as well off as in state **X**′. (The obvious "redistribution" is of course **X**″ itself.) Now, in

[1] Arrow, *op. cit.*, pp. 44–45.

$\mathbf{X}'$ there are 4 units of commodity 1 and 2 units of commodity 2. Effect the following redistribution: Give 2.4 units of commodity 1 and 0.7 unit of commodity 2 to Mr. *A*. There then remain 1.6 units of commodity 1 and 1.3 units of commodity 2 for Mr. *B*. Then both *A* and *B* are better off than they were in $\mathbf{X}''$. Then, by the Scitovsky criterion, since it is possible to redistribute the goods in state $\mathbf{X}''$ in such a way that everybody is at least as well off as in state $\mathbf{X}'$, and it is also possible to redistribute the goods in state $\mathbf{X}'$ so that everybody is at least as well off as in $\mathbf{X}''$, $\mathbf{X}'$ and $\mathbf{X}''$ are socially indifferent.

Given the assumed preferences, both *A* and *B* are better off in state $\mathbf{X}'''$ than in state $\mathbf{X}''$. But if the 3.5 units of commodity 1 and 2.4 units of commodity 2 present in state $\mathbf{X}''$ are redistributed such that *A* has (2.1,1.0) and *B* has (1.4,1.4), then both *A* and *B* are better off than in state $\mathbf{X}'''$. Therefore, by the Scitovsky criterion, $\mathbf{X}''$ and $\mathbf{X}'''$ are socially indifferent. Thus, transitivity is violated.

In summary, then, the compensation principle in any of its various formulations does not represent a logically consistent technique for *extending* the scope of the Pareto ranking. To the extent that it is logically consistent with arbitrary preference rankings of consumers, it is identical to the Pareto ranking itself. It is apparently not possible to use aggregate real income as a basis for a social ranking if the fundamental ethical postulate is assumed to hold; the distribution of income cannot be ignored.

A widely used device for ranking states of the economy in terms of levels of output alone is Koopmans' *efficiency* ranking.[1] It should be noted that this ranking is not a social ranking in the sense that we have used the term in this chapter, but it does provide a convenient description or characterization of states in terms of a property that is intimately related to social welfare. Given a fixed vector of inputs, the set of all feasible output vectors is constructed. Within this set, an output vector is said to be *efficient* (in Koopmans' sense) if there does not exist an output vector in the feasible set that is weakly larger than the output vector in question; that is, $\mathbf{y}'$ in the set S of feasible output vectors is said to be efficient if there does not exist a vector $\mathbf{y}''$ belonging to S such that $\mathbf{y}'' \geq \mathbf{y}'$.†

Koopmans' efficiency ranking of output vectors is related to Pareto optimality in the following way: If every consumer in the community is

[1] T. C. Koopmans, Analysis of Production as an Efficient Combination of Activities, in T. C. Koopmans (ed.), *Activity Analysis of Production and Allocation*, John Wiley & Sons, Inc., New York, 1951.

† It will be recalled from Chap. 1 that $\mathbf{y}'' \geq \mathbf{y}'$ means $y_i'' \geq y_i'$ for every i and $y_k'' > y_k'$ for some k.

selfish, and if, for every commodity, there exists a consumer not satiated with respect to that commodity, then any Pareto-optimal state of the economy must be efficient in Koopmans' sense, although the converse, of course, does not hold. Like the Pareto ranking, Koopmans' efficiency ranking is a partial ranking, certain of the output vectors being non-comparable in terms of Koopmans' criterion in most sets of states.

The concept of a Pareto-optimal state thus implicitly involves on the production side the notion of Koopmans' efficiency (if selfishness and nonsatiation hold), while on the distribution side there is no attainable state that is unanimously at least as preferred by all consumers and strictly preferred by at least one consumer. Of particular importance to economists is the fact that there exists a close relationship between the concept of equilibrium of the competitive mechanism and Pareto optimality. The next section is concerned with this relationship.

4-5 PARETO OPTIMALITY AND COMPETITIVE EQUILIBRIUM

The notion that the competitive mechanism possesses certain "desirable" features relative to other methods of organizing the production and distribution of goods and services is present in most of the writings of the classical and neoclassical economists. It is only recently, however, that the study of comparative economic systems has been formulated in a rigorous manner; consequently there still remain many unsolved problems concerning this field. With respect to the competitive system, work done in the 1930s by Lerner and Lange, among others, led to the pathbreaking study by Arrow in the early 1950s. While some significant extensions of Arrow's work have been published, the essential concepts are present in Arrow's original paper, and we shall follow the argument of that paper in most of the discussion in this section.[1]

Consider any mechanism for organizing the production and distribution of goods and services, e.g., the competitive mechanism, central controls, etc. Following Hurwicz, we shall define a *Pareto-satisfactory*

[1] Kenneth J. Arrow, An Extension of the Basic Theorems of Classical Welfare Economics, in J. Neyman (ed.), *Proceedings of the Second Berkeley Symposium on Mathematical Statistics and Probability*, pp. 507–532, University of California Press, Berkeley, 1951. Extensions of Arrow's results appear in Kenneth J. Arrow and Gerard Debreu, Existence of an Equilibrium for a Competitive Economy, *Econometrica*, vol. 22, pp. 265–290, 1954; Gerard Debreu, Valuation Equilibrium and Pareto Optimum, *Proceedings of the National Academy of Sciences of the U.S.A.*, vol. 40, pp. 588–592, 1954; David Gale, The Law of Supply and Demand, *Mathematica Scandinavia*, vol. 3, pp. 155–169, 1955; and Gerard Debreu, *Theory of Value*, John Wiley & Sons, Inc., New York, 1959.

mechanism as one which possesses the following properties:[1]

1. Every equilibrium position of the mechanism is a Pareto-optimal state of the economy.
2. Given any Pareto-optimal state of the economy, under an appropriate choice of parameters, that Pareto-optimal state can be achieved as an equilibrium position of the mechanism.

Arrow's *Berkeley Symposium* paper proves that under a broad set of conditions, the competitive mechanism is a Pareto-satisfactory mechanism, i.e., every equilibrium position of a competitive system is a Pareto-optimal state of the economy, and given an arbitrary Pareto-optimal state of the economy, there exists a set of resource endowments for consumers and a price vector such that given these resource endowments and price vector, the competitive economy will be at equilibrium at that Pareto-optimal state. (Hurwicz refers to property 1 as an "efficiency" property and to property 2 as an "unbiasedness" property. "Efficiency" is here used in a sense different from that of Koopmans' efficiency discussed in the last section.)

Arrow's proof of the Pareto-satisfactory nature of the competitive mechanism is sometimes summarized loosely by the statements that "every competitive equilibrium is Pareto-optimal" and "every Pareto-optimal position is competitive equilibrium," but the second of these two statements is somewhat misleading, as a reading of the previous paragraph indicates. It is possible for a world containing monopolistic elements to attain Pareto-optimal states—the competitive mechanism is not the only method by which such socially preferable states of the economy can be reached.

An illustration of this (due to Hurwicz) is the following: Assume three individuals in a society, Mr. *A*, Mr. *B*, and Mr. *C*. Mr. *A* has two watches, Mr. *B* has \$20, and Mr. *C* has 5 cents. We assume selfishness and that Mr. *A* prefers money to watches, Mr. *B* prefers one watch to \$20, and Mr. *C* prefers one watch to 5 cents. If the market for watches operates competitively, so that one price prevails in the market, and demand and supply are equated, the price will be 5 cents per watch, with Mr. *A* ending up with 10 cents, Mr. *B* with one watch and \$19.95, and Mr. *C* with

[1] Leonid Hurwicz, Optimality and Informational Efficiency in Resource Allocation Processes, *Mathematical Methods in the Social Sciences, 1959:* Stanford University Press, Stanford, 1960. Hurwicz adds the condition of "essential single-valuedness," i.e., for given values of the parameters, if equilibrium is not unique, all equilibrium positions must be Pareto-indifferent. This condition will not be needed in our discussion, but it might be noted that the competitive mechanism satisfies "essential single-valuedness."

one watch. It is easy to verify that this equilibrium position is a Pareto-optimal state. Alternatively, assume that Mr. *A* is a perfectly discriminating monopolist. Then the equilibrium position of the economy will be one in which Mr. *A* charges Mr. *B* $20 for one watch and Mr. *C* 5 cents for one watch. The resulting distribution is Pareto-optimal since, in effect, Mr. *A* eliminates all the "consumer surplus" in the market. Hence the perfectly discriminating monopoly has led to a Pareto-optimal state.

It might be noted that the unbiasedness property of Pareto-satisfactory mechanisms (property 2 above) asserts that every Pareto-optimal state can be "reached" by the mechanism. That the competitive mechanism satisfies this property in the example above can be seen with respect to the discriminating monopoly equilibrium position by a redistribution of initial holdings so that Mr. *A* enters the market with $20.05, Mr. *B* with one watch, and Mr. *C* with one watch. Then no trading will occur at any set of prices; further, for any price of watches less than or equal to 5 cents per watch, we have competitive equilibrium for this set of initial holdings.

Before presenting Arrow's proof of the Pareto-satisfactory character of the competitive mechanism, it might be well to consider the intuitive appeal of the proposition graphically. In the next few pages we shall deal with the pure trade case involving two individuals, Mr. *A* and Mr. *B*, and two commodities, 1 and 2, using the Edgeworth box diagram discussed in Chap. 3. By the term *pure trade* we mean that there is assumed to be no production in the economy, so that the only economic activity is that of trading commodities.[1] Mr. *A* is assumed to enter the market with x_{1A}^0 units of commodity 1 and x_{2A}^0 units of commodity 2, while Mr. *B* is assumed to have initial holdings of x_{1B}^0 units of commodity 1 and x_{2B}^0 units of commodity 2. Both Mr. *A* and Mr. *B* are assumed to be selfish so that indifference curves for each of these individuals can be drawn independently of the holdings of the other. Figure 4-3 shows the normal case already depicted in Chap. 3.

In Fig. 4-3, the joint initial-holdings point (the initial state of the economy) is the point $\mathbf{X}^0$. Through the point $\mathbf{X}^0$ are drawn indifference curves for Mr. *A* and Mr. *B*, labeled I_1^A and I_1^B, respectively. The shaded area in the diagram is the set of holdings of commodities 1 and 2 that are Pareto-superior to the point $\mathbf{X}^0$; that is, they are feasible joint-holdings points (the joint holdings are consistent with the amounts of the commodities available), and each individual is at least as well off as at the point $\mathbf{X}^0$, with at least one individual better off. (The point $\mathbf{X}'$ is Pareto-indifferent to $\mathbf{X}^0$.) The set of all Pareto-optimal points is drawn from

[1] The discarding of commodities as an economic activity is admitted in certain cases. See the discussion of free disposal in Chap. 2 and in the succeeding pages.

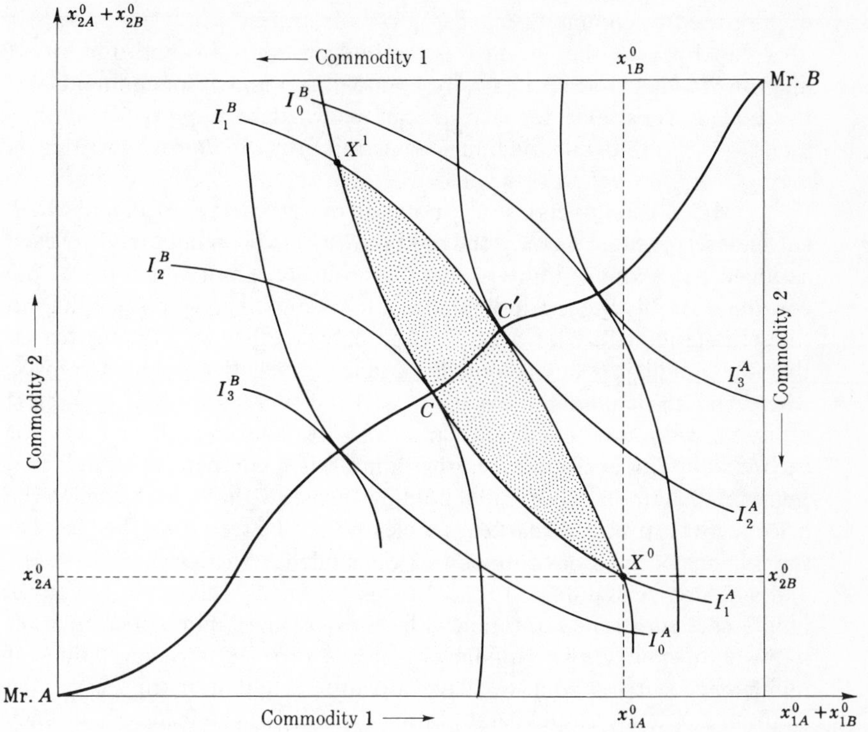

FIGURE 4-3

Mr. *A*'s origin to Mr. *B*'s origin. In particular, that segment of the curve lying in the shaded area consists of all those Pareto-optimal states that are Pareto-superior to the state $\mathbf{X}^0$. (All other Pareto-optimal states are noncomparable in terms of the Pareto criterion with respect to the state $\mathbf{X}^0$.) The Pareto-optimal points lying in the shaded region and on the boundary of this region (CC' in Fig. 4-3) have the property that each individual is at least as well off at any point of CC' as he was given the initial allocation $\mathbf{X}^0$. Since CC' thus denotes the set of all possible positions to which each individual would willingly go from the initial position $\mathbf{X}^0$, CC' is called the *contract curve* relative to $\mathbf{X}^0$.

A competitive equilibrium in the pure trade case can be shown on the Edgeworth box diagram by drawing a straight line through the initial-holdings point $\mathbf{X}^0$, this line representing the budget constraints for both Mr. *A* and Mr. *B* for some choice of prices of commodities 1 and 2. If the line is properly drawn (and if the conditions for existence of equilibrium are met), that point at which Mr. *A* maximizes utility subject to his budget constraint will coincide with the point at which Mr. *B* maximizes utility subject to his budget constraint, in which case supply equals demand for each of the two commodities, as Fig. 4-4 illustrates.

In Fig. 4-4, the line $B(\mathbf{p})$ is the budget constraint both for Mr. A and for Mr. B. Given prices p_1 for commodity 1 and p_2 for commodity 2, the budget constraint for Mr. A can be written as $p_1(x_{1A} - x_{1A}^0) + p_2(x_{2A} - x_{2A}^0) \leqq 0$, and the budget constraint for Mr. B can be written as $p_1(x_{1B} - x_{1B}^0) + p_2(x_{2B} - x_{2B}^0) \leqq 0$.

Mr. A can thus choose any point on or to the left of $B(\mathbf{p})$, and Mr. B can choose any point on or to the right of $B(\mathbf{p})$. Mr. A and Mr. B are each assumed to maximize utility, i.e., to choose that point which places the consumer on his highest indifference curve consistent with remaining in the set determined by his budget constraint, together with the restriction that final holdings of any commodity cannot be negative. At the point $\bar{\mathbf{X}}$, where Mr. A's final holdings are $(\bar{x}_{1A},\bar{x}_{2A})$ and Mr. B's are $(\bar{x}_{1B},\bar{x}_{2B})$, these utility-maximization conditions are met. In addition, the market for each commodity is cleared, i.e., the point $\bar{\mathbf{X}}$ is a competitive equilibrium point relative to the set of initial holdings given by the point $\mathbf{X}^0$, when the price vector is $\mathbf{p}$. That markets are cleared can be seen from the fact that the number of units of commodity 1 demanded by Mr. B is $(x_{1A}^0 - \bar{x}_{1A})$ and similarly for commodity 2. In this "normal" case (strictly convex indifference curves, no saturation with respect to any commodities by either individual), competitive equilibrium occurs only at tangency points of indifference curves. But we have already seen that in this case, the contract curve, the set of Pareto-optimal points, is the locus of tangency points of indifference curves, i.e., each competitive equilibrium position is Pareto-optimal.

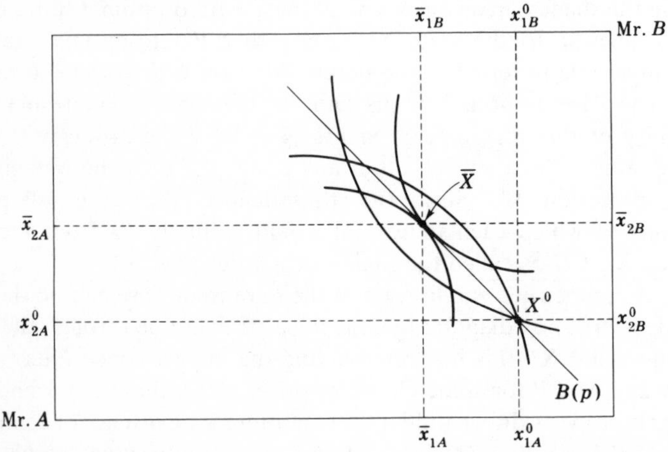

FIGURE 4-4

Similarly, assume that the economy is at a Pareto-optimal point in the "normal" case. It is a matter of complete indifference to us how this position was attained—whether by government decree, perfectly discriminating monopoly, or any other device. To be at a Pareto-optimal point means that the economy is at a tangency point of indifference curves. If we now choose a set of initial holdings for Mr. A and Mr. B identical to those at the Pareto-optimal point, the fact that a tangency exists means that we can draw a budget line $B(\mathbf{p})$ through this point in such a way that both Mr. A and Mr. B will remain at the point if they maximize utility subject to the budget constraint $B(\mathbf{p})$, and because of the tangency condition, markets are cleared, i.e., the Pareto-optimal point can be reached by the competitive mechanism. Thus the Pareto-satisfactory character of the competitive mechanism is seen to have a strong intuitive appeal in the case considered—the "normal" case of pure trade theory.

When the assumptions of nonsatiation and strict convexity of indifference curves are relaxed, we obtain what might be referred to as "nonnormal" cases. In particular, if indifference curves with straight line segments are permitted, the contract curve might be thick, as shown in Fig. 4-5*a*, or might follow the boundary of the Edgeworth box diagram, as illustrated in Fig. 4-5*b*.

In Fig. 4-5*a*, the crosshatched area is the set of Pareto-optimal points. In Fig. 4-5*b*, the set of Pareto optima is the left and upper boundary of the Edgeworth box diagram. While the cases shown in Fig. 4-5 are not the "normal" ones usually depicted, they are not excluded, for example, on the basis of the axiom system for existence of competitive equilibrium as formulated by Debreu and considered in the previous chapter. Further some graphing of price lines in Fig. 4-5 should be sufficient to convince the reader that the Pareto-satisfactory nature of the competitive mechanism can be established even in these "abnormal" cases.

The competitive mechanism is not necessarily Pareto-satisfactory when the nonsatiation assumption is relaxed. For example, in Fig. 4-6, it is assumed that both Mr. A and Mr. B possess bliss points in the interior of the Edgeworth box diagram, these bliss points being denoted by $\hat{\mathbf{X}}_A$ and $\hat{\mathbf{X}}_B$, respectively.

In Fig. 4-6, the set of Pareto optima consists only of those points representing tangencies of indifference curves between the two bliss points $\hat{\mathbf{X}}_A$ and $\hat{\mathbf{X}}_B$. This may be established by considering any point to the left of $\hat{\mathbf{X}}_A$. $\hat{\mathbf{X}}_A$ is clearly Pareto-superior to any such point, and a similar argument applies to any point to the right of $\hat{\mathbf{X}}_B$. Is the competitive mechanism Pareto-satisfactory in this case? The answer is that it is, if we admit the possibility of negative prices. A negative price for a commodity means that a consumer is paid for accepting units of the commodity or,

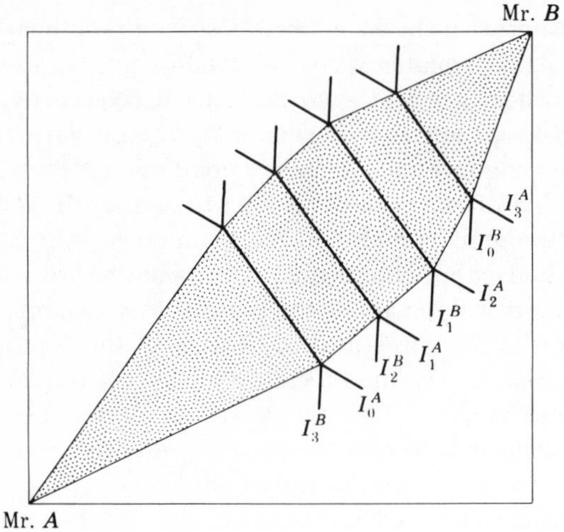

(a)

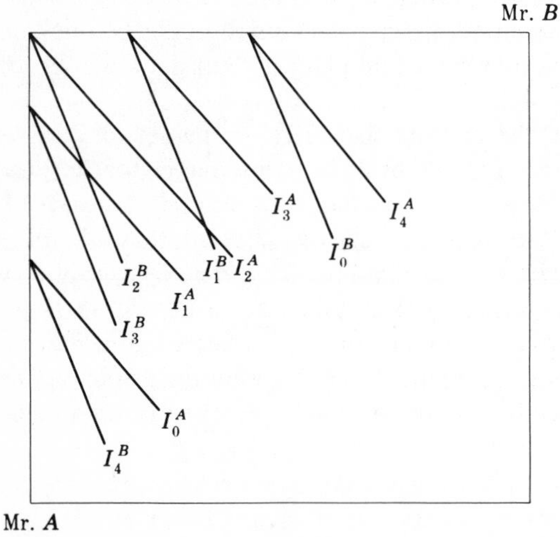

(b)

FIGURE 4-5

alternatively, that it costs something to dispose of unwanted units of the commodity. Consider the point $\mathbf{X}^0$, which is a Pareto-optimal point—a movement in any direction away from $\mathbf{X}^0$ can make one consumer better off only by making the other worse off. Let $B(\mathbf{p})$ be the budget constraint associated with prices p_1 and p_2. Clearly, if these prices were positive, both Mr. A and Mr. B would move to their bliss points, which lie within the set of points attainable for them. If this were the case, then markets would not be cleared; in fact, there would be excess supplies of both commodity 1 and commodity 2. On the other hand, if p_1 and p_2 were both negative, then the budget constraint for Mr. *A* would restrict him to points on or to the *right* of $B(\mathbf{p})$, and Mr. *B* would be restricted to points on or to the *left* of $B(\mathbf{p})$. Given this restriction, $\mathbf{X}^0$ turns out to be a competitive equilibrium position. Hence any Pareto-optimal point can be achieved as a competitive equilibrium position for an appropriate choice of initial holdings, if negative prices are permitted. It may also be verified that the only possible competitive equilibrium positions consistent with the indifference curves as drawn are positions that lie on the contract curve so that property 1 of Pareto-satisfactory mechanisms holds in this case as well, if negative prices are permitted.

As we have seen in Chap. 3, much of the work in the theory of competitive equilibrium positions is carried out in terms of models that require that prices be nonnegative. Nonnegativity of prices can be ensured in the competitive framework if we make the rather unrealistic assumption of free disposal of commodities. It will be recalled that by *free disposal* is meant, roughly, that arbitrary amounts of any good can be discarded without cost in terms of the use of productive resources. Strictly speaking, the disposal of commodities is a productive activity, and it is clear from the discussion in Chap. 3 that only commodities that have nonpositive prices will be discarded. In the case depicted in Fig. 4-6, nonnegative prices are thus consistent with equilibrium in the free-disposal case only if the prices of both commodities are zero. But this conflicts with the definition of equilibrium given earlier, i.e., at least one price must be nonzero. Hence, the proof of Pareto satisfactoriness of the competitive mechanism must exclude the case of bliss points in the feasible set for all consumers.

A further difficulty that arises when satiation is assumed possible is pictured in Fig. 4-7; as the diagram indicates, Mr. *B* has a bliss point in

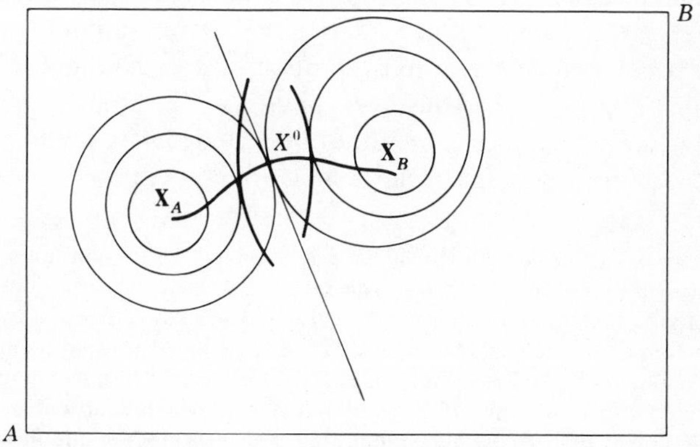

FIGURE 4-6

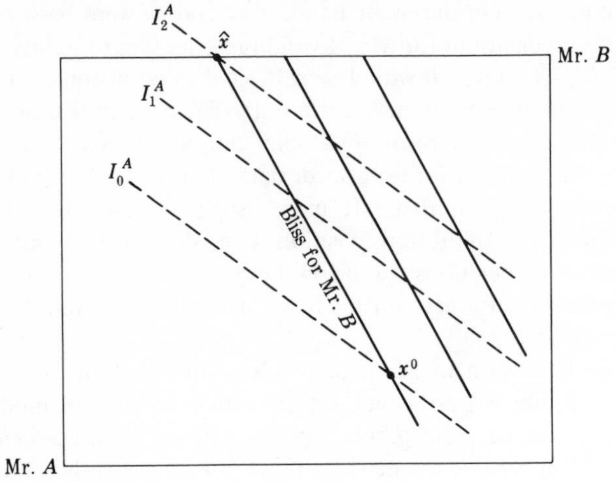

FIGURE 4-7

the feasible set, while Mr. *A* is not satiated with respect to either commodity in the feasible set.

Both Mr. *A* and Mr. *B* are assumed to have straight-line indifference curves, with the line through $\mathbf{X}^0$ and $\hat{\mathbf{X}}$ denoting bliss for Mr. *B*. The set of Pareto optima for this case is the set of points lying on the upper boundary of the Edgeworth box from $\hat{\mathbf{X}}$ to the origin for Mr. *B*. It is straightforward to verify that any Pareto-optimal state can be achieved as an equilibrium of the competitive mechanism; the efficiency property (property 1) does not hold in general, however. Consider the initial-holdings point $\mathbf{X}^0$, where Mr. *B* is at his bliss level and Mr. *A* is on the indifference curve I_0^A. If positive prices p_1 and p_2 are chosen so that the budget line $B(\mathbf{p})$ coincides with the indifference curve I_0^A, then $\mathbf{X}^0$ is a competitive equilibrium for the price vector, since both Mr. *A* and Mr. *B* maximize utility by staying at $\mathbf{X}^0$ and markets are cleared. Since $\mathbf{X}^0$ is not a Pareto-optimal point (in particular, $\hat{\mathbf{X}}$ is Pareto-superior to it), property 1 does not hold. We thus conclude that if one or more consumers possess a bliss point in the feasible set, straight-line indifference curves must be excluded if we are to prove the Pareto-satisfactory character of the competitive system.[1]

[1] Gale, *op. cit.*, p. 169, points out that if there is "saving," i.e., a consumer does not spend his entire budget, then in general the efficiency property does not hold for the competitive mechanism. The example he gives is that of a two-person, one-commodity economy in which Mr. *A* is assumed to hold x units of the commodity and Mr. *B* to hold no units. Further, he assumes that Mr. *A* is satiated with $x - c$ units of the commodity, while Mr. *B* desires at least c units. Gale argues that a possible equilibrium (with "saving") is one in which Mr. *A* consumes $x - c$ units (and "saves" c units by discarding them) and Mr. *B*

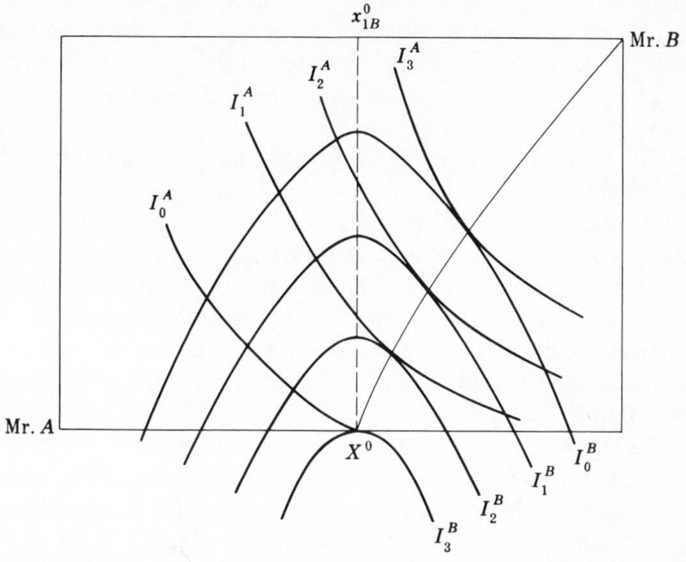

FIGURE 4-8

Even if bliss points for consumers are excluded, satiation with respect to particular commodities can cause difficulties in the proof of the Pareto-satisfactory character of competitive equilibrium, as is indicated by Arrow's "exceptional" case, shown in Fig. 4-8.

In Fig. 4-8, Mr. B is assumed to be satiated with respect to commodity 1 at the point x^0_{1B}, while Mr. A holds nothing but commodity 1. If $\mathbf{X}^0$ is the initial joint-holdings point, it is clear that $\mathbf{X}^0$ is a Pareto-optimal state, as is indicated by the contract curve which passes through $\mathbf{X}^0$. However, as Sec. 3-2 made clear, there is no price line through $\mathbf{X}^0$ such that both Mr. A and Mr. B will wish to remain at that point; consequently, the unbiasedness property fails for the competitive mechanism in this case. The devices employed in the various axiom systems for existence of equilibrium to eliminate this case have been discussed in Sec. 3-8. Here we

---

consumes zero units. This is not Pareto-optimal, of course. If price falls to zero, then Mr. B will consume c units, this being within his budget possibilities if price is at this level; hence price (if it is meaningful to discuss price in a one-commodity world) is assumed positive. The difficulty with Gale's example is that it is not consistent with profit maximization in production. As has been noted above, discarding of surplus units of a commodity can occur only if the price of the commodity is nonpositive; when free disposal is assumed, then the commodity must have a zero price. Gale imposes no requirement relative to the free-disposal assumption with respect to production, so it is not clear just what role the assumption plays in his model. The term "saving" as used by Gale is not "saving" as used by most economists.

simply note that in order to ensure that Pareto-optimal states can always be "reached" by the competitive mechanism, it must be assumed that all participants in the market possess some units of a commodity that is desired by someone else; no person can be excluded from the possibility of trading. In terms of Fig. 4-8, this would mean moving Mr. *A* away from the boundary of the Edgeworth box, by providing him with some units of commodity 2.

A final example of an "abnormal" case in which the competitive mechanism is not necessarily Pareto-satisfactory is presented in Fig. 4-9. In Fig. 4-9, it is assumed that commodities 1 and 2 are indivisible, so that only the points shown as "lattice points" on the diagram are feasible. Preferences are defined over all points in the diagram, but because of the nature of the two commodities, consumers are permitted to choose only lattice points in maximizing utility.

In Fig. 4-9, $\mathbf{X}^0$ represents the initial joint-holdings point for Mr. *A* and Mr. *B*. Then, given the budget line $B(\mathbf{p})$, the utility-maximizing holdings point for Mr. *A* and Mr. *B* consistent with market clearing and consistent with the requirement that final holdings be feasible (joint holdings must occur at a lattice point) is the point $\mathbf{X}'$. However, $\mathbf{X}'$ is not a Pareto-optimal state, since $\mathbf{X}''$ is Pareto-superior to it—Mr. *A* is on a higher indifference curve and Mr. *B* is on the same indifference curve as compared with $\mathbf{X}'$. Since $\mathbf{X}'$ is a competitive equilibrium position given the initial-holdings point $\mathbf{X}^0$ and the price vector $\mathbf{p}$, the efficiency property of the competitive system is violated. Thus, in general, the presence of indivisible commodities is incompatible with the Pareto-satisfactory character of the competitive mechanism.

A brief summary of the preceding discussion might be given as follows: To assert that the competitive mechanism is a Pareto-satisfactory

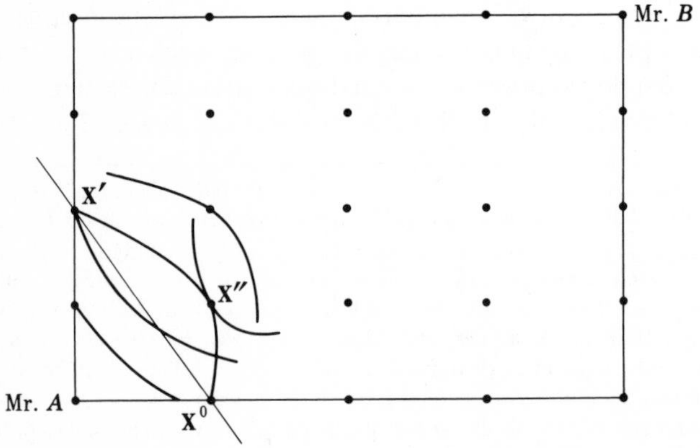

FIGURE 4-9

mechanism is to say that (1) every competitive equilibrium occurs at a Pareto-optimal state and (2) every Pareto-optimal state can be achieved by the competitive mechanism as an equilibrium position for an appropriate choice of resource endowments for consumers and a price vector. In the "normal" case usually depicted, the Pareto-satisfactory character of the competitive system is intuitively clear; however, certain "abnormal" cases must be excluded if the proposition is to be proved in general. These "abnormal" cases include the case in which several consumers have bliss points lying in the feasible set, the case in which some one consumer has a bliss point and indifference curves contain straight line segments, Arrow's "exceptional" case in which some consumer is not able to trade because he holds no units of any commodity that is desired by other consumers, and the case of indivisible commodities.

We now summarize the proof given by Arrow of the Pareto-satisfactory character of the competitive mechanism. In contrast to the graphical analysis presented above, in what follows we shall incorporate production into the framework of the analysis. For simplicity, the problem associated with converting inputs into outputs will not be treated explicitly; instead, following Arrow's original formulation, it is assumed that the amounts of inputs available are taken as given and that there is defined for the economy a *transformation set* T, where T is the set consisting of all technologically feasible *output* vectors for the economy for the given amounts of inputs. By this device, we eliminate all intermediate products and basic resources from consideration and deal only with final products. Figure 4-10 presents a typical transformation set in two dimensions. (Note that as contrasted with the diagrams of the previous chapters dealing with production, commodities 1 and 2 are here both final products and any point in T is a feasible vector of outputs of these two commodities, given the fixed amounts of inputs. y_i denotes output of the ith final product.)

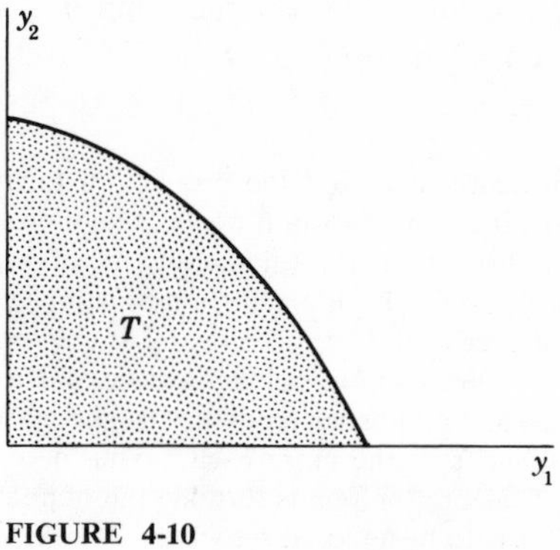

FIGURE 4-10

As in the earlier chapters, let x_{ij} denote the amount of the ith commodity allocated to the jth consumer, where $i = 1, \ldots, n$ and $j = 1, \ldots, m$. The fact that the number of final commodities will not be as great as the number of commodities, including human and nonhuman resources and services used in the production process, is ignored in this notation. The axiom system employed by Arrow is the following:

Assumption 1: $x_{ij} \geqq 0$ for all i and j. (Since we consider only final products, negative holdings or consumption of commodities is excluded.)

Assumption 2: Each individual's preference ordering over states of the economy (here taken to be listings of final products allocated to consumers) is characterized by selfishness, i.e., his preference ranking is defined over the commodity bundles he receives and is not influenced by the amounts of commodities assigned to other consumers.

Assumption 3: Each individual's preference ranking is characterized by strong convexity, i.e., for all j, given two commodity bundles $\mathbf{x}'^j$ and $\mathbf{x}''^j$, if $\mathbf{x}'^j \ \mathrm{I}_j \ \mathbf{x}''^j$, then for all $0 < t < 1$, $[t\mathbf{x}'^j + (1 - t)\mathbf{x}''^j] \ \mathrm{P}_j \ \mathbf{x}''^j$. Further it is assumed that these preferences can be represented by a continuous utility function u^j, with the characteristic that if $u^j(\mathbf{x}'^j) = u^j(\mathbf{x}''^j)$, then, for all $0 < t < 1$, $u^j[t\mathbf{x}'^j + (1 - t)\mathbf{x}''^j] > u^j(\mathbf{x}''^j)$. By this assumption, lexicographic orderings are excluded and straight line and/or thick indifference curves are excluded.

Assumption 4: The transformation set T is nonempty, convex, and compact and is contained in the positive orthant of euclidean space. [At least one output vector is feasible (T nonempty). If $\mathbf{y}', \mathbf{y}'' \in T$, then for all $0 \leqq t \leqq 1$, $(t\mathbf{y}' + (1 - t)\mathbf{y}'') \in T$ (T convex). The distance between any two points of T is finite, and T contains its limit points (T compact); every point in T has nonnegative components (T is contained in the positive orthant of euclidean space).[1]]

Assumption 5: If $\mathbf{y}'$ belongs to T and $\mathbf{y}''$ is a vector such that $0 \leqq y_i'' \leqq y_i'$ for all $i = 1, 2, \ldots, n$, then $\mathbf{y}''$ belongs to T. (This is the free-disposal assumption. In effect, it states that if it is possible to

[1] The precise relationship between convexity of T and the production functions for particular outputs is not known; it can be shown, however, that if every output is produced under constant returns to scale, and additivity of production processes is assumed, then T is convex. If all production functions are quasi-concave and homogeneous of degree k $(0 < k \leqq 1)$, then T is convex.

The statement that T contains its limit points means that T is a closed set. A limit point of T is defined as a point such that every neighborhood of the point contains points of T distinct from the point itself. Thus every interior point of T is a limit point of T, as are the points forming the boundary of T. T must contain its boundary if it is to be a closed set.

produce at some level, it is always possible to produce at a lower level, e.g., by discarding any surplus output.)

Assumption 6: Every commodity is perfectly divisible.[1]

Within the framework of these assumptions, the notions of competitive equilibrium positions and Pareto-optimal states of the economy are defined as follows:

Definition 1: A price vector $\bar{\mathbf{p}}$ and an output vector $\bar{\mathbf{y}} \in T$ and a state of the economy $\bar{\mathbf{X}}$ are said to constitute a competitive equilibrium if the following conditions hold:

1. For each j, $\bar{\mathbf{x}}^j$ uniquely maximizes $u^j(\mathbf{x}^j)$ subject to the constraint that

$$\sum_{i=1}^{n} \bar{p}_i x_{ij} \leq \sum_{i=1}^{n} \bar{p}_i \bar{x}_{ij}$$

2. For all $\mathbf{y} \in T$,

$$\sum_{i=1}^{n} \bar{p}_i y_i \leq \sum_{i=1}^{n} \bar{p}_i \sum_{j=1}^{m} \bar{x}_{ij} = \sum_{i=1}^{n} \bar{p}_i \bar{y}_i$$

(This is a more restrictive definition of competitive equilibrium than any of those used in Chap. 3, made possible by the stronger assumptions employed by Arrow. Condition 1, the utility maximization condition for consumers, states unique maximization because of the strong convexity assumption on preference orderings. Condition 2 is the profit maximization condition over feasible output vectors. It asserts that firms cannot make more profits than can be made by producing the aggregate amounts demanded by consumers.)

Definition 2: A state $\mathbf{X}^*$ is said to be a Pareto-optimal state (relative to T) if there exists $\mathbf{y}^* \in T$ such that $\mathbf{y}^* = \sum_{j=1}^{m} \mathbf{x}^{*j}$, and there exists no state $\mathbf{X}'$ such that $\mathbf{y}' = \sum_{j=1}^{m} \mathbf{x}'^j$, $\mathbf{y}' \in T$, and $u^j(\mathbf{x}'^j) \geq u^j(\mathbf{x}'^j)$ for all j, the strict inequality holding for at least one j ($j = 1, 2, \ldots, m$).

THEOREM 1: If assumptions 1 to 6 hold, then any competitive equilibrium state of the economy $\bar{\mathbf{X}}$, associated with a price vector $\bar{\mathbf{p}}$, is a Pareto-optimal state (relative to T).

[1] This assumption is not stated explicitly in the *Second Berkeley Symposium* paper, but, as the situation graphed in Fig. 4-9 makes clear, is needed to establish that the competitive system is Pareto-satisfactory. The assumption is implicit in Arrow's proof of this proposition.

Before giving the proof of Theorem 1, it should be pointed out that Arrow's assumptions 1 to 6 are sufficient to guarantee that there always exists a Pareto-optimal state (relative to T) (T is assumed to be closed and bounded and preferences are continuous), but not sufficient to guarantee that a competitive equilibrium exists. In particular, these assumptions do not rule out Arrow's "exceptional" case graphed in Fig. 4-8. It is largely because of this difficulty that renewed interest was shown in solving the problem of stating axiom systems sufficient to guarantee existence of equilibrium as evidenced in the writings of Arrow and Debreu, Debreu, Gale, McKenzie, etc., which were considered in some detail in Chap. 3.

The proof of Theorem 1 is straightforward: Assume that $(\bar{\mathbf{X}},\bar{\mathbf{y}}),\bar{\mathbf{y}} \in T$, is a competitive equilibrium for a price vector $\bar{\mathbf{p}}$, but that $\bar{\mathbf{X}}$ is not a Pareto-optimal state. Then there exists $(\mathbf{X}',\mathbf{y}'),\mathbf{y}' \in T$ such that $u^j(\mathbf{x}'^j) \geqq u^j(\bar{\mathbf{x}}^j)$ for every j, and $u^k(\mathbf{x}'^k) > u^k(\bar{\mathbf{x}}^k)$ for some k. By the definition of a competitive equilibrium, this implies that

$$\sum_{i=1}^{n} \bar{p}_1 x'_{ik} > \sum_{i=1}^{n} \bar{p}_i \bar{x}_{ik} \quad \text{and} \quad \sum_{i=1}^{n} \bar{p}_i x'_{ij} \geqq \sum_{i=1}^{n} \bar{p}_i \bar{x}_{ij} \qquad \text{for every } j$$

This in turn implies that

$$\sum_{i=1}^{n} \bar{p}_i \sum_{j=1}^{m} x'_{ij} > \sum_{i=1}^{n} \bar{p}_i \sum_{j=1}^{m} \bar{x}_{ij}$$

which contradicts the profit maximization condition, since $\mathbf{y}'$ is assumed to belong to T. Hence if $(\bar{\mathbf{X}},\bar{\mathbf{y}})$ is a competitive equilibrium position, $\bar{\mathbf{X}}$ is a Pareto-optimal state.

The most striking feature of the proof of Theorem 1 is its utter simplicity, which is accounted for primarily by the assumption of strongly convex preferences, but, as has been noted previously, the theorem can be proved under more general conditions if appropriate assumptions are made to cover the problems posed by the existence of bliss points. We shall not attempt to deal with that extension here.[1] From the point of view of the fundamentals of welfare economics, certainly the most important of Arrow's assumptions is the selfishness assumption. Generally speaking, if the preferences of any consumer depend upon the commodity bundles assigned to other consumers, the method of decentralized decision making involved in the competitive mechanism does not lead to optimal results—instead, typically, some sort of coercion such as government interference is required to ensure optimality. While the theorem breaks down if commodities are indivisible, the existence of rental markets for commodities falling into this category makes this restriction perhaps less troublesome than it appears at first glance. Finally, it might be noted

[1] See Debreu, *Theory of Value*, pp. 94–95.

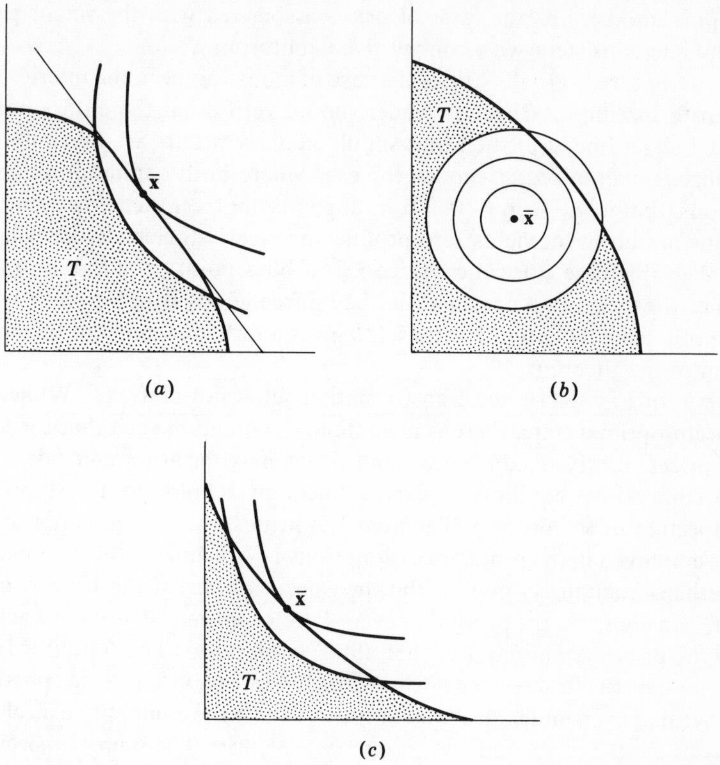

FIGURE 4-11

that the difficulties posed for the theorem by the existence of bliss points as depicted in Fig. 4-6 are taken care of implicitly by imposing no restriction that the price vector $\bar{\mathbf{p}}$ be nonnegative in the strict sense—a price vector consisting entirely of zeros is permissible. Theorem 1 is illustrated graphically for the case of one consumer and two commodities in Fig. 4-11.

The situation graphed in Fig. 4-11*a* is the "normal" case of production theory (but, to add some generality, the transformation set is taken to have a straight line segment along its boundary), when preference sets are assumed to be strictly convex. The equilibrium price vector $\bar{\mathbf{p}}$ has been chosen so that the budget line $B(\bar{\mathbf{p}})$ touches the indifference curve at $\bar{\mathbf{x}}$, this line also representing the highest isoprofit line attainable at this set of prices when production is restricted to points in the set T. It will be noted that while there are a number of profit-maximizing points (since T is not strictly convex), there is only one Pareto-optimal point, $\bar{\mathbf{x}}$. It also is true that $\bar{\mathbf{x}}$ is the unique competitive equilibrium position (at no other point in Fig. 4-11*a* will markets be cleared and the profit and utility maximization conditions be met for any set of prices). Similarly, the *slope* of

$B(\bar{\mathbf{p}})$ is unique, i.e., the ratio of prices associated with the vector $\bar{\mathbf{p}}$ is the only one consistent with competitive equilibrium.

Figure 4-11*b* illustrates the case of a bliss point in the interior of the transformation set T. The reader should verify that there does not exist any budget line $B(\bar{\mathbf{p}})$ such that simultaneously profits are maximized and utility is maximized, except in the case where both commodities are free goods, that is, $p_1 = p_2 = 0$. If both goods are free, then any point in the transformation set yields zero profits, and clearly the consumer will move to $\bar{\mathbf{x}}$ in this case. Further, since $\bar{\mathbf{x}}$ is a bliss point, it is Pareto-optimal. Since the case of all commodities being free goods is not excluded by the hypothesis of Theorem 1, Fig. 4-11*b* gives another example of the application of the theorem.

In Fig. 4-11*c*, the transformation set is not convex. While $\bar{\mathbf{x}}$ is a Pareto-optimal state, there is no state in the diagram such that for any set of prices, utility maximization and profit maximization coincide. Since no competitive equilibrium exists, Theorem 1 holds vacuously. As an inspection of the proof of Theorem 1 indicates, the only assumptions that are employed in the proof are assumptions 1, 2, 3, and 6—the theorem holds (perhaps vacuously) under arbitrary specifications of the transformation set. In contrast, the proof that every Pareto-optimal state can be achieved by the price system requires that all of assumptions 1 to 6 hold. In fact, because of the "exceptional" case depicted in Fig. 4-8, it is not possible to prove that even under all the assumptions 1 to 6 the competitive mechanism possesses the unbiasedness property. Hence, Theorem 2 specifically excludes this case:

THEOREM 2: If assumptions 1 to 6 are satisfied, and if the "exceptional" case is excluded, then given any Pareto-optimal state of the economy $\mathbf{X}^*$, there exists a price vector $\mathbf{p}^*$, $\mathbf{p}^* \geqq 0$, and an output vector $\mathbf{y}^* \in T$ such that $(\mathbf{X}^*, \mathbf{p}^*, \mathbf{y}^*)$ constitute a competitive equilibrium.[1]

The "exceptional" case can be excluded by including in the set of assumptions a requirement that every consumer in state $\mathbf{X}^*$ consume a positive amount of some nonfree good.

Theorem 2 can be illustrated for the one-consumer, two-commodity case with production as in Fig. 4-12.

Figure 4-12*a* shows that "normal" case in which the unique Pareto-optimal point $\mathbf{x}^*$ can be reached by a true competitive equilibrium, given that prices are chosen so that the budget line is given by $B(\mathbf{p}^*)$. No new problems arise here, since the set of prices that equates supply and demand is clearly a positive set. In Fig. 4-12*b*, the consumer is assumed to have a

[1] If at least one consumer is not at a bliss point at $\mathbf{X}^*$, then Theorem 2 can be strengthened by specifying that $\mathbf{p}^* \geq 0$ (at least one component of $\mathbf{p}^*$ is strictly positive).

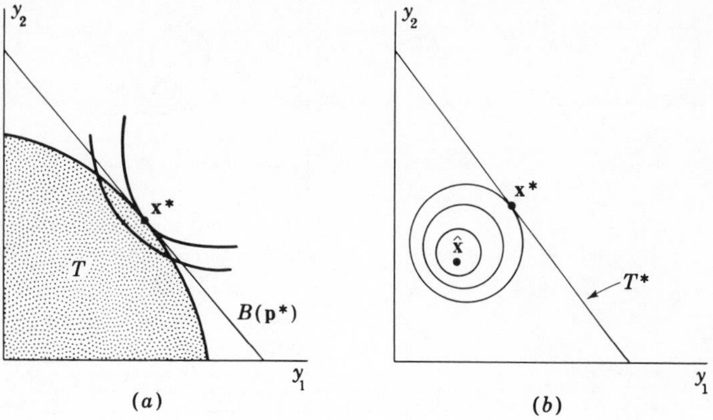

FIGURE 4-12

bliss point denoted by $\hat{\mathbf{x}}$. In the absence of the free-disposal assumption, the transformation set for the economy might be the straight line T^*, and if prices are chosen both negative in such a way that $B(\mathbf{p}^*)$ coincides with T^*, then $\mathbf{x}^*$ will be the competitive equilibrium position for that set of prices, since every point on T^* gives the same (negative) profits and the consumer is constrained to be on or to the right of T^*. The free-disposal assumption means that if T^* is feasible, so is the entire triangle, with the upper boundary given by T^*. Consequently, if both prices are zero, profit maximization and utility maximization will coincide at the point $\hat{\mathbf{x}}$. As was noted earlier, if the price vector associated with competitive equilibrium is to contain some positive component, at least one consumer must not be at his bliss point.

As contrasted with Theorem 1, the proof of Theorem 2 is quite complex and will not be given in detail here. The basic ideas underlying the proof may be summarized quite simply, however, at least in the "normal" case graphed in Fig. 4-12*a*. In effect, at least for the "normal" case, Theorem 2 states that given two sets (the transformation set T and the set of points at least as preferred as the point $\mathbf{x}^*$), there is some way of passing a line through $\mathbf{x}^*$ so that the sets are separated, i.e., all of T falls on one side of the line (or on the line), and all of the "at least as preferred as $\mathbf{x}^*$" set falls on the other side of the line (or on the line). (We ignore the complications introduced by the "exceptional" case and the existence of bliss points, to simplify the explanation.) Such a line, in the case of a one-consumer, two-commodity world, is simultaneously the budget line of the consumer and the highest isoprofit line feasible for the producer, so that the relationship of this "separating line" (or "separating hyperplane" in higher dimensions) to competitive equilibrium is straightforward.

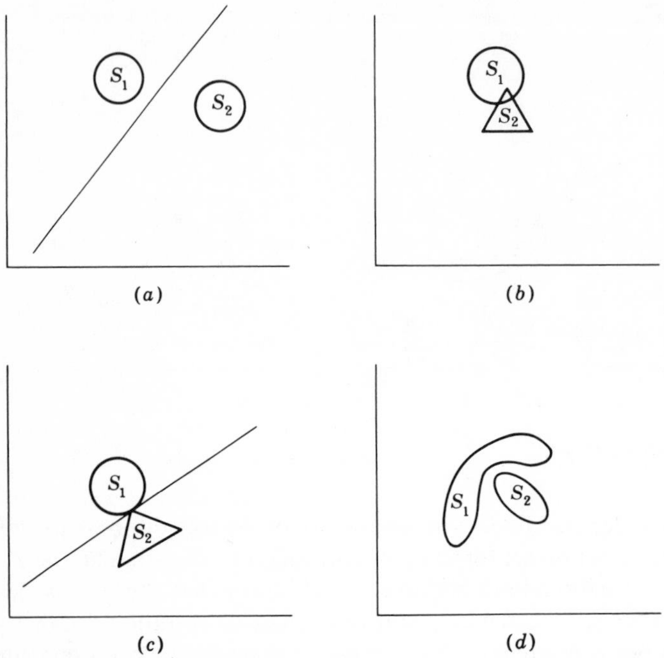

FIGURE 4-13

It is not surprising, then, that the main mathematical tool employed in the proof of Theorem 2 is what is known as a *separation theorem*, a theorem asserting sufficient conditions for the existence of a hyperplane to separate two sets (a separating line in two dimensions, a separating plane in three dimensions, etc.). While extremely general theorems have been developed in this branch of mathematics, we shall summarize here only the theorem most important for our purposes: In euclidean space, any two disjoint convex sets may be separated by a hyperplane. Figure 4-13 illustrates this theorem.

In Fig. 4-13*a* and *c*, S_1 and S_2 are convex and disjoint (if it is assumed that the point at which S_1 and S_2 "touch" in Fig. 4-13*c* belongs only to one of the two sets), and separating lines are sketched in. In Fig. 4-13*b*, S_1 and S_2 are convex but not disjoint; hence the theorem does not apply. In Fig. 4-13*d*, S_1 is not convex, again being outside the scope of the theorem.

The application of the separation theorem for euclidean spaces to the problem of proving the unbiasedness property of competitive equilibrium positions will be given for the case of a one-consumer economy in which the consumer is not satiated in T. The general case is proved in Arrow's paper.

For the one-consumer case, a Pareto-optimal state is a vector $\mathbf{x}^* \in T$ such that $u(\mathbf{x}^*) \geqq u(\mathbf{x})$ for every $\mathbf{x} \in T$. Given such a point $\mathbf{x}^*$, we wish to show that there exists a hyperplane

$$H = \left\{\mathbf{x} \mid \sum_{i=1}^{n} p_i^* x_i = c, \mathbf{p}^* \geqq 0\right\}$$

such that this hyperplane separates the transformation set T from the set S of points at least as preferred as $\mathbf{x}^*$.

In order to apply the separation theorem, S and T must be disjoint sets; however, $\mathbf{x}^*$ belongs to both S and T. Consider then a set $S' = \{\mathbf{x} \mid u(\mathbf{x}) > u(\mathbf{x}^*)\}$. Using a proof of Arrow's, it can be shown that S convex implies S' convex as well, a result that is intuitively obvious in two-dimensional space.

For S' to be convex means that given $\mathbf{z}', \mathbf{z}'' \in S'$, and for $0 \leqq t \leqq 1$, $u[t\mathbf{z}' + (1 - t)\mathbf{z}''] > u(\mathbf{x}^*)$. Assume, without loss of generality, that $u(\mathbf{x}^*) < u(\mathbf{z}') \leqq u(\mathbf{z}'')$. $u[t\mathbf{z}' + (1 - t)\mathbf{z}'']$ may be considered a function of t, where $0 \leqq t \leqq 1$. Call this function $f(t)$. Since $f(t)$ is a continuous real-valued function on a closed and bounded interval (continuous because u is assumed continuous by assumption 3), f takes on its minimum value at some point t_0 in the interval [0,1]. Suppose $0 < t_0 < 1$. It follows that we can choose numbers t_1, t_2 such that $0 < t_1 < t_0 < t_2 < 1$ and $f(t_1) = f(t_2) \geqq f(t_0)$. But, combining assumption 3 with $f(t_1) = f(t_2)$ and setting $t = (t_0 - t_2)/(t_1 - t_2)$, we have $f(t_0) > f(t_1)$. Therefore, $f(t)$ must be a minimum for $t_0 = 0$ or $t_0 = 1$. But since it was assumed that $u(\mathbf{z}') \leqq u(\mathbf{z}'')$, $t_0 = 1$, then $u[t\mathbf{z}' + (1 - t)\mathbf{z}''] \geqq u(\mathbf{z}') > u(\mathbf{x}^*)$, for $0 \leqq t \leqq 1$. Thus S' is convex.

By assumption 4, T is convex; by the argument above, S' is convex as well. Further, since $\mathbf{x}^*$ is a Pareto-optimal state, $u(\mathbf{x}) > u(\mathbf{x}^*)$ implies $\mathbf{x} \notin T$; hence S' and T are disjoint. Thus there exists a hyperplane separating S' and T; that is, given assumptions 1 to 6 there exists $\mathbf{p} \geqq 0$ such that

$$\mathbf{x} \in S' \text{ implies } \sum_{i=1}^{n} p_i x_i \geqq c \qquad \text{and} \qquad \mathbf{x} \in T \text{ implies } \sum_{i=1}^{n} p_i x_i \leqq c$$

If we assume that $\mathbf{x}^*$ is not a bliss point, then S' is nonempty. And, since $u(\mathbf{z}) > u(\mathbf{x}^*)$ implies $u[t\mathbf{z} + (1 - t)\mathbf{x}^*] > u(\mathbf{x}^*)$ for all $0 < t < 1$, if S' is nonempty, then S' is infinite. We can thus find a sequence $(\mathbf{x}_n) \in S'$ converging to $\mathbf{x}^*$ such that

$$\sum_{i=1}^{m} p_i^* x_i \geqq c$$

for each element in the sequence, thus

$$\sum_{i=1}^{m} p_i^* x_i^* \geqq c$$

Since $\mathbf{x}^* \in T$,

$$\sum_{i=1}^{m} p_i^* x_i^* \leqq c$$

thus we have

$$\sum_{i=1}^{m} p_i^* x_i^* = c$$

Thus $\mathbf{x}^*$ lies on H.

The following two conditions are thus met: If $\mathbf{x}^*$ maximizes $u(\mathbf{x})$ in T and $\mathbf{x}^*$ is not a bliss point, then

1. $u(\mathbf{x}) > u(\mathbf{x}^*)$ implies $\sum_{i=1}^{m} p_i^* x_i^* \leqq \sum_{i=1}^{m} p_i^* x_i$

2. $\mathbf{x} \in T$ implies $\sum_{i=1}^{m} p_i^* x_i \leqq \sum_{i=1}^{m} p_i^* x_i^*$

It can further be shown that condition 1 holds even when $u(\mathbf{x}) = u(\mathbf{x}^*)$. This follows directly from assumption 3. (If $\mathbf{x}^*$ is a bliss point, then the price vector $\mathbf{p} = \mathbf{0}$ will lead to the same conclusions, i.e., conditions 1 and 2.) This establishes the Arrow theorem 2 for a one-consumer economy.[1]

To summarize the past few pages concerning the Arrow results: Under the assumption of strongly convex preferences, Arrow has shown that every competitive equilibrium position is a Pareto-optimal state of the economy, if indivisibilities are absent. Given a Pareto-optimal state, under the free-disposal assumption, there exist a set of nonnegative prices and a set of initial holdings such that a competitive equilibrium can be established at that state, if the exceptional case is excluded.

We remarked earlier that Arrow's theorems have been extended by several authors in certain ways: first, by showing that under axioms sufficient to establish the existence of equilibrium, Arrow's results still hold; second, by weakening Arrow's assumptions with respect to strong convexity of preferences and by including explicitly problems of converting inputs into outputs and the supply of inputs to the productive sector (when strong convexity is replaced by convexity of preferences, Theorem 1

[1] Condition 1 does not look quite like a statement of utility maximization. However, if the "exceptional case" is ruled out, condition 1 implies utility maximization. See Arrow, An Extension of the Basic Theorems of Classical Welfare Economics, *op. cit.*, lemmas, p. 513.

may be proved if each consumer is not at a bliss point); and last, by increasing the dimensionality of the problem. Chapter 3 included a discussion of the first two of these points together with some comments on Debreu's proof of existence of equilibrium for a countably infinite number of commodities. Here we discuss briefly the Debreu extension of Arrow's optimality results to include the infinite-dimensional case.[1]

The assumptions employed by Debreu are essentially the same as those employed by Arrow, except that the strong convexity of preferences assumption is replaced by convexity of preferences (i.e., instead of the condition $\mathbf{x}'^j \, \mathrm{I}_j \, \mathbf{x}''^j$ implies $[t\mathbf{x}'^j + (1 - t)\mathbf{x}''^j] \, \mathrm{P}_j \, \mathbf{x}'^j$, Debreu uses the condition $\mathbf{x}'^j \, \mathrm{P}_j \, \mathbf{x}''^j$ implies $[t\mathbf{x}'^j + (1 - t)\mathbf{x}''^j] \, \mathrm{P}_j \, \mathbf{x}''^j$, both for $0 < t < 1$). The analysis is carried on within a framework of individual consumption and production sets in which conversion of inputs into outputs is treated explicitly, and the proof is given for arbitrary linear spaces rather than simply for finite-dimensional euclidean space. The principal mathematical tool employed in the Debreu proof is the Hahn-Banach theorem, which extends the separation theorem stated for euclidean space to arbitrary linear spaces.

The substantive contribution that is contained in Debreu's paper is the extension of the Arrow theorems relating competitive equilibrium to Pareto optimality to the case where individuals have infinite planning horizons, i.e., when consumers make choices today taking into account not only their preferences over current consumption possibilities but also the implications of these choices for future consumption possibilities, and likewise for firms. In addition, by another interpretation of variables of Debreu's model, consumption and production choices may be made with respect to commodities located at different points in space. There are important problems associated with these concepts,[2] and Debreu's discussion of the issues involved is largely in formal terms; nonetheless, in essence, the Debreu theorems state that even if the number of variables in the competitive model is made infinite, the two Arrow theorems—every competitive equilibrium is Pareto-optimal and every Pareto-optimal state is a potential competitive equilibrium—still hold, with the same qualifications that characterize the model with a finite number of variables. In short, increasing the dimensionality of the model from an arbitrary finite number of commodities to an infinite number really does not change the basic results at all—only the method of proof is affected.

[1] Debreu, Valuation Equilibrium and Pareto Optimum, *Proceedings of the National Academy of Sciences of the U.S.A.*, vol. 40, pp. 588–592, 1954.

[2] See T. C. Koopmans, Allocation of Resources and the Price System, *Three Essays on the State of Economic Science*, pp. 64ff, McGraw-Hill Book Company, New York, 1957.

The Debreu extension of Arrow's theorems to the case of infinite planning horizons by consumers still restricts those results to *static* equilibrium positions of a competitive economy. When we attempt to consider the welfare properties of a competitive system operating through time, not only are important new difficulties introduced into the analysis but, more basically, it is not even clear that unambiguous criteria can be developed to compare time paths of states of the economy under various methods of organizing the economy. The source of difficulty is easy to identify: choices by consumers today influence the production possibilities feasible in the future, so that choices available to consumers in the future are determined in large part by such previous decisions. Recall that the fundamental axiom of welfare economics asserts that individuals' preferences are to count; as long as we deal with a static framework, there is no difficulty in identifying *which* individuals are to be taken into account; in a dynamic setting, however, all future generations are affected to some degree by choices today: should their (unknown) preferences be taken into account in welfare theory?

In conclusion it might bear repeating that the theorem asserting that any Pareto optimum may be attained as a competitive equilibrium requires not only that prices be appropriately set, but also that appropriate imputation of resources be made. In a context of pure trade, as illustrated by an Edgeworth diagram, we saw that in order to characterize all Pareto optima as competitive equilibrium positions, we had to be free to choose initial endowments as well as prices. In our discussion of the contract curve we noted that the subset of all Pareto optima that made up the contract curve with respect to a given endowment had the property that these allocations alone could be attained through free negotiations between the two parties. With respect to the given initial endowment, only the allocations comprising the contract curve could be reached by contracts willingly entered into by both parties.

If we insist that all contracts made have been entered into willingly by both parties, then the set of Pareto-optimal positions lying outside the contract curve diminishes in importance, since these positions would never be realized. Thus, taking resource endowments as given, there arises the interesting question of the relationship between the allocations comprising the contract curve and competitive equilibrium positions.

Referring back to Fig. 4-3, it is apparent that there are points along CC' that are not positions of competitive equilibrium, given the endowment $\mathbf{X}^0$. Experimentation with Fig. 4-3 would lead us to the correct conclusion that any competitive equilibrium, given the initial endowment $\mathbf{X}^0$, lies along CC'. Thus it appears that whereas every competitive equilibrium position given $\mathbf{X}^0$ lies in CC', there are points in CC' that are not positions of competitive equilibrium.

It is a theorem of Edgeworth that, as the number of individuals having the same indifference map as Mr. *A* increases and the number of individuals having the same indifference map as Mr. *B* increases, the contract curve "shrinks" until it coincides with the set of competitive equilibria.[1] Very roughly speaking, the introduction of more traders (each of whom is either a type *A* or a type *B*) presents the opportunity of recontracting, that is, for some number of *A*'s to take aside some number of *B*'s and make private "deals" to the exclusion of the other participants.

Edgeworth's result, which holds for the case of two commodities and two types of traders, has been generalized to the case of many commodities and many types of consumers by invoking the notion of the *core* of an economy, which is defined as follows: Let $\mathbf{x}^1, \ldots, \mathbf{x}^m$ be the commodity bundles allocated to the m consumers, respectively, in an attainable state of the economy. Then $\sum_{j=1}^{m} (\mathbf{x}^j - \mathbf{r}^j)$ is an element of the aggregate production set $\bar{Y}$, where $\mathbf{r}^j$ denotes the initial endowment. Now suppose there is some subset S of consumers such that for some other allocation $\hat{\mathbf{x}}^1, \ldots, \hat{\mathbf{x}}^m$ we have

$$\sum_{j \in S} (\hat{\mathbf{x}}^j - \mathbf{r}^j) \in \bar{Y} \tag{1}$$

and

$$\begin{aligned} &\hat{\mathbf{x}}^j \, \mathrm{R}_j \, \mathbf{x}^j \qquad \text{for all } j \in S \\ &\hat{\mathbf{x}}^j \, \mathrm{P}_j \, \mathbf{x}^j \qquad \text{for some } j \in S \end{aligned} \tag{2}$$

This being the case, the set S is said to block the allocation. The *core* of an economy is defined to be those allocations that are blocked by no set of consumers. (It might help in grasping the notion of a blocking set to point out that any allocation in the core of an economy has to be a Pareto optimum, for otherwise the set of all consumers would form a blocking set.[2]) In the case where the number of traders is viewed as nondenumerably infinite, every state in the core of the economy is a competitive equilibrium position as well as a Pareto-optimal allocation.

[1] F. Y. Edgeworth, *Mathematical Psychics*, Kegan Paul, London, 1881; reprinted by Kelley and Milman, New York, 1954. For a very clear exposition of the Edgeworth theory, see Peter K. Newman, *The Theory of Exchange*, chap. 5, Prentice-Hall, Inc., Englewood Cliffs, N.J., 1965.

[2] A partial bibliography on theorems relating to the core of an economy is given by the following three papers and the references contained therein: R. J. Aumann, Markets with a Continuum of Traders, *Econometrica*, vol. 32, pp. 1–17, 1964; Gerard Debreu and Herbert Scarf, A Limit Theorem on the Core of an Economy, *International Economic Review*, vol. 4, pp. 235–246, 1963; Gerard Debreu, On a Theorem of Scarf, *Review of Economic Studies*, vol. 30, pp. 177–180, 1963.

FIVE

COMPETITIVE EQUILIBRIUM: STABILITY

5-1 INTRODUCTION

In Chaps. 3 and 4, the questions of the existence and uniqueness of competitive equilibrium positions and the welfare properties of the competitive mechanism have been discussed. Briefly, under the assumptions of selfishness on the part of consumers and independence of production possibilities on the part of producers, divisibility of commodities, and certain convexity and closure and boundedness properties of the consumption and production sets, together with a guarantee that every consumer can participate in the trading process, competitive equilibrium positions exist, and they represent Pareto-optimal states of the economy. Further, any Pareto-optimal state can be achieved as an equilibrium position of the competitive mechanism, if a proper redistribution of wealth is made. In this chapter, we consider the further question as to whether, if equilibrium is disturbed by some change in the economic environment, there will be a tendency for the system to return to some equilibrium position. Questions of this sort involve a study of the *stability* properties of the competitive mechanism and, as contrasted with our previous discussions, lead to an examination of the behavior of the competitive mechanism when it is out of equilibrium.

Study of the stability properties of equilibrium positions is essential to the theory of the competitive mechanism because it is only when stability has been verified that the competitive mechanism can be regarded as a workable device for generating optimal solutions to the problems of allocating resources to producers and distributing output among consumers. The parameters of the competitive model, tastes and resource holdings of consumers and production possibilities available to producers, are volatile, and the optimality properties of the competitive mechanism would hold little interest if, when equilibrium is disturbed by some change in these parameters, the system had no tendency to converge to equilibrium.

In order to examine the manner in which prices and quantities demanded and supplied react when the economic system is out of equilibrium, it is necessary to extend the framework of our analysis to incorporate an explicit adjustment process governing the changes over time in these variables. In most of this chapter, the *tâtonnement* adjustment process is utilized; the last section of the chapter deals with non-*tâtonnement* adjustment processes. Because time enters into our analysis in a crucial manner, we refer to this as *dynamic* stability analysis. Before taking this up, however, we shall summarize the concept of *static* stability as applied to the competitive mechanism. Static stability analysis involves no explicit framework for determining how prices and quantities demanded and supplied change over time when equilibrium is disturbed. As Samuelson has pointed out, "In principle [this] procedure is clearly wrong . . . ,"[1] but there is a close connection between the results of static stability analysis and those of dynamic stability analysis that makes it important to study static stability.

Finally, a distinction may be drawn between *local* dynamic stability and *global* dynamic stability; most of this chapter will be concerned with the first of these, but there is a brief discussion of global stability in Sec. 5.6.

5-2 STATIC STABILITY

Two notions of static stability appear in the writings of the neoclassical economists, these being referred to as *Marshallian* stability and *Walrasian* stability. While our primary concern in this section will be with Walrasian static stability, a brief discussion of the difference between these two types of static stability seems in order. A market is said to possess *Marshallian stability* if, when quantity is larger than the equilibrium level, the supply price associated with this quantity exceeds the demand price associated with this quantity, and the opposite holds when quantities are less than the equilibrium level. A market is said to possess *Walrasian stability* if, when price is higher than the equilibrium level, the quantity demanded at this price is less than the quantity supplied at this price, and the opposite holds for prices less than the equilibrium level. The diagrams in Fig. 5-1 illustrate Marshallian and Walrasian static stability.

In Fig. 5-1*a*, given an arbitrary quantity x_0, $x_0 > \bar{x}$, supply price is $S_p(x_0)$ and demand price is $D_p(x_0)$. Since $S_p(x_0) > D_p(x_0)$ for all $x_0 > \bar{x}$

[1] Paul A. Samuelson, *The Foundations of Economic Analysis*, p. 273, Harvard University Press, Cambridge, Mass., 1955.

Marshallian stability – excess quantities
Walrasian stability – excess price

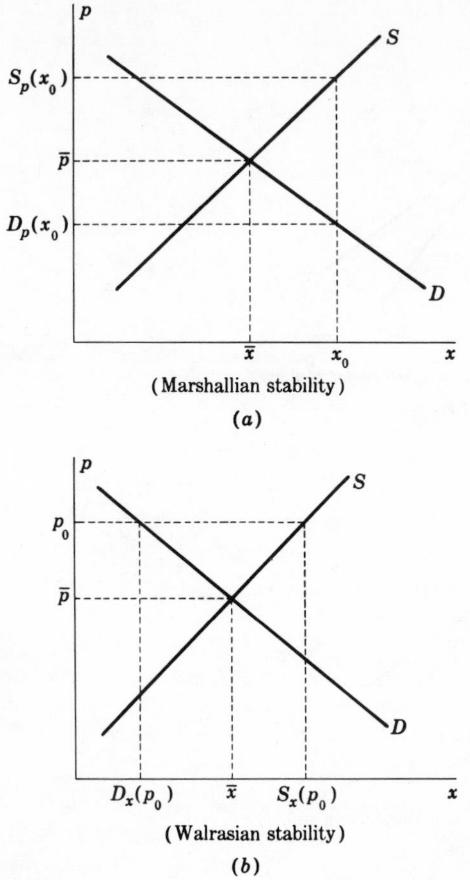

FIGURE 5-1

(and the opposite holds for $x_0 < \bar{x}$), the market is stable in the Marshallian sense. Similarly, in Fig. 5-1*b*, given an arbitrary price p_0, $p_0 > \bar{p}$, the quantity demanded is $D_x(p_0)$. Since $S_x(p_0) > D_x(p_0)$ for all $p_0 > \bar{p}$ (and the opposite holds for $p_0 < \bar{p}$), the market possesses Walrasian stability.

Examples of markets that are (1) Marshallian-stable but not Walrasian-stable, and (2) Walrasian-stable but not Marshallian-stable, are provided in Fig. 5-2.

Other than providing a perhaps convenient description of possible market situations in the case of a one-commodity world, it is difficult to find anything further to recommend the use of either the Marshallian or Walrasian concepts of static stability. In particular, it might be asked why the term "stability" is applied at all to the cases covered by the two definitions given above. In common parlance, "stability" is a term used to

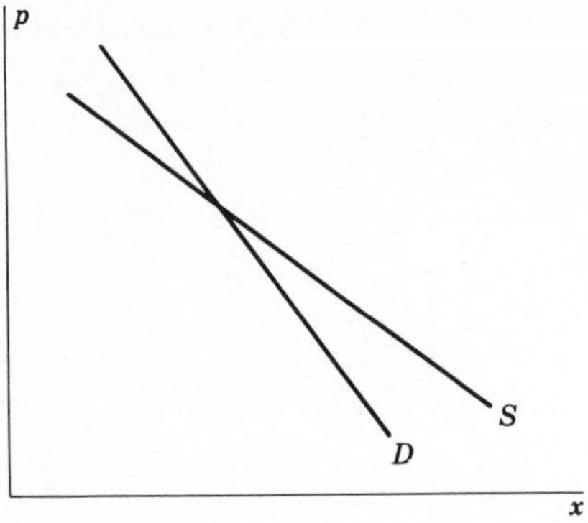

(Marshallian stable but not Walrasian stable)

(a)

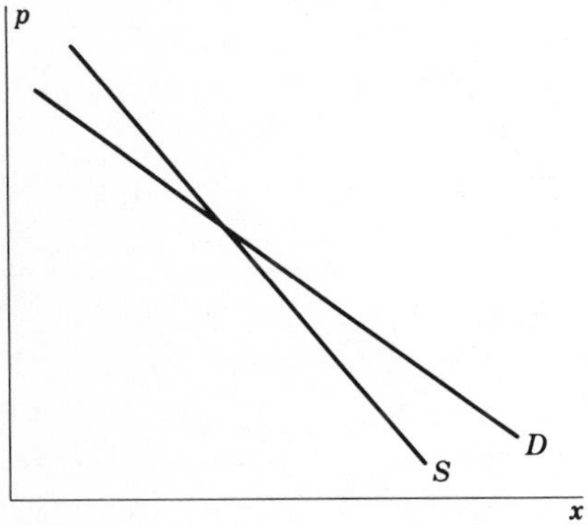

(Walrasian stable but not Marshallian stable)

(b)

FIGURE 5-2

refer to that characteristic of a system that involves the way in which the system reacts to changes imposed upon it; however, neither the Marshallian nor the Walrasian static stability concepts have anything to say about the market reaction when price and quantity are not at their equilibrium levels. Instead, we are simply presented with definitions of stability that are divorced from any explicit adjustment process. This is not to say that it is impossible to find adjustment processes that lead to stability conditions as given in the definitions of Marshallian and Walrasian stability; in fact, the notion of "true" dynamic stability arises out of a formalization of Walras' attempts to construct such a process, and Marshall, Edgeworth, and Walras were well aware of the need for the introduction of adjustment processes to justify the stability concepts we have mentioned.

The Walrasian static stability concept has been generalized to the case of multiple markets, i.e., to general equilibrium situations, by Hicks, and it is to this contribution that we turn next.[1] In the one-market case, we have stability in the static sense of Walras if at prices above equilibrium, excess demand is negative (supply exceeds demand) and at prices below equilibrium, excess demand is positive. In Hicks' formulation, the effects of a change in one price on the prices of other commodities in the general equilibrium situation are taken into account. Thus Hicks defines an equilibrium position to be *imperfectly stable* if excess demand for any commodity is negative when its price is above equilibrium (excess demand positive when price is below equilibrium), given that all other prices are adjusted so that the markets for all other commodities are cleared. A competitive equilibrium position is said to be *perfectly stable* (or *Hicksian stable*) if excess demand for any commodity is negative when its price is above the equilibrium level (and positive when price is below equilibrium), given that any arbitrary set of prices may be adjusted, the others being held fixed, as long as the markets for those commodities whose prices are adjusted are cleared. It will be noted that for the case of one commodity, both perfect and imperfect stability are identical to Walrasian static stability.

Hicks has derived necessary and sufficient conditions for the existence of perfect stability for the case in which excess demand functions are assumed to be differentiable.[2] The derivation of these conditions is straightforward and is presented here.

Assume the economy has $n + 1$ commodities that are produced and consumed. These commodities are numbered $0, 1, \ldots, n$. Let z_i denote the aggregate excess demand for the ith commodity, where $i = 0, \ldots, n$. Then

$$z_i = \sum_{j=1}^{m} [x_{ij}(\mathbf{p}) - x_{ij}^0] - \sum_{k=1}^{l} y_{ik}(\mathbf{p}) = F_i(\mathbf{p})$$

where x_{ij} is the final holding (or consumption) of the ith commodity by the jth consumer, x_{ij}^0 is the initial holding of the ith commodity by the jth consumer, y_{ik} is the amount of the ith commodity supplied by the kth producer, and $\mathbf{p} = (p_0, p_1, \ldots, p_n)$ is the price vector. Because of the homogeneity property of the aggregate demand and supply functions, that is, $F_i(\lambda\mathbf{p}) = F_i(\mathbf{p})$ for any positive λ and all i, we can arbitrarily set one

[1] J. R. Hicks, *Value and Capital*, 2d ed., Oxford University Press, London, 1946; see especially the mathematical appendix.

[2] Throughout this chapter, excess demand functions will be assumed to be single-valued and continuous, with differentiability often assumed as well. These represent rather severe restrictions on the demand and supply correspondences discussed in Chap. 3. Section 5 of this chapter contains a brief discussion of the relationship of these assumptions to those found in the existence discussion in Chap. 3.

price equal to 1 and treat the other prices as "normalized" prices. Here we set $p_0 = 1$ and view each remaining price as the number of units of commodity 0 that can be exchanged for one unit of the commodity in question. We refer to commodity 0 as *numéraire;* as the discussion in Chap. 3 concerning *numéraire* commodities indicates, such a commodity is not money in the usual sense of the term, but instead is an arbitrarily chosen commodity that acts as a measuring stick of value and provides satisfactions directly to the consumer and not simply indirectly as a medium of exchange or unit of account. We can write our system of excess demand functions as

$$\begin{aligned} z_0 &= F_0(1, p_1, \ldots, p_n) \\ z_1 &= F_1(1, p_1, \ldots, p_n) \\ &\cdots\cdots\cdots\cdots\cdots \\ z_n &= F_n(1, p_1, \ldots, p_n) \end{aligned}$$

where we impose the condition that, in equilibrium, $z_i = 0$ for each $i = 0, \ldots, n$. (The case of excess supply at equilibrium is not covered by the analysis of this chapter; thus implicitly we are dealing only with situations in which for each commodity there is at least one consumer who is not satiated with respect to that commodity.)

A stronger assumption will also be made, namely that *Walras' law* holds. By Walras' law we mean the statement that for any choice of the price vector $\mathbf{p}$, the following equality is satisfied:

$$\sum_{i=0}^{n} p_i z_i = 0$$

Walras' law holds if and only if the budget constraint of each consumer is satisfied as an equality for any choice of $\mathbf{p}$. This can be seen from the fact that the budget constraint for the jth consumer is written as

$$\sum_{i=0}^{m} p_i[x_{ij} - x_{ij}^0] - \sum_{k=1}^{l} s^{kj} \sum_{i=0}^{n} p_i y_{ik} \leqq 0$$

where $s^{kj} \sum_{i=0}^{n} p_i y_{ik}$ is the share of the profits of the kth firm that is assigned to the jth consumer. Summing the budget constraints over j, we obtain

$$\sum_{j=1}^{m} \sum_{i=0}^{n} p_i[x_{ij} - x_{ij}^0] - \sum_{k=1}^{l} s^{kj} \sum_{i=0}^{n} p_i y_{ik} \leqq 0$$

But, since each element in the sum is nonpositive, the sum equals zero if and only if each of the budget constraints is exactly satisfied. Further, assuming that all profits are distributed to consumers $\left(\sum_{j=1}^{m} s^{kj} = 1 \text{ for } k = 1, \ldots, l\right)$, we obtain $\sum_{i=0}^{n} p_i z_i = 0$ for any choice of $\mathbf{p}$ if and only if the

See eq'n on previous pg.

budget constraint of each consumer is satisfied as an equality for any choice of $\mathbf{p}$.

In particular, when Walras' law holds, we have that

$$\sum_{i=1}^{n} p_i z_i = -p_0 z_0$$

and, by the convention that $p_0 = 1$,

$$\sum_{i=1}^{n} p_i z_i = -z_0$$

Thus, given any price vector $\mathbf{p}$, excess demand for the 0th commodity is determined by the levels of excess demand for the remaining commodities. Consequently, we need only consider n excess demand functions in deriving conditions for Hicksian stability, not the entire $n + 1$.

We wish to determine the effects on excess demand in any market as a consequence of a change in the price of that commodity. For concreteness, we choose the market for the first commodity in our investigation of the conditions for Hicksian stability. Following Hicks, these effects are first studied assuming no change in any price except p_1 and then under the assumption that each possible subset of prices is allowed to adjust in such a way that if any price (other than p_1) changes, the market for that commodity must be cleared. For Hicksian perfect stability, the sign of dz_1/dp_1 must be negative for any such changes in prices. The determination of necessary and sufficient conditions for Hicksian perfect stability is most easily seen if we differentiate totally each of the n excess demand functions with respect to p_1, giving

$$\frac{dz_1}{dp_1} = F_{11}\frac{dp_1}{dp_1} + \cdots + F_{1n}\frac{dp_n}{dp_1}$$

$$\cdots\cdots\cdots\cdots\cdots\cdots\cdots\cdots$$

$$\frac{dz_n}{dp_1} = F_{n1}\frac{dp_1}{dp_1} + \cdots + F_{nn}\frac{dp_n}{dp_1}$$

where $F_{ir} = \partial F_i/\partial p_r$ for $i, r = 1, \ldots, n$, these partial derivatives being evaluated at the equilibrium set of prices.

By the conditions imposed in investigating Hicksian stability, we have

$$\frac{dp_i}{dp_1} = 0 \qquad \text{if } \frac{dz_i}{dp_1} \neq 0$$

and $\qquad\qquad\qquad\qquad$ for $i = 2, \ldots, n$

$$\frac{dz_i}{dp_1} = 0 \qquad \text{if } \frac{dp_i}{dp_1} \neq 0$$

[For any commodity (other than commodity 1) whose price changes, the change in price must be such that the market for that commodity is cleared.]

Assume, then, that we ignore the effects on all other prices of a change in p_1, in which case $dp_i/dp_1 = 0$ for $i = 2, \ldots, n$. In this case, we have $dz_1/dp_1 = F_{11}$, and, since for perfect stability it must be that $dz_1/dp_1 < 0$, it follows that $F_{11} < 0$, when perfect stability obtains. But we chose commodity 1 arbitrarily in our derivation of the Hicks conditions, so by a simple renumbering of commodities we can arrive at the conclusion that Hicksian stability requires that $F_{ii} < 0$ for all i, that is, the aggregate excess demand curve for each commodity must be downward sloping.

In general, we may rewrite our system of equations in matrix notation as follows:

$$\begin{bmatrix} \dfrac{dz_1}{dp_1} \\ \dfrac{dz_2}{dp_1} \\ \cdot \\ \cdot \\ \cdot \\ \dfrac{dz_n}{dp_1} \end{bmatrix} = \begin{bmatrix} F_{11} & F_{12} & \cdots & F_{1n} \\ F_{21} & F_{12} & \cdots & F_{2n} \\ \cdots & \cdots & \cdots & \cdots \\ F_{n1} & F_{n2} & \cdots & F_{nn} \end{bmatrix} \begin{bmatrix} 1 \\ \dfrac{dp_2}{dp_1} \\ \cdot \\ \cdot \\ \cdot \\ \dfrac{dp_n}{dp_1} \end{bmatrix}$$

so that

$$\frac{dz_1}{dp_1} = \sum_{r=1}^{n} F_{1r} \frac{dp_r}{dp_1}$$

In particular, if we allow p_2 only to vary when p_1 changes, the condition for Hicksian stability may be obtained by solving the following two equations:

$$\frac{dz_1}{dp_1} = F_{11} + F_{12} \frac{dp_2}{dp_1}$$

$$0 = F_{21} + F_{22} \frac{dp_2}{dp_1}$$

or

$$\frac{dz_1}{dp_1} = \frac{F_{11}F_{22} - F_{12}F_{21}}{F_{22}}$$

Since, for Hicksian perfect stability, $dz_1/dp_1 < 0$, and we have already seen that $F_{22} < 0$ if Hicksian perfect stability holds, we have derived a second condition for Hicksian stability, that is, $F_{11}F_{22} - F_{12}F_{21} > 0$. By a renumbering of commodities, this implies $F_{ii}F_{rr} - F_{ir}F_{ri} > 0$ for all $i \neq r$. By a continuation of this procedure, it can be established that Hicksian perfect stability holds if and only if the principal minors of the matrix $[F_{ir}]$ alternate in sign, i.e.,

$$F_{ii} < 0 \text{ for all } i \qquad \begin{vmatrix} F_{ii} & F_{ir} \\ F_{ri} & F_{rr} \end{vmatrix} > 0 \text{ for all } i \neq r$$

$$\begin{vmatrix} F_{ii} & F_{ir} & F_{is} \\ F_{ri} & F_{rr} & F_{rs} \\ F_{si} & F_{sr} & F_{ss} \end{vmatrix} < 0 \text{ for } i \neq r \neq s, \text{ etc.}$$

A rigorous proof of this assertion is as follows: Assume that prices $p_2, p_3, \ldots, p_s$ are permitted to vary as p_1 changes, holding $p_{s+1}, \ldots, p_n$ fixed. The choice of prices $p_2, \ldots, p_s$ as those that vary constitutes no restriction, since by a renumbering of commodities, any arbitrary set of commodities can be covered by the argument. The same comment, of course, applies to the choice of p_1 and z_1 as the variables to consider in deriving conditions for Hicksian perfect stability. By this choice, we have

$$\frac{dp_{s+1}}{dp_1} = \cdots = \frac{dp_n}{dp_1} = 0$$

and

$$\frac{dz_2}{dp_1} = \cdots = \frac{dz_s}{dp_1} = 0$$

and thus the following equation system holds:

$$\begin{bmatrix} \dfrac{dz_1}{dp_1} \\ 0 \\ \cdot \\ \cdot \\ \cdot \\ 0 \end{bmatrix} = \begin{bmatrix} F_{11} & F_{12} & \cdots & F_{1s} \\ F_{21} & F_{22} & \cdots & F_{2s} \\ \cdots & \cdots & \cdots & \cdots \\ F_{s1} & F_{s2} & \cdots & F_{ss} \end{bmatrix} \begin{bmatrix} 1 \\ \dfrac{dp_2}{dp_1} \\ \cdot \\ \cdot \\ \cdot \\ \dfrac{dp_s}{dp_1} \end{bmatrix} \tag{1}$$

and

$$\begin{bmatrix} F_{21} \\ F_{31} \\ \cdot \\ \cdot \\ \cdot \\ F_{s1} \end{bmatrix} = - \begin{bmatrix} F_{22} & F_{23} & \cdots & F_{2s} \\ F_{32} & F_{33} & \cdots & F_{3s} \\ \cdots & \cdots & \cdots & \cdots \\ F_{s2} & F_{s3} & \cdots & F_{ss} \end{bmatrix} \begin{bmatrix} \dfrac{dp_2}{dp_1} \\ \dfrac{dp_3}{dp_1} \\ \cdot \\ \cdot \\ \cdot \\ \dfrac{dp_s}{dp_1} \end{bmatrix} \tag{2}$$

where (2) follows from (1).

If (2) is solved for the vector dp_i/dp_1, we obtain

$$
\begin{bmatrix} \dfrac{dp_2}{dp_1} \\[2ex] \dfrac{dp_3}{dp_1} \\[1ex] \cdot \\ \cdot \\ \cdot \\ \dfrac{dp_s}{dp_1} \end{bmatrix} = -\frac{1}{\Delta} \begin{bmatrix} \Delta_{22} & \Delta_{32} & \cdots & \Delta_{s2} \\[1ex] \Delta_{23} & \Delta_{33} & \cdots & \Delta_{s3} \\[1ex] & \cdots \cdots \cdots \cdots \\[1ex] \Delta_{2s} & \Delta_{3s} & \cdots & \Delta_{ss} \end{bmatrix} \begin{bmatrix} F_{21} \\[2ex] F_{31} \\[1ex] \cdot \\ \cdot \\ \cdot \\ F_{s1} \end{bmatrix}
$$

(handwritten margin note: $X^{-1} = \left[\dfrac{x_{ij}}{|X|}\right]^{T}$, "cofactor")

where Δ is the determinant of the matrix $[F_{ir}]$ for $i, r = 2, \ldots, s$, and Δ_{ir} is the cofactor associated with the entry F_{ir} in $[F_{ir}]$. In a more convenient form for our purposes, we can write

$$
\frac{dp_i}{dp_1} = -\frac{1}{\Delta} \sum_{r=2}^{s} \Delta_{ri} F_{r1} \qquad \text{for } i = 2, \ldots, s
$$

Since

$$
\frac{dz_1}{dp_1} = \sum_{i=1}^{s} F_{1i} \frac{dp_i}{dp_1},
$$

we have

$$
\frac{dz_1}{dp_1} = F_{11} - \frac{1}{\Delta} \sum_{i=2}^{s} F_{1i} \sum_{r=2}^{s} F_{r1} \Delta_{ri}
$$

Next consider the determinant of the matrix in (1), that is, the determinant of $[F_{ir}]$ for $i, r = 1, \ldots, s$. Let us denote this determinant by Δ^*. Expanding this determinant by cofactors along the first row, we obtain

$$
\Delta^* = F_{11}\Delta + \sum_{r=2}^{s} F_{1r} \Delta_{1r}^*
$$

where Δ_{ir}^* is the cofactor associated with the element in the ith row and rth column of $[F_{ir}]$, $i, r = 1, \ldots, s$. But each Δ_{ir}^* is in turn a determinant whose value can be determined by the same process of expanding through the use of cofactors. In particular, if we expand each of the Δ_{ir}^* determinants along the first column of each determinant, our expression for Δ^* becomes

$$
\Delta^* = F_{11}\Delta - \sum_{r=2}^{s} F_{1r} \sum_{i=2}^{s} F_{i1} \Delta_{ir}
$$

Thus, it follows that $dz_1/dp_1 = \Delta^*/\Delta$ and consequently $dz_1/dp_1 < 0$ if and only if $\Delta^*/\Delta < 0$. But Δ^* and Δ are adjacent principal minors of the matrix $[F_{ir}]$ for $i, r = 1, \ldots, n$. We have already seen that the first-order principal minors of this matrix are negative, so the necessary and sufficient condition for Hicksian perfect stability is that every even-ordered principal minor of $[F_{ir}]$, $i, r = 1, \ldots, n$, must be positive and every odd-order principal minor must be negative. This completes the proof of the conditions for Hicksian perfect stability.[1]

Hicks has shown that the only possible source of instability of the competitive mechanism (in terms of his definition of stability) is asymmetric income effects.[2] The reason for this is apparent when the relationship between the aggregate excess demand functions F_i and individual consumer and producer excess demand functions is recalled: We have

$$F_i(1, p_1, \ldots, p_n) = \sum_{j=1}^{m} [x_{ij}(1, p_1, \ldots, p_n) - x_{ij}^0] - \sum_{k=1}^{l} y_{ik}(1, p_1, \ldots, p_n) \qquad \text{for all } i = 0, \ldots, n$$

Thus

$$F_{ir} = \frac{\partial F_i}{\partial p_r} = \sum_{j=1}^{m} \frac{\partial x_{ij}}{\partial p_r} - \sum_{k=1}^{l} \frac{\partial y_{ik}}{\partial p_r} \qquad \text{for } i, r = 1, 2, \ldots, n$$

By Slutsky's equation,

$$\frac{\partial x_{ij}}{\partial p_r} = S_{ir}^j - \left[(x_{rj} - x_{rj}^0) + \sum_{k=1}^{l} s^{kj} y_{rk}\right] \frac{\partial x_{ij}}{\partial I_j}$$

where S_{ir}^j is the substitution term for the jth consumer with respect to commodities i and r (that is, $S_{ir}^j = \partial x_{ij}/\partial p_r$, when all other prices are held constant and income is adjusted in such a way that utility is held constant for the jth consumer) and $\partial x_{ij}/\partial I_j$ is the change in x_{ij} when income changes, all prices being held constant. Assume that income effects are symmetrical with respect to consumers in the sense that

$$\frac{\partial x_{ij}}{\partial I_j} = \frac{\partial x_{iq}}{\partial I_q} = \frac{\partial x_i}{\partial I} \qquad \text{for all } j, q = 1, \ldots, m, \text{ and } i = 0, \ldots, n$$

Then we can write

$$F_{ir} = \sum_{j=1}^{m} S_{ir}^j - \frac{\partial x_i}{\partial I} \sum_{j=1}^{m} \left[(x_{rj} - x_{rj}^0) + \sum_{k=1}^{l} s^{kj} y_{rk}\right] - \sum_{k=1}^{l} \frac{\partial y_{ik}}{\partial p_r}$$

[1] Since the choice of commodity 0 for *numéraire* was arbitrary, true Hicksian stability should be independent of choice of *numéraire*. Thus the conditions for "complete" Hicksian stability should be that the principal minors of every $n \times n$ matrix of partial derivatives of excess demand that can be formed from the $n + 1$ commodities should alternate in sign. See Peter K. Newman, Some Notes on Stability Conditions, *Review of Economic Studies*, vol. 72, pp. 1–9, 1959.

[2] Hicks, *op. cit.*

But, in equilibrium, when all profits are distributed to consumers,

$$\sum_{j=1}^{m}\left[(x_{rj} - x_{rj}^0) + \sum_{k=1}^{l} s^{kj} y_{rk}\right] = 0 \qquad \text{for all } r = 0, \ldots, n$$

i.e., in the aggregate, income terms vanish. As Hicks shows, however, for each consumer the matrix of substitution terms is symmetric and negative definite of rank n, which means that the principal minors of each of the individual substitution matrices alternate in sign; consequently the aggregate matrix $\left[\sum_{j=1}^{m} S_{ir}^{j}\right]$ has principal minors that alternate in sign as well.[1] Similarly, at a regular maximum of profits, the matrix $[-\partial y_{ir}/\partial p_r]$ is negative definite; thus the aggregate matrix $\left[-\sum_{k=1}^{l} (\partial y_{ir}/\partial p_r)\right]$ has principal minors that alternate in sign. We thus conclude that the principal minors of the matrix $[F_{ir}]$, i, $r = 1, \ldots, n$, alternate in sign if income effects are symmetric with respect to consumers, i.e., instability of competitive equilibrium in the Hicksian sense occurs only if income effects are asymmetric.

5-3 DYNAMIC STABILITY: THE *TÂTONNEMENT* PROCESS

As contrasted with the taxonomic character of static stability analysis, the study of dynamic stability of equilibrium positions rests upon an explicit adjustment mechanism that governs the manner in which prices and quantities demanded and supplied change over time in response to a disturbance of equilibrium. The Walrasian *tâtonnement* adjustment mechanism can be described as follows.

Assume that at the beginning of the marketing day, a "referee" announces a price vector to the market participants (producers and consumers) and that following this announcement, each participant fills out a ticket listing the amounts of each commodity that he intends to demand or supply at this price vector. If supply in the aggregate equals demand in the aggregate for each commodity, then the participants make contracts

[1] An $n \times n$ *symmetric* matrix $A = [a_{ij}]$ is said to be *negative definite* if, for any choice of the numbers $h_1, \ldots, h_n$ (not all $h_i = 0$), the following inequality is satisfied: $\sum_{i=1}^{n}\sum_{j=1}^{n} a_{ij}h_ih_j < 0$. Clearly, if $A^1 = [a_{ij}^1]$, $A^2 = [a_{ij}^2], \ldots, A^m = [a_{ij}^m]$, and if each is negative definite, so is $A^1 + A^2 + \cdots + A^m$. A is negative definite if and only if the principal minors of A alternate in sign. Similarly, a matrix $A = [a_{ij}]$ is said to be positive definite if, for any choice of $h_1, \ldots, h_n$ (not all $h_i = 0$), $\sum_i\sum_j a_{ij}h_ih_j > 0$; A is positive definite if and only if the principal minors of A are all positive.

at the equilibrium set of prices and an equilibrium is achieved. If, on the other hand, there is positive excess demand for some commodity, the referee raises the price of that commodity, while if there is positive excess supply, the price of the commodity is lowered. No trading is permitted at the nonequilibrium set of prices; instead, tickets are once again collected at the adjusted set of prices and aggregate excess demand for each commodity is recalculated. This process continues until an equilibrium position is reached, at which time trading takes place. If the process converges to an equilibrium position, the process is said to be dynamically stable; if not, it is dynamically unstable. It should be noted that it will be assumed throughout our discussion that the axioms listed in Chap. 3 are satisfied, so that the issue of the existence of equilibrium positions is not relevant. Instead, we are concerned with whether those equilibrium positions that exist are attainable under a *tâtonnement* adjustment mechanism if we start at a disequilibrium set of prices.

This interpretation of stability can be formalized so that explicit conditions for dynamic stability can be derived: As above, let $F_i(1, p_1, \ldots, p_n)$ denote the aggregate excess demand for the ith commodity, where $i = 0, \ldots, n$. Then, according to the mechanism described above, the time path of prices $p_1, \ldots, p_n$ can be described by the following system of differential equations:

$$\dot{p}_1 = \frac{dp_1}{dt} = g_1[F_1(1, p_1, \ldots, p_n)]$$

$$\dot{p}_2 = \frac{dp_2}{dt} = g_2[F_2(1, p_1, \ldots, p_n)]$$

$$\cdots\cdots\cdots\cdots\cdots\cdots\cdots\cdots$$

$$\dot{p}_n = \frac{dp_n}{dt} = g_n[F_n(1, p_1, \ldots, p_n)]$$

where $\dot{p}_i = dp_i/dt$ and g_i is some increasing ("sign preserving") function of excess demand F_i for $i = 1, \ldots, n$. Further, if $\bar{\mathbf{p}} = (1, \bar{p}_1, \ldots, \bar{p}_n)$ is an equilibrium price vector, then $g_i(F_i(\bar{p})) = 0$ for all i, that is, if the system is in equilibrium, then prices do not change.

In the spirit of the Walrasian scheme outlined above, the economy is said to possess stability in the dynamic sense if, given an arbitrary initial set of prices announced or "called out" by the referee, these prices to be denoted by $\mathbf{p}^0$, where $\mathbf{p}^0 = (1, p_1^0, \ldots, p_n^0)$, then in the limit as t approaches infinity, the price vector $\mathbf{p}$ approaches some equilibrium price vector $\bar{\mathbf{p}}$. It will be noted that in this definition of stability, the possibility of multiple equilibria has not been excluded. However, because of the possibility of multiple equilibria, it is necessary to distinguish between stability of a system of equilibrium positions and stability of a particular equilibrium position. This is formalized in the following definitions [let $\Psi(\mathbf{p}^0;t)$ denote the time path of prices $\mathbf{p}$, determined by the above set of differential equations, given the initial set of prices $\mathbf{p}^0$]:

1. If, for any $\mathbf{p}^0$, $\lim_{t\to\infty} \Psi(\mathbf{p}^0;t) = \bar{\mathbf{p}}$ for some equilibrium price vector $\bar{\mathbf{p}}$, then we say that the system of equilibrium positions possesses *stability of the system* or, briefly, *system stability*.
2. A particular equilibrium position with its associated price vector $\bar{\mathbf{p}}$ is said to be *globally stable* if, given any $\mathbf{p}^0$, $\lim_{t\to\infty} \Psi(\mathbf{p}^0;t) = \bar{\mathbf{p}}$.
3. A particular equilibrium position with its associated price vector $\bar{\mathbf{p}}$ is said to be *locally stable* if, for $\mathbf{p}^0$ belonging to a sufficiently small neighborhood of $\bar{\mathbf{p}}$, $\lim_{t\to\infty} \Psi(\mathbf{p}^0;t) = \bar{\mathbf{p}}$.

The graphs on the following pages illustrate the derivation of excess demand functions for the case of a two-commodity pure trade world. Figure 5-3 presents the case of a unique equilibrium position relative to the initial-holdings point indicated, while Fig. 5-4 presents the case of multiple equilibria. As the discussion in Chap. 3 indicates, the occurrence of a unique equilibrium position must be regarded, in general, as somewhat exceptional, since the conditions required to guarantee the existence of unique equilibrium positions are considerably stronger than those required to guarantee existence itself. When a unique equilibrium position exists, the concept of global stability becomes applicable, and it should be clear that the case depicted in Fig. 5-3 is one in which the equilibrium position is in fact globally stable. This is true because if any price for commodity 1 less than \$1 is chosen, excess demand is positive; thus (by our adjustment model) price rises over time, converging to \$1. Similarly, if any initial price for commodity 1 greater than \$1 is chosen by the referee, excess demand is negative and price falls toward \$1 over time. Since the existence of global stability implies the existence of local stability, the equilibrium position pictured is locally stable as well. Finally, when global stability occurs, it is easy to verify that system stability occurs as well, so that all three of the definitions of stability are satisfied for the case depicted in Fig. 5-3.

In contrast, consider Fig. 5-4. Three equilibrium positions are shown, occurring at $p_1 = \frac{1}{4}$, $p_1 = 1$, and $p_1 = 4$ (p_0 is taken to be 1). Because we have more than one equilibrium point, no equilibrium can be globally stable (e.g., what if we choose the initial price to be one of the three equilibrium prices?); on the other hand, the reader should verify that values of p_1 of $\frac{1}{4}$ and 4 are associated with locally stable equilibrium positions (for what neighborhoods?), while p_1 of 1 is associated with an

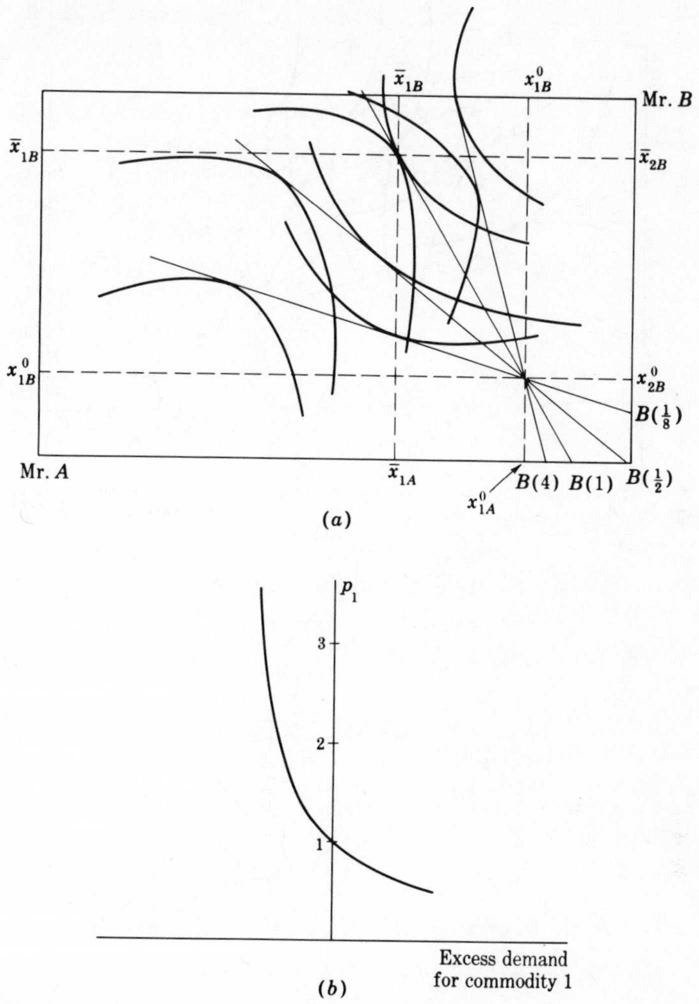

FIGURE 5-3

unstable equilibrium. The *system* of equilibrium positions, however, is stable, since whatever initial price is chosen for commodity 1, the adjustment process will drive p_1 toward either $\frac{1}{4}$, 1, or 4.

Certain properties of matrices are taken up in the next section, following which local dynamic stability of equilibrium positions is discussed, together with the relationship of local dynamic stability to static stability. System stability and global stability of the competitive mechanism are taken up in Secs. 5-6 and 5-7.

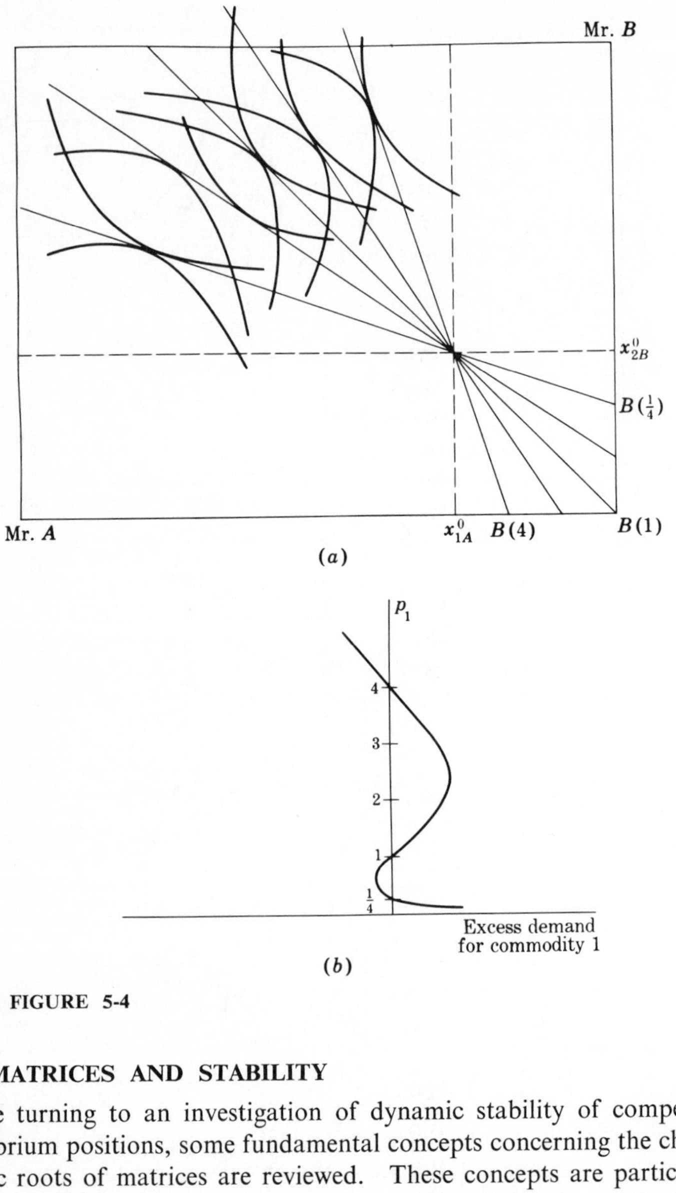

FIGURE 5-4

5-4 MATRICES AND STABILITY

Before turning to an investigation of dynamic stability of competitive equilibrium positions, some fundamental concepts concerning the characteristic roots of matrices are reviewed. These concepts are particularly useful in the study of the local stability properties of equilibrium positions, to be discussed in Sec. 5-5.

Given an arbitrary $n \times n$ matrix $\mathbf{A}$, the *characteristic equation* of $\mathbf{A}$ is the determinantal equation $|\mathbf{A} - \lambda \mathbf{I}| = 0$. The real or complex numbers λ satisfying this equation are referred to as the *characteristic roots* (*characteristic values, eigenvalues*, etc.) of $\mathbf{A}$. Associated with each characteristic

principle minor: determinent of submatrix when corresponding rows & columns are deleted root of **A** is a nonzero vector **x**, called a *characteristic vector* of **A**, satisfying $\mathbf{Ax} = \lambda\mathbf{x}$. The characteristic equation of **A** may be rewritten as $\lambda^n + k_1\lambda^{n-1} + k_2\lambda^{n-2} + \cdots + k_n = 0$, where $k_i = (-1)^i$ times the sum of all ith-order principal minors of **A** for $i = 1, \ldots, n$. (The expression on the left in this equation is referred to as the *characteristic polynomial* of **A**.) If a particular characteristic value occurs only once (is unrepeated), then it is referred to as a *simple* characteristic root of **A**. If **A** is a real matrix (i.e., all entries of **A** are real numbers), then if there exists a complex characteristic root of **A**, with value $a + bi$, where $i = \sqrt{-1}$, some other characteristic root of **A** will be the *complex conjugate* of this root, with value $a - bi$. For any complex number $a + bi$, the real number a is referred to as the *real part* of $a + bi$, and the real number b is referred to as the *imaginary part* of $a + bi$. For reasons to be made clear below, if, for any $n \times n$ matrix **A**, every characteristic root of **A** has the real part negative, then **A** is called a *stable matrix*. Among the many theorems that exist concerning stable matrices, the following two are particularly basic and important:

ROUTH-HURWITZ THEOREM

A real $n \times n$ matrix **A** is stable if and only if the following conditions are satisfied [recall that $k_i = (-1)^i$ times the sum of all i^{th}-order principal minors of **A**]:

1. $k_i > 0$ for every $i = 1, \ldots, n$.
2. The following determinantal conditions hold:

$$\begin{vmatrix} k_1 & k_3 \\ 1 & k_2 \end{vmatrix} > 0 \quad \begin{vmatrix} k_1 & k_3 & k_5 \\ 1 & k_2 & k_4 \\ 0 & k_1 & k_3 \end{vmatrix} > 0 \quad \cdots \quad \begin{vmatrix} k_1 & k_3 & \cdots & 0 \\ 1 & k_2 & \cdots & 0 \\ \cdots & \cdots & \cdots & \cdots \\ 0 & 0 & & k_n \end{vmatrix} > 0$$

where $k_i = 0$ for $i > n$.

LYAPUNOV THEOREM

A real $n \times n$ matrix **A** is stable if and only if there exists a symmetric positive definite matrix **B** such that $\mathbf{BA} + \mathbf{A'B}$ is negative definite.[1] (**A'** is the *transpose* of **A**, that is, if $\mathbf{A} = [a_{ij}]$, $\mathbf{A'} = [a_{ji}]$.)

Of particular importance in economics is a more restricted notion of stability as applied to matrices, the notion of *D stability*. A matrix **A**

[1] Proofs of the Routh-Hurwitz and Lyapunov theorems may be found in F. R. Gantmacher, *The Theory of Matrices*, vol. II, Chelsea Publishing Co., New York, 1960.

is said to be *D stable* if the product **DA** is stable (real parts of characteristic roots of **DA** negative) for any positive diagonal matrix **D**, that is, $\mathbf{D} = [d_{ij}]$ is such that $d_{ii} > 0$ for all i and $d_{ij} = 0$ for $i \neq j$. Equivalent conditions for D stability of matrices are not known, but the following theorems are easily established:

SUFFICIENT CONDITION FOR *D* STABILITY (ARROW-MCMANUS)[1]

If there exists a positive diagonal matrix **C** such that $\mathbf{CA} + \mathbf{A'C}$ is negative definite, then **A** is D stable.

PROOF: Consider **DA**, where **D** is an arbitrary positive diagonal matrix. To show **DA** stable, it is sufficient to find a positive definite symmetric matrix **B** such that $\mathbf{B(DA)} + \mathbf{(DA)'B}$ is negative definite. (This follows from the Lyapunov theorem.) Let $\mathbf{B} = \mathbf{CD}^{-1}$. Since **D** is positive diagonal, $\mathbf{D}^{-1}$ is positive diagonal as well; consequently, $\mathbf{D} = \mathbf{D}'$ and $\mathbf{D}^{-1} = (\mathbf{D}^{-1})'$. Further, because **C** and **D** are positive diagonal, **B** is positive diagonal, hence symmetric positive definite. Thus $(\mathbf{CD}^{-1})(\mathbf{DA}) + (\mathbf{DA})'(\mathbf{CD}^{-1}) = \mathbf{CA} + \mathbf{A'C}$, which is negative definite by hypothesis. Therefore, **A** is D stable.

NECESSARY CONDITION FOR *D* STABILITY

If **A** is a D-stable matrix, then every principal minor of **A** of even order is nonnegative, and every principal minor of **A** of odd order is nonpositive, and at least one nonzero principal minor of **A** of every order exists. (The proof follows directly from the Routh-Hurwitz theorem.)

Related to D-stable matrices are *totally stable* matrices. An $n \times n$ matrix **A** is said to be *totally stable* if every submatrix of **A** whose determinant is a principal minor of **A** is D stable. Metzler has proved the following:[2]

NECESSARY CONDITION FOR TOTAL STABILITY

If **A** is a totally stable matrix, then **A** is a *Hicksian* matrix, i.e., every even-order principal minor of **A** is positive and every odd-order principal minor of **A** is negative. (The proof follows directly from the Routh-Hurwitz theorem.)

Certain special cases arise of particular interest to economists, in which total stability can be established. The most important of these are the following:

[1] Kenneth J. Arrow and Maurice McManus, A Note on Dynamic Stability, *Econometrica*, vol. 26, pp. 297–305, 1958.

[2] Lloyd Metzler, Stability of Multiple Markets: The Hicks Conditions, *Econometrica*, vol. 13, pp. 277–292, 1945.

SUFFICIENT CONDITIONS FOR TOTAL STABILITY

1. If a real $n \times n$ matrix $\mathbf{A}$ is quasinegative definite, that is, $\mathbf{A} + \mathbf{A}'$ is negative definite, then $\mathbf{A}$ is totally stable.

PROOF: $\mathbf{A} + \mathbf{A}'$ negative definite means that for any nonzero vector $\mathbf{x}$, $\mathbf{x}'(\mathbf{A} + \mathbf{A}')\mathbf{x} < 0$, which implies that $\mathbf{x}'\mathbf{A}\mathbf{x} < 0$ for any nonzero vector $\mathbf{x}$. Consider any submatrix $\mathbf{A}^*$ of $\mathbf{A}$, where $\mathbf{A}^*$ is formed by deleting certain rows and the corresponding columns from $\mathbf{A}$. Then for that submatrix, $\mathbf{x}^{*\prime}\mathbf{A}^*\mathbf{x}^* < 0$, where $\mathbf{x}^*$ is an arbitrary nonzero vector with as many elements as the number of rows (columns) of $\mathbf{A}^*$. (The inequality holds because the expression is equivalent to setting the appropriate elements of the vector $\mathbf{x}$ equal to zero.) But $\mathbf{A}^*$ is D-stable, because $\mathbf{A}^* + \mathbf{A}^{*\prime}$ is negative definite; thus the Arrow-McManus sufficiency condition for D stability is satisfied. (The identity matrix $\mathbf{I}$ fills the role of the positive diagonal matrix $\mathbf{C}$ in the Arrow-McManus condition.) Thus $\mathbf{A}$ is totally stable.

2. If a real $n \times n$ matrix $\mathbf{A}$ has a negative diagonal and is quasidominant diagonal, then $\mathbf{A}$ is totally stable. (A matrix $\mathbf{A}$ is said to be *quasidominant diagonal* if there exist positive numbers $c_1, \ldots, c_n$ such that $c_i\,|a_{ii}| > \sum_{j \neq i} c_j\,|a_{ij}|$ for every $i = 1, \ldots, n$, or if there exist positive numbers $b_1, \ldots, b_n$ such that $b_i\,|a_{ii}| > \sum_{j \neq i} b_j\,|a_{ji}|$ for every $i = 1, \ldots, n$.)

PROOF: Following McKenzie,[1] it is first shown that a quasidominant diagonal matrix is nonsingular, from which stability follows quite easily. Assume that A is quasidominant diagonal and is singular. Then, given any positive diagonal matrix $\mathbf{D}$, there exists a nonzero vector $\mathbf{x}$ such that $\mathbf{x}'\mathbf{D}\mathbf{A} = 0$. Let x_k be chosen so that $x_k = \max |x_i|$, and let $d_{ii} = c_i$, as in the definition above. Then

$$\sum_{j=1}^{n} d_{jj} a_{ji} x_j = 0 \qquad \text{for } i = 1, \ldots, n$$

in particular,

$$\sum_{j=1}^{n} d_{jj} a_{jk} x_j = 0$$

[1] See Lionel W. McKenzie, The Matrix with Dominant Diagonal and Economic Theory, *Proceedings of a Symposium on Mathematical Methods in the Social Sciences*, Stanford University Press, Palo Alto, Calif., 1960, pp. 277–292. McKenzie uses a more general notion of quasidominant diagonal matrices than that given here.

which implies

$$d_{kk}a_{kk}x_k = -\sum_{j\neq k} d_{jj}a_{jk}x_j$$

Hence

$$d_{kk}\,|a_{kk}|\,x_k \leqq \sum_{j\neq k} d_{jj}\,|a_{jk}|\,|x_j| \leqq \sum_{j\neq k} d_{jj}\,|a_{jk}|\,x_k$$

which violates the assumption that A is quasidominant diagonal. A quasidominant diagonal matrix **A** with negative diagonal is shown to be stable as follows:

Consider $\mathbf{A} - \lambda\mathbf{I}$ with typical diagonal element $a_{ii} - \lambda$. Then

$$|a_{ii} - \lambda| = \sqrt{(a_{ii} - R(\lambda))^2 + I(\lambda)^2} \geqq |a_{ii} - R(\lambda)|$$

where $R(\lambda)$ and $I(\lambda)$ are the real and imaginary parts of λ. Given that $a_{ii} < 0$, then $R(\lambda) \geqq 0$ implies $|a_{ii} - R(\lambda)| \geqq |a_{ii}|$; thus if **A** is quasidominant diagonal, $\mathbf{A} - \lambda\mathbf{I}$ is quasidominant diagonal as well, hence nonsingular. This means that λ is not a characteristic root of **A**, that is, every characteristic root of **A** has negative real part, so that **A** is a stable matrix.

It is clear from the definition of a quasidominant diagonal matrix that if **A** is quasidominant diagonal, then so is any submatrix of **A** formed by deleting certain columns of **A** together with the corresponding rows (in fact, the same c_i or b_i constants will "work" for any submatrix if they establish the quasidominant diagonal property for the matrix itself).

To show that **A** is D-stable if **A** is quasidominant diagonal (with diagonal elements negative), let $c_1, \ldots, c_n$ be chosen such that

$$c_i\,|a_{ii}| > \sum_{j\neq i} c_j\,|a_{ij}| \qquad i = 1, \ldots, n$$

Given any positive diagonal matrix **D**, let $c_i^* = c_i/d_{ii}$. It is clear that $c_1^*, \ldots, c_n^*$ satisfies $c_i^*\,|d_{ii}a_{ii}| > \sum_{j\neq i} c_j^*\,|d_{jj}a_{ij}|$ for $i = 1, \ldots, n$; hence **DA** is stable. This, together with the remarks above, establishes that **A** is totally stable.

The relationship between these results and the local stability of competitive equilibrium positions is examined next.

5-5 LOCAL DYNAMIC STABILITY

The *tâtonnement* adjustment mechanism described in Sec. 5-3 reduces to the following equation system:

$$\dot{p}_i = g_i(F_i(1, p_1, \ldots, p_n)) \qquad \text{for } i = 1, \ldots, n \tag{3}$$

where $\dot{p}_i = dp_i/dt$ and g_i is an arbitrary-increasing function of F_i, with $g_i(F_i(\bar{\mathbf{p}})) \equiv g_i(0) = 0$.

Assume that in a sufficiently small neighborhood about an equilibrium price vector $\bar{\mathbf{p}}$, the excess demand functions possess partial derivatives of every order and the g_i functions possess derivatives of every order. Then, in a Taylor-series expansion in which terms of higher order than the first are ignored, the equation system (3) can be approximated by

$$\dot{p}_i = g_i(F_i(\bar{\mathbf{p}})) + g_i' \sum_{r=1}^{n} F_{ir}(p_r - \bar{p}_r) \qquad \text{for } i = 1, \ldots, n \tag{3'}$$

where

$$F_{ir} = \frac{\partial F_i}{\partial p_r} \qquad \text{for } i, r = 1, \ldots, n$$

these partial derivatives being evaluated at $\bar{\mathbf{p}}$. Further, since $F_i(\bar{\mathbf{p}}) = 0$, the system can be reduced to

$$\dot{p}_i = g_i' \sum_{r=1}^{n} F_{ir}(p_r - \bar{p}_r) \qquad \text{for } i = 1, \ldots, n \tag{4}$$

To solve (4), it is convenient to reduce it to homogeneous form by introducing the change in variables $P_i = p_i - \bar{p}_i$ for each i; thus P_i is the deviation of p_i from its equilibrium value. Because $\bar{p}_i$ is a constant for each i, (4) can be rewritten as

$$\dot{P}_i = g_i' \sum_{r=1}^{n} F_{ir} P_r \qquad \text{for } i = 1, \ldots, n \tag{5}$$

For the case $n = 1$, the solution is given by $P_1 = P_1^0 e^{g' F_{11} t}$, where P_1^0 is the initial deviation of p_1 from its equilibrium value. Similarly, in the case $n > 1$, a general solution to the system can be obtained by assuming that a particular solution is given by $P_i = c_i e^{\lambda t}$ for $i = 1, \ldots, n$, for some constants c_i and λ. Substituting in (5) we obtain

$$\begin{aligned} c_1 \lambda e^{\lambda t} &= g_1' F_{11} c_1 e^{\lambda t} + \cdots + g_1' F_{1n} c_n e^{\lambda t} \\ &\cdots\cdots\cdots\cdots\cdots\cdots \\ c_n \lambda e^{\lambda t} &= g_n' F_{n1} c_1 e^{\lambda t} + \cdots + g_n' F_{nn} c_n e^{\lambda t} \end{aligned} \tag{6}$$

Factoring out $e^{\lambda t}$ and collecting terms, (6) reduces to

$$\begin{bmatrix} g_1' F_{11} - \lambda & g_1' F_{12} & \cdots & g_1' F_{1n} \\ \cdot & & & \\ \cdot & & & \\ \cdot & & & \\ g_n' F_{n1} & g_n' F_{n2} & \cdots & g_n' F_{nn} - \lambda \end{bmatrix} \begin{bmatrix} c_1 \\ \cdot \\ \cdot \\ \cdot \\ c_n \end{bmatrix} = \begin{bmatrix} 0 \\ \cdot \\ \cdot \\ \cdot \\ 0 \end{bmatrix} \tag{7}$$

A solution to (7) exists for a nontrivial vector of c_i terms only if the determinant of the matrix on the left is zero; hence the constants λ are the characteristic roots of the matrix $[g_i'F_{ij}]$. For simplicity of notation, let $g_i' = b_i$. Because each of the g_i functions is assumed to be an increasing function of the corresponding F_i, b_i is positive for each i. The interpretation given to b_i is that of a "speed of adjustment" of the ith price, since the larger is b_i, the larger is the change in the ith price with respect to time for a given value of excess demand for the ith commodity. If we let $\mathbf{A} = [F_{ij}]$ and $\mathbf{B} = [b_i]$ ($\mathbf{B}$ is a diagonal matrix with b_i in the ith-diagonal position), then each constant λ is a characteristic root of the matrix $\mathbf{BA}$.

If every λ is simple (unrepeated), then the general solution to (5) is given by a linear combination of particular solutions, that is,

$$P_i(t) = \sum_{r=1}^{n} \alpha_{ir} e^{\lambda_r t} \qquad \text{for } i = 1, \ldots, n \tag{8}$$

If any root of $\mathbf{BA}$ is repeated, then in the solution of (5), the exponential term involving that root is multiplied by a polynomial in t of degree at most one less than the number of times the root is repeated, i.e., the general solution to (5) is given by

$$P_i(t) = \sum_{r=1}^{s} Q_{ir}(t) e^{\lambda_r t} \qquad \text{for } i = 1, \ldots, n \tag{8$'$}$$

where $s \leqq n$ is the number of simple roots of $\mathbf{BA}$ and $Q_{ir}(t)$ is a polynomial in t of degree at most one less than the number of times the rth characteristic root of $\mathbf{BA}$ is repeated and λ_r is the rth simple root of $\mathbf{BA}$.†

Local stability of system (3) occurs if, in the neighborhood of $\bar{p}$ in which the linear approximation (5) holds, $\lim_{t\to\infty} P_i(t) = 0$ [$\lim_{t\to\infty} p_i(t) = \bar{p}_i$ for all $i = 1, \ldots, n$].

Because exponential terms dominate polynomials, the existence of repeated roots has no effect on the asymptotic behavior of P_i. It is clear then from either (8) or (8′) that if the coefficients of the exponential terms can take on arbitrary values, and if each characteristic root of $\mathbf{BA}$ is real, local stability occurs if and only if each characteristic root is negative. More generally, if $\lambda_r = a_r + b_r i$, we have $e^{\lambda_r t} = e^{a_r t} \cdot e^{b_r i t}$. Since $|e^{b_r i t}| = 1$, the asymptotic behavior of P_i is determined by the real parts of the characteristic roots of $\mathbf{BA}$, and a necessary and sufficient condition for local stability of (3) for any $\mathbf{p}^0$ lying in a neighborhood of $\bar{\mathbf{p}}$ for which the linear approximation (5) holds is that the real parts of all

† The coefficients α_{ir} and the coefficients appearing in $Q_{ir}(t)$ are determined by the initial conditions, i.e., the vector $\mathbf{p}^0$.

characteristic roots of **BA** be negative.[1] The relevance of the Routh-Hurwitz and Lyapunov theorems to the study of local dynamic stability is obvious.

It has been continuously emphasized in the early parts of this book that the economist's ignorance of the specific values of the parameters of the economic system forces him to construct theories that hold under rather general conditions, and this difficulty arises in the study of stability of equilibrium as well. In particular, little is known concerning the speeds at which various prices adjust, and as a consequence, theorems relating stability to various assumptions concerning the nature of excess demand functions are particularly useful if they hold for arbitrary (positive) speeds of adjustment of prices. For this reason, economists have been interested in situations characterized by D stability or total stability as defined in Sec. 5-4. Utilizing the properties of the excess demand functions, the sufficient conditions for total stability (conditions 1 and 2 of Sec. 5-4) can be applied to the following cases.[2]

THEOREM 1: In a pure trade world, if there is no trade at equilibrium, then equilibrium is locally stable for any speeds of adjustment of prices.

THEOREM 2: If all commodities are gross substitutes, then equilibrium is locally stable for any speeds of adjustment of prices.

The proof of Theorem 1 follows directly from the properties of substitution terms in a pure trade world. In the matrix $\mathbf{A} \equiv [F_{ir}]$, a typical element can be written as

$$F_{ir} \equiv \frac{\partial F_i}{\partial p_r} = \sum_{j=1}^{m} S_{ir}^j - \sum_{j=1}^{m} (x_{rj} - x_{rj}^0) \frac{\partial x_{ij}}{\partial I_j}$$

where S_{ir}^j is the substitution term for the jth consumer, x_{rj} is the amount of the rth commodity consumed by the jth consumer, x_{rj}^0 is the initial holdings of the rth commodity by the jth consumer, and I_j is the income of the jth consumer. If there is no trade at equilibrium, $x_{rj} - x_{rj}^0 = 0$ for every $r = 0, \ldots, n$ and every $j = 1, \ldots, m$; thus

$$F_{ir} = \sum_{j=1}^{m} S_{ir}^j$$

[1] See Gantmacher, *op. cit.*, for a proof of this proposition.

[2] Stronger theorems are available concerning these cases, due to Arrow and Hurwicz, and Arrow, Block, and Hurwicz. See Sec. 5-6 of this chapter and Kenneth J. Arrow and Leonid Hurwicz, The Stability of the Competitive Equilibrium I, *Econometrica*, vol. 26, pp. 522–552, 1958, and Kenneth J. Arrow, H. Block, and Leonid Hurwicz, The Stability of the Competitive Equilibrium II, *Econometrica*, vol. 27, pp. 82–109, 1959.

and consequently **A** is symmetric and negative definite. By condition 1 of Sec. 5-4, this implies that **A** is totally stable; hence equilibrium of the equation system (3) is locally stable for any speeds of adjustment of prices.

Among the cases covered by Theorem 1 are (1) the case of a one-consumer economy, (2) the case in which all consumers are identical in terms of preferences and initial holdings, and (3) the case in which the initial holdings of consumers are such that a Pareto optimum exists at the initial-holdings point.

To prove Theorem 2, we need to use either Walras' law or the fact that excess demand functions are homogeneous of degree zero in prices:

Walras' law:

$$\sum_{i=0}^{n} p_i F_i = 0 \qquad \text{for every price vector } \mathbf{p} = (p_0, \ldots, p_n) \tag{W}$$

Homogeneity:

$$F_i(\mu p_0, \ldots, \mu p_n) = F_i(p_0, \ldots, p_n) \qquad \text{for any } \mu > 0 \tag{H}$$

Differentiating (W) with respect to p_r gives

$$\sum_{i=0}^{n} p_i F_{ir} + F_r = 0 \qquad \text{for } r = 0, \ldots, n$$

In particular, evaluating this expression at $p_i = \bar{p}_i$ for each i, we obtain

$$\sum_{i=0}^{n} \bar{p}_i F_{ir} = 0 \qquad \text{for } r = 0, \ldots, n \tag{W$'$}$$

Similarly, using Euler's theorem, (H) yields, at equilibrium,

$$\sum_{r=0}^{n} \bar{p}_r F_{ir} = 0 \qquad \text{for } i = 0, \ldots, n \tag{H$'$}$$

We define the *gross substitute* case as one in which $F_{ii} < 0$ for every $i = 0, \ldots, n$ and $F_{ij} > 0$ for $i \neq j, i, j = 0, \ldots, n$. Choosing commodity 0 as *numéraire*, and utilizing (W′), we obtain

$$\sum_{i=1}^{n} \bar{p}_i F_{ir} = -\bar{p}_0 F_{0r} < 0 \qquad \text{for } r = 1, \ldots, n$$

so that

$$\bar{p}_r F_{rr} < -\sum_{i \neq r} \bar{p}_i F_{ir} \qquad \text{for } r = 1, \ldots, n$$

or

$$-\bar{p}_r F_{rr} > \sum_{i \neq r} \bar{p}_i F_{ir} \qquad \text{for } r = 1, \ldots, n$$

By the assumptions concerning the signs of the elements F_{ir}, this implies that

$$\bar{p}_r |F_{rr}| > \sum_{i \neq r} \bar{p}_i |F_{ir}| \qquad \text{for } r = 1, \ldots, n$$

But this means that in the gross substitute case, the matrix $\mathbf{A} = [F_{ir}]$ has a quasidominant diagonal and hence, by condition 2 of Sec. 5-4, is totally stable.[1]

Theorems 1 and 2 are the fundamental results that have been obtained in the study of local stability properties of the competitive mechanism. It is of some interest to note that because of Metzler's result cited in Sec. 5-4, these cases in which local stability has been proved are also characterized by Hicksian stability, and in addition, stability is invariant under any choice of *numéraire*. That Hicksian stability need not characterize an equilibrium position that is stable under any set of speeds of adjustment is shown in a matrix with sign pattern $\begin{bmatrix} - & + \\ - & 0 \end{bmatrix}$. Such a matrix is *D*-stable but not Hicksian. Furthermore, Hicksian stability is not sufficient for local dynamic stability, as the following matrix illustrates;

$$\begin{bmatrix} -1 & +1 & -14 \\ -1 & -1 & +1 \\ 0 & -1 & -1 \end{bmatrix}$$

[1] Strictly speaking this proof requires the assumption that $\bar{p}_i > 0$ for every i; that this holds in the gross substitute case has been proved by Arrow, Block, and Hurwicz, *op. cit.* The proof above is taken from an unpublished paper by McManus: Maurice McManus, *The Arrow and Hurwicz and Hahn Theorem*, Stanford University, Palo Alto, Calif. (mimeograph), 1958. It will be noted that (H′) could have been used rather than (W′) in the proof. In addition, it should be pointed out that a proof of total stability can be constructed for a somewhat broader case, that of *weak gross substitutes*, that is, $F_{ii} < 0$ for every i, and $F_{ir} \geqq 0$ for every $i \neq r$, $i, r = 0, \ldots, n$, if an indecomposability assumption is imposed. (A matrix $\mathbf{B}$ is said to be indecomposable if it cannot be permuted into a matrix of the form $\begin{bmatrix} \mathbf{B}_1 & \mathbf{B}_{12} \\ \mathbf{0} & \mathbf{B}_2 \end{bmatrix}$, where $\mathbf{B}_1$ and $\mathbf{B}_2$ are square blocks and $\mathbf{0}$ is a block of zeros.) Finally, it might be noted that in a qualitatively specified competitive world, the dominant diagonal argument can be used to prove stability only when $\mathbf{A}$ is (weak) gross substitute.

It is easy to verify, however, that Hicksian stability is sufficient for D stability for the cases in which there are two or three commodities (including *numéraire*). In addition, an interesting property of matrices that are Hicksian has been discovered by Fisher and Fuller;[1] if $\mathbf{A}$ is Hicksian, then $\mathbf{DA}$ is stable for some positive diagonal $\mathbf{D}$, that is, if equilibrium is characterized by Hicksian stability, it is locally stable for *some* speeds of adjustment of prices.

For completeness, we note the following cases in which local stability of equilibrium occurs under any set of speeds of adjustment of prices; precisely what economic content may be given to the assumptions is not clear.

THEOREM 3: If $\mathbf{A} \equiv [F_{ir}]$ is quasinegative definite, then equilibrium is locally stable under any speeds of adjustment of prices.

THEOREM 4: If $\mathbf{A} \equiv [F_{ir}]$ is quasidominant diagonal, then equilibrium is locally stable under any speeds of adjustment of prices.

THEOREM 5: If $\mathbf{A} \equiv [F_{ir}]$ is indecomposable and satisfies conditions 1 to 4 below, then equilibrium is locally stable under any speeds of adjustment of prices.[2]

Condition 1: $F_{ij}F_{ji} \leqq 0$ for every $i \neq j,\ i, j = 1, \ldots, n$.
Condition 2: $i_1 \neq i_2 \neq \cdots \neq i_s,\ F_{i_1i_2} \neq 0,\ F_{i_2i_3} \neq 0, \ldots, F_{i_{s-1}i_s} \neq 0$ implies $F_{i_si_1} = 0$ for any $s > 2$.
Condition 3: $F_{ii} \leqq 0$ for every i and $F_{kk} < 0$ for some k.
Condition 4: There exists a nonzero term in the expansion of $|\mathbf{A}|$.

Theorems 3 and 4 follow directly from conditions 1 and 2 of Sec. 5-4. The proof of Theorem 5 utilizes the Routh-Hurwitz and Lyapunov theorems. For the cases covered by Theorems 3 to 5, stability is, in general, not independent of the choice of *numéraire*, and in the case of matrices satisfying the conditions of Theorem 5, Hicksian stability need not characterize equilibrium.

[1] M. Fisher and A. Fuller, On the Stabilization of Matrices and the Convergence of Linear Iterative Processes, *Proceedings of the Cambridge Philosophical Society*, vol. 54, pp. 417–425, 1958.

[2] J. Quirk and R. Ruppert, Qualitative Economics and the Stability of Equilibrium, *Review of Economic Studies*, vol. 32, pp. 311–326, 1965. A matrix satisfying these conditions is called a *sign-stable* matrix, since any matrix with the sign conditions specified is stable for any values of the entries in the matrix.

In addition to the cases covered by Theorems 3 to 5, Morishima has shown that Hicksian stability and local dynamic stability are equivalent when the following conditions are satisfied:[1]

THEOREM 6: If $\mathbf{A} \equiv [F_{ir}]$ satisfies conditions 1 to 3 below, and $F_{ij} \neq 0$ for every i, j, then $\mathbf{A}$ is stable if and only if $\mathbf{A}$ is Hicksian:

Condition 1: $F_{ii} < 0$ for every $i = 1, \ldots, n$
Condition 2: sign F_{ij} = sign F_{ji} for every i, j
Condition 3: sign $F_{ij}F_{jk}$ = sign F_{ik} for every $i \neq j \neq k$

The proof of Theorem 6 utilizes a generalization of the *Frobenius theorem*, to be discussed in Chap. 6. While Theorem 6 formalizes a certain aspect of the general equilibrium model considered by Hicks in *Value and Capital*, as contrasted with the earlier results there is no guarantee that when conditions 1 to 3 are satisfied, the competitive equilibrium will be locally stable; in fact, as Arrow and Hurwicz have shown, if conditions 1 to 3 are expanded to include the *numéraire* commodity as well, then equilibrium will *not* be locally stable.[2]

In all the situations considered in this section, it has been assumed that excess demand functions are differentiable. This is a stronger assumption concerning the economic environment than those employed in the earlier chapters, although precisely what further restrictions on consumer preferences, consumption and production sets, etc., are in fact involved is not completely clear.[3] In particular, of course, this means that excess demand functions must be single-valued and continuous. The need to restrict any stability analysis to cases involving single-valued and continuous excess demand functions arises because, in general, solutions to differential equation systems in which functions are discontinuous cannot be guaranteed and, as Arrow and Hurwicz remark with respect

[1] Michio Morishima, On the Laws of Change of the Price System in an Economy Which Contains Complementary Commodities, *Osaka Economic Papers*, vol. 1, pp. 101–113, 1952.

[2] Arrow and Hurwicz, The Stability of the Competitive Equilibrium I. A generalization of their result is given in L. Bassett, H. Habibagahi, and J. Quirk, Qualitative Economics and Morishima Matrices, *Econometrica*, 1967.

[3] A necessary condition for everywhere-differentiable demand functions for a consumer in the pure trade case is that there exists a one-to-one mapping of excess demands and normalized price vectors. This is apparently not sufficient, however.

to correspondences, "... [in this case] the precise meaning of the adjustment equations becomes problematical."[1]

While the restrictions imposed by the differentiability assumption are not known, the following theorem, due to Gale, guarantees the existence of single-valued continuous excess demand functions for consumers:[2]

GALE THEOREM

If, for the jth consumer, R_j, the consumer's preference ranking, is continuous, and if R_j is strictly convex, and if the consumer holds positive amounts of each commodity, then the excess demand functions for the jth consumer are single-valued and continuous.[3]

Producer demand functions will be single-valued and continuous if each production set is closed and bounded from above and is strictly convex. More generally, if the aggregate production set is closed and is bounded from above and is strictly convex, and if each consumer's preference ordering and initial holdings satisfy the hypothesis of Gale's theorem, then aggregate excess demand functions for each commodity will be single-valued and continuous.

The strict-convexity assumptions outlaw the case of perfect substitutes (and perfect complements as well) in consumption and constant returns to scale in production in the aggregate. It is the last of these restrictions that is the least appealing, since constant returns to scale is taken as the "standard" case of many analyses of the competitive system.

[1] Arrow and Hurwicz, The Stability of the Competitive Equilibrium I.

[2] David Gale, The Law of Supply and Demand, *Mathematica Scandinavia*, vol. 3, pp. 155–169, 1955.

[3] It will be recalled that the assumption that R_j is continuous is equivalent to the assumptions that, given any $\mathbf{x}^j \in \bar{X}^j$, the set of commodity bundles at least as preferred as $\mathbf{x}^j$ is closed, and the set of commodity bundles at most as preferred as $\mathbf{x}^j$ is closed. Strict convexity of the preference ordering means that for any t, $0 < t < 1$, $\mathbf{x}^j$, $\mathbf{x}'^j \in \bar{X}^j$, $\mathbf{x}^j \, \mathrm{I}_j \, \mathbf{x}'^j$ implies $[t\mathbf{x}^j + (1 - t)\mathbf{x}'^j] \, \mathrm{P}_j \, \mathbf{x}'^j$. Various weakenings of the assumption that each consumer holds positive stocks of all commodities have been made, e.g., each consumer holds a stock of some "always desired" good or the economy is "irreducible," but to establish single-valuedness and continuity, it is essential to include the convexity and continuity conditions on the preference ordering. A theorem equivalent to Gale's under the assumption of positive holdings of some "always desired" good appears in Kenneth J. Arrow and Gerard Debreu, Existence of an Equilibrium for a Competitive Economy, *Econometrica*, vol. 22, pp. 265–290, 1954. In a certain sense, strict convexity is too strong, since in the case of perfect complements (and price positive), single-valued demand functions exist even though the indifference curves have straight line segments.

Thus, for example, McKenzie argues that, whatever is assumed about individual production units, free entry should ensure that in the aggregate constant returns prevail, and he proves his existence theorem under the assumption that the aggregate production set has this characteristic.[1]

To indicate the difficulties for stability analysis of the constant returns case, consider a two-commodity, one-person world in which the production set is characterized by constant returns. Figure 5-5 illustrates this case.

In Fig. 5-5*a*, the conditions of Gale's theorem are assumed to hold with respect to the preference ordering of the consumer, but constant returns is assumed with respect to the production set. Assuming labor is taken as *numéraire*, three budget lines are plotted, for prices of wheat of $\frac{3}{2}$, 1, and $\frac{1}{2}$. The demand function for wheat by the consumer, $D(p_w)$, is single-valued and continuous; on the other hand, the supply function of the producer, $S(p_w)$, is a correspondence, being equal to 0 for $p_w < 1$, any amount greater than or equal to 0 for $p_w = 1$, and infinite for $p_w > 1$. While a unique equilibrium is defined ($\bar{w}$ units being taken off the market at $p_w = 1$), the excess demand function is undefined for $p_w > 1$. Because it is undefined for $p_w > 1$, it makes no sense at all to talk about adjustment equations for price above the equilibrium level. Thus stability analysis of the usual type is inapplicable to cases in which constant returns to scale characterizes the aggregate production set. Hence, to ensure meaningful adjustment equations of the type discussed here, it is necessary to specify strictly decreasing returns to scale with respect to the aggregate production function, which is a serious restriction on the scope of stability analysis as contrasted with the analysis of equilibrium positions with respect to their existence and optimality, or, alternatively, it is necessary to admit the presence of fixed factors.[2]

In addition to the assumption of strict convexity of preference orderings and of the aggregate production set, Arrow and Hurwicz assume that at equilibrium, demand and supply exactly balance, i.e., at equilibrium there is no excess supply of any commodity. In the more general case discussed in Chaps. 3 and 4, the equilibrium conditions may be written as $F_i(\mathbf{p}) \leqq 0$, where if $F_i(\mathbf{p}) < 0$, then $p_i = 0$.

[1] Lionel W. McKenzie, On the Existence of a General Equilibrium for a Competitive Market, *Econometrica*, vol. 27, pp. 54–71, 1959

[2] While the strict-convexity assumptions impose restrictions on the competitive model not present in the existence and optimality proofs (with certain exceptions; e.g., Arrow assumes strict convexity of preferences in his optimality proofs), this is not the case with respect to the assumption of positive holdings of all goods (positive holdings of an "always desired good," etc.), some condition of this sort being required in the proofs of existence, as is clear from the discussion in Chap. 3.

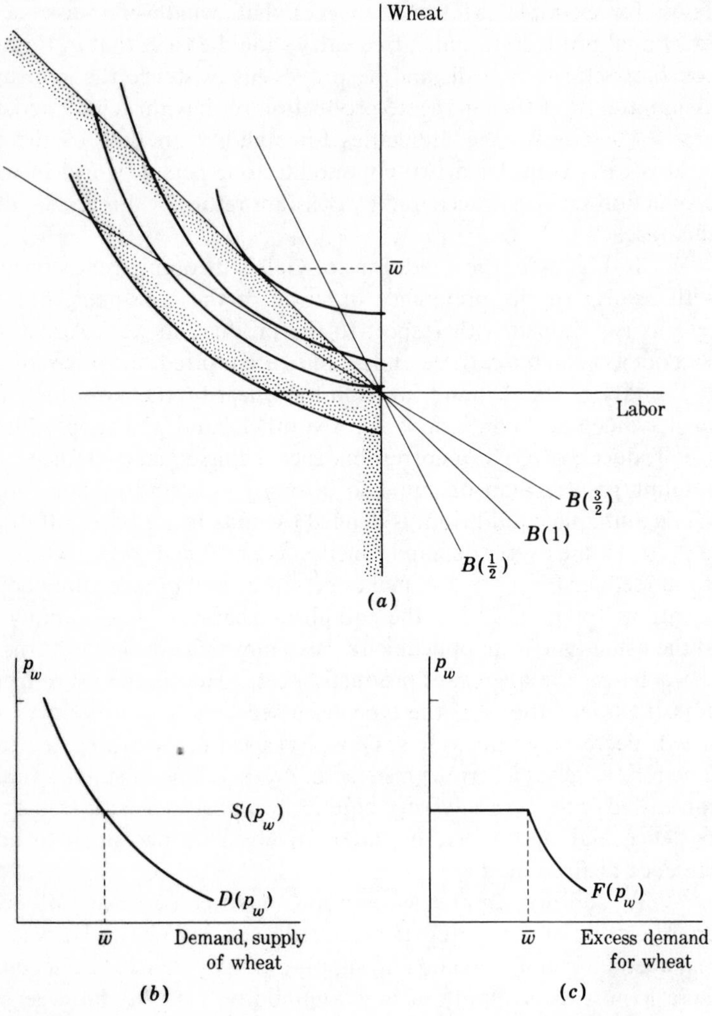

FIGURE 5-5

5-6 GLOBAL DYNAMIC STABILITY

Local stability of equilibrium positions, as discussed in the previous section, guarantees that equilibrium will be restored if a sufficiently small disturbance to equilibrium occurs. However, there is no assurance of a return to equilibrium in the face of "large" disturbances. For certain special cases, Arrow and Hurwicz have proved global stability of the competitive equilibrium, i.e., whatever the magnitude of the disturbance to equilibrium, equilibrium will be restored under the *tâtonnement* mechanism in these cases. Their proofs utilize the following fundamental theorem on global stability.[1]

LIAPUNOV GLOBAL STABILITY THEOREM

Let $\bar{\mathbf{p}}$ denote an equilibrium price vector and $F(\mathbf{p})$ denote the vector of aggregate excess demands at the arbitrary price vector $\mathbf{p}$. The equilibrium price vector $\bar{\mathbf{p}}$ is globally stable if there exists a *distance function* $D(\mathbf{p} - \bar{\mathbf{p}})$ such that

$$\frac{dD(\mathbf{p} - \bar{\mathbf{p}})}{dt} < 0 \qquad \text{for any } \mathbf{p} \neq \bar{\mathbf{p}}$$

or if there exists a distance function $D^*(F(\mathbf{p}))$ such that

$$\frac{dD^*\,(F(\mathbf{p}))}{dt} < 0 \qquad \text{for any } \mathbf{p} \neq \bar{\mathbf{p}}$$

Several distance functions are used in the Arrow-Hurwicz and Arrow-Block-Hurwicz papers, including the euclidean distance functions, that is,

$$D(\mathbf{p} - \bar{\mathbf{p}}) = \sum_{i=0}^{n} (p_i - \bar{p}_i)^2$$

and

$$D^*(F(\mathbf{p})) = \sum_{i=0}^{n} (F_i(\mathbf{p}))^2$$

The *tâtonnement* adjustment mechanism is employed, under the assumption that in the expression $p_i = g_i(F_i(\mathbf{p}))$ for $i = 1, \ldots, n$, the functions $g_i(F_i(\mathbf{p}))$ are simply $F_i(\mathbf{p})$. Thus speeds of adjustment are assumed equal to 1 in all markets.[2]

Theorem 7 generalizes the proof of local stability in the "no trade at equilibrium" case to the global situation:

THEOREM 7: If equilibrium is unique in the pure trade case and if there is no trade at equilibrium, then equilibrium is globally stable.

PROOF: Each consumer is assumed to satisfy the weak axiom of revealed preference. As earlier comments have indicated, this is weaker than the assumption of regular utility maximization by consumers. For the jth consumer, this means that given two price vectors $\mathbf{p}'$ and $\mathbf{p}''$,

[1] Wolfgang Hahn, *Theory and Application of Liapunov's Direct Method*, Prentice-Hall, Inc., Englewood Cliffs, N.J., 1963.

[2] Because the cases considered by Arrow and Hurwicz all involve totally stable equilibrium positions, this involves no loss of generality. Speeds of adjustment equal to 1 for all prices can be set by choosing the units in which commodities are measured appropriately.

and given the commodity bundles $\mathbf{x}'^j$ and $\mathbf{x}''^j$, where $\mathbf{x}'^j$ is chosen at the prices $\mathbf{p}'$ and $\mathbf{x}''^j$ is chosen at the prices $\mathbf{p}''$ ($\mathbf{x}'^j \neq \mathbf{x}''^j$), the following inequalities are satisfied:

$$\sum_{i=0}^{n} p_i' x_{ij}' \geq \sum_{i=0}^{n} p_i' x_{ij}'' \Rightarrow \sum_{i=0}^{n} p_i'' x_{ij}' > \sum_{i=0}^{n} p_i'' x_{ij}''$$

Equivalently, in terms of excess demand, where $z_{ij}' = x_{ij}' - x_{ij}^0$, $z_{ij}'' = x_{ij}'' - x_{ij}''^0$,

$$\sum_{i=0}^{n} p_i' z_{ij}' \geq \sum_{i=0}^{n} p_i' z_{ij}'' \Rightarrow \sum_{i=0}^{n} p_i'' z_{ij}' > \sum_{i=0}^{n} p_i'' z_{ij}'' \qquad (z_j' \neq z_j'')$$

Consider

$$\frac{dD(\mathbf{p} - \bar{\mathbf{p}})}{dt} = \frac{d}{dt} \sum_{i=0}^{n} (p_i - \bar{p}_i)^2 = 2 \sum_{i=0}^{n} (p_i - \bar{p}_i) \dot{p}_i$$

$$= 2 \sum_{i=0}^{n} p_i F_i(\mathbf{p}) - 2 \sum_{i=0}^{n} \bar{p}_i F_i(\mathbf{p})$$

By Walras' law,

$$\sum_{i=0}^{n} p_i F_i(\mathbf{p}) = 0$$

hence

$$\frac{dD}{dt} < 0 \qquad \text{if } \sum_{i=0}^{n} \bar{p}_i F_i(\mathbf{p}) > 0$$

In terms of the notation above,

$$F_i(\mathbf{p}) = \sum_{j=1}^{m} z_{ij}(\mathbf{p})$$

By the "no trade at equilibrium" assumption, $z_{ij}(\bar{\mathbf{p}}) = 0$ for every $i = 0, \ldots, n$ and every $j = 1, \ldots, m$. Let $\mathbf{p}'' = \bar{\mathbf{p}}$ and let $\mathbf{p}' = \mathbf{p}$, where $\mathbf{p}$ is an arbitrary price vector. Then

$$\sum_{i=0}^{n} p_i z_{ij}' = 0 \qquad \text{by the budget constraint}$$

$$\sum_{i=0}^{n} p_i z_{ij}'' = 0 \qquad \text{since } z_{ij}'' \equiv z_{ij}(\bar{\mathbf{p}}) = 0$$

hence

$$\sum_{i=0}^{n} p_i z_{ij}' \geq \sum_{i=0}^{n} p_i z_{ij}'',$$

which implies

$$\sum_{i=0}^{n} \bar{p}_i z_{ij}' > 0 \qquad \text{for each } j = 1, \ldots, m$$

Thus

$$\sum_{i=0}^{n} \bar{p}_i F_i(p) = \sum_{i=0}^{n} \bar{p}_i \sum_{j=1}^{m} z'_{ij} > 0$$

if equilibrium is unique. (Cases in which no trade occurs at equilibrium have been noted in Sec. 5-5.)

The proof of Theorem 7 suggests another case in which global stability occurs:

THEOREM 8: If aggregate excess demand functions obey the weak axiom of revealed preference, and if equilibrium is unique, then equilibrium is globally stable.

It should be noted that the assumption that revealed preference holds in the aggregate does not follow from the assumption that the weak axiom holds for every consumer. Wald, who first introduced the assumption (as applied in the aggregate), remarked that it did not follow from individual utility maximization, but that the assumption was violated only in "statistically improbable cases."[1] In particular, the following example illustrates the kind of "offsetting" preferences under which the weak axiom does not hold in the aggregate.

In Fig. 5-6 the initial holdings of Mr. 1 and Mr. 2 are both given by the vector (1,1). Taking the commodity measured along the horizontal axis as *numéraire*, two budget lines are plotted for prices of the other commodity, of 1 and $\frac{2}{3}$, respectively. In the first situation (price equal to 1), Mr. 1 chooses the vector $A = (\frac{1}{4}, 1\frac{3}{4})$, and Mr. 2 chooses the vector $C = (2,0)$. Aggregate demand is thus $(2\frac{1}{4}, 1\frac{3}{4})$, the point $A + C$ plotted in Fig. 5-7. In the second situation (price equal to $\frac{2}{3}$), both Mr. 1 and Mr. 2 are assumed to obey the weak axiom of revealed preference (for example, B is chosen in a situation where A is not available, and similarly for C with respect to D), leading to the choice of bundles $B = (\frac{1}{2}, 1\frac{1}{4})$ and $D = (1\frac{1}{4}, \frac{7}{8})$. The resulting aggregate demand point $B + D = (1\frac{3}{4}, 2\frac{1}{8})$ violates the weak axiom of revealed preference with respect to the point $A + C$: $A + C$ was chosen when $B + D$ was available, and the weak axiom states that $B + D$ can only be chosen in a case in which $A + C$ is not available. The assumption that each consumer's preferences satisfy

[1] Abraham Wald, Über einige Gleichungssysteme der mathematischen Okonomie, *Zeitschrift für Nationalokonomie*, vol. 7, pp. 637–670, 1936; English translation, On Some Systems of Equations of Mathematical Economics, *Econometrica*, vol. 19, pp. 368–403, 1951.

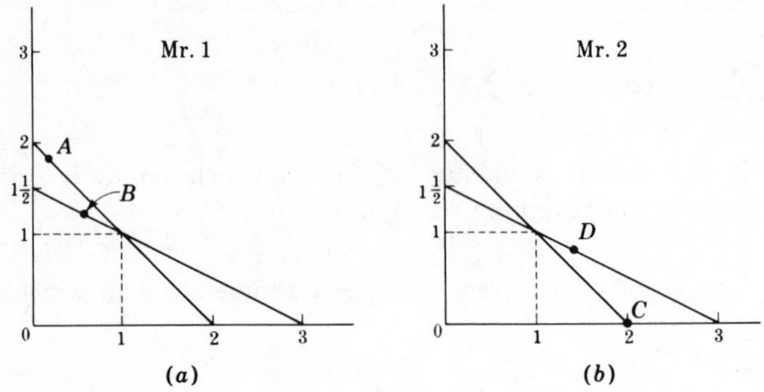

FIGURE 5-6

the weak axiom of revealed preference does not lead to the conclusion that the market excess demand functions have the same property. On the other hand, there are cases in which this does occur: as Arrow and Hurwicz point out, the aggregate excess demand functions will obey the weak axiom in the case of a one-person economy and in the case of identical individuals, and no doubt much broader classes of cases in which the axiom applies in the aggregate could be constructed.

Assume, then, that the weak axiom holds in the aggregate. At equilibrium we have $\bar{z}_i = F_i(\bar{\mathbf{p}}) = 0$ for all $i = 0, \ldots, n$, so that for any $\mathbf{p}$, $\sum_{i=0}^{n} p_i \bar{z}_i = 0$. In particular, assume that at some arbitrary $\mathbf{p}$, the vector $\mathbf{z}$ represents excess demand in the aggregate, i.e., is "chosen" at the price vector $\mathbf{p}$. Because the budget constraints are satisfied as an equality by each consumer at utility-maximizing points, we have

$$\sum_{i=0} p_i z_i = 0$$

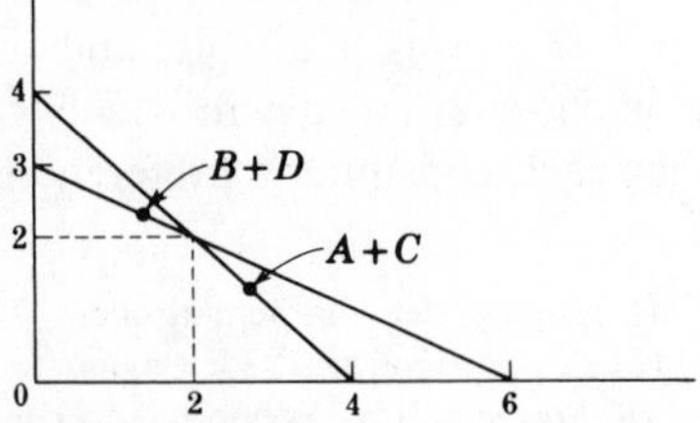

FIGURE 5-7

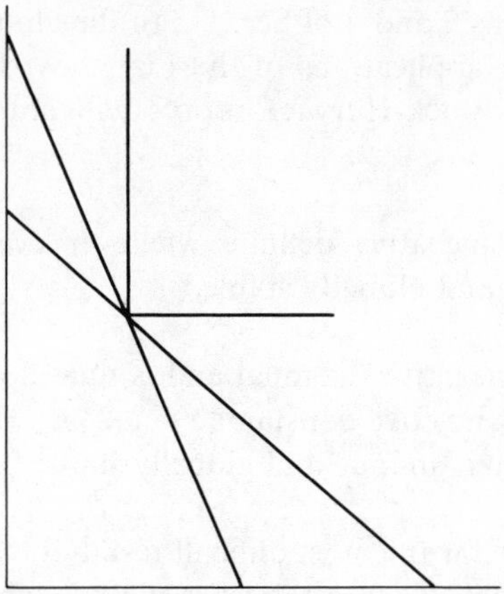

FIGURE 5-8

Thus

$$\sum_{i=0}^{n} p_i \bar{z}_i \leqq \sum_{i=0}^{n} p_i z_i$$

which, by the weak axiom assumed to hold in the aggregate, implies

$$\sum_{i=0}^{n} \bar{p}_i \bar{z}_i < \sum_{i=0}^{n} \bar{p}_i z_i$$

which in turn implies

$$\sum_{i=0}^{n} \bar{p}_i z_i \left(= \sum_{i=0}^{n} \bar{p}_i F_i \right) > 0 \qquad \text{for } z \neq \bar{z}$$

Thus equilibrium is globally stable if unique.

Theorems 7 and 8 establish global stability if equilibrium is unique; the weak axiom is not enough, however, to guarantee uniqueness, as the case depicted in Fig. 5-8 illustrates.

When a "kink" occurs in indifference curves, no unique equilibrium price vector need exist. Arrow and Hurwicz have shown, however, that the set of equilibrium price vectors is always convex when the weak axiom holds in the aggregate [i.e., if $\bar{\mathbf{p}}^1$ and $\bar{\mathbf{p}}^2$ are equilibrium price vectors, then $\alpha\bar{\mathbf{p}}^1 + (1 - \alpha)\bar{\mathbf{p}}^2$ is also an equilibrium price vector for any $0 < \alpha < 1$]. Further, given any initial price vector, the *tâtonnement* mechanism leads to convergence to some equilibrium price vector if the weak axiom holds in the aggregate.[1]

[1] Kenneth J. Arrow and Leonid Hurwicz, Some Remarks on the Equilibria of Economic Systems, *Econometrica*, vol. 28, pp. 640–646, 1960.

Generalizations of Theorems 3 and 4 of Sec. 5-5 to the global case involve relatively straightforward applications of the Liapunov theorem on global stability. The Arrow-Block-Hurwicz proofs will not be reproduced here.

THEOREM 9: If $\mathbf{A} \equiv [F_{ir}]$ is quasinegative definite wherever evaluated, then equilibrium is unique and globally stable.[1]

THEOREM 10: If $\mathbf{A} \equiv [F_{ir}]$ has a negative diagonal and is quasidominant diagonal for a given set of positive constants $c_1, \ldots, c_n$ wherever evaluated, then equilibrium is unique and globally stable.[2]

The most important and by far the most difficult result obtained by Arrow, Block, and Hurwicz is that which establishes global stability of equilibrium in the gross substitute case. Prior to their work, Metzler had proved that in the gross substitute case, local dynamic stability occurs under all speeds of adjustment of prices if and only if Hicksian stability characterizes equilibrium.[3] Hahn, McManus, Morishima, and McKenzie[4] have all done work on local stability in the gross substitute case. Negishi[5] has summarized the literature. Theorem 11 gives the Arrow-Block-Hurwicz result:

THEOREM 11: If all commodities are gross substitutes, then equilibrium is unique and globally stable.[6]

In order to handle cases of large disturbances of equilibrium, an alternative definition of the term "gross substitute" is adopted: Given two price vectors $\mathbf{p}'$ and $\mathbf{p}''$, where $p_i' = p_i''$ for all $i \neq k$, $p_k' > p_k''$, then the system of excess demand functions is said to satisfy the gross substitute assumption (in the large) if $F_i(\mathbf{p}') > F_i(\mathbf{p}'')$ for $i \neq k$, $i = 0, \ldots, n$.

[1] Arrow, Block, and Hurwicz, The Stability of the Competitive Equilibrium II, Theorem 4.

[2] *Ibid.*, theorem 3.

[3] Metzler, *op. cit.*

[4] Frank Hahn, Gross Substitutes and the Dynamic Stability of General Equilibrium, *Econometrica*, vol. 26, pp. 169–170, 1958; McManus, *op. cit.*; Michio Morishima, Notes on the Theory of Stability of Multiple Exchange, *Review of Economic Studies*, vol. 24, pp. 203–208, 1957; McKenzie, The Matrix with Dominant Diagonal and Economic Theory.

[5] Takashi Negishi, The Stability of the Competitive Equilibrium. A Survey Article, *Econometrica*, vol. 30, pp. 635–670, 1962.

[6] Arrow, Block, and Hurwicz, *op. cit.*, theorem 1.

The proof of Theorem 11 is too involved to reproduce here; however, the procedure is the following: (1) uniqueness of equilibrium is first established; (2) it is shown that the weak axiom of revealed preference holds in the gross substitute case as between any two price vectors as long as one is the equilibrium price vector $\bar{\mathbf{p}}$ (or any positive multiple of $\bar{\mathbf{p}}$); (3) by Theorem 8, this establishes global stability.[1]

We shall return to the gross substitute case in the next chapter, where the comparative statics properties of this case will be reviewed. There is no other case of comparable generality in general equilibrium theory concerning which as much is known as in the gross substitute case. In a certain sense, it practically exhausts the comparative statics content of general equilibrium analysis, at least in terms of cases that have a straightforward economic interpretation.

5-7 SYSTEM STABILITY: THE TWO-COMMODITY CASE

In addition to the cases in which local stability has been proved (Sec. 5-5) and global stability has been proved (Sec. 5-6), there remains an interesting special case in which Arrow and Hurwicz have proved *system stability*—the case of two commodities: *numéraire* and one other. In this case, it turns out that for any disturbance of equilibrium, the system will converge to *some* equilibrium position. Figure 5-9 illustrates different excess demand functions for the non-*numéraire* commodity in a two-commodity world.

Figures 5-9*a*, *b*, and *c* are cases consistent with the theorem that system stability characterizes any two-commodity world, while Fig. 5-9*d* shows a case that is not possible in such a world. In Fig. 5-9*a*, equilibrium is unique and *globally stable;* in Fig. 5-9*b*, *system stability* is shown (the equilibrium prices $\bar{p}_1$, $\bar{p}_2$, and $\bar{p}_5$ are locally stable), as is the case in Fig. 5-9*c* (but no equilibrium price is locally stable!). Figure 5-9*b* illustrates the fact that if there are a finite number of equilibrium prices in a two-commodity world, then this number must be odd, stable equilibrium points alternating with unstable points, the two "end" equilibria being locally stable. This is formalized in Theorem 12:

THEOREM 12: In the case of two commodities, in the absence of satiation the set of equilibrium price vectors possesses system stability.[2]

[1] A particularly simple statement of the theorem is given by Negishi, *op. cit*. It might be further noted that it can be shown in addition that given any positive initial price vector $\mathbf{p}^0$, $\mathbf{p}(t)$ remains nonnegative for all t in approaching equilibrium.

[2] Arrow, Block, and Hurwicz, *op. cit.*, theorem 6.

The proof of system stability in the two-commodity cases generalizes from the case of one individual to the case of many individuals. Assume first that there is only one individual in the economy and there are two goods, commodity 1 and *numéraire*. Let $\bar{p}^j$ denote the price of commodity 1 at which equilibrium occurs (commodity 0 always has a price of 1). An equilibrium exists, because the assumptions of Arrow and Hurwicz are stronger than those employed by Debreu and others, in existence proofs; further, it is assumed that the weak axiom of revealed preference holds for each consumer and that equilibrium is unique. (It should be noted that for a consumer the weak axiom of revealed preference and utility maximization are equivalent in the case of a two-commodity world, because integrability problems only arise with three or more commodities.) This is illustrated in Fig. 5-10.

Equilibrium in the one-individual case means that the individual's final holdings are equal to his initial holdings; the assumption that the weak axiom holds means that indifference curves are strictly convex; in addition, it will be assumed that equilibrium is unique, so that the only (normalized) equilibrium budget constraint is that represented by $B(\bar{p}^j)$.

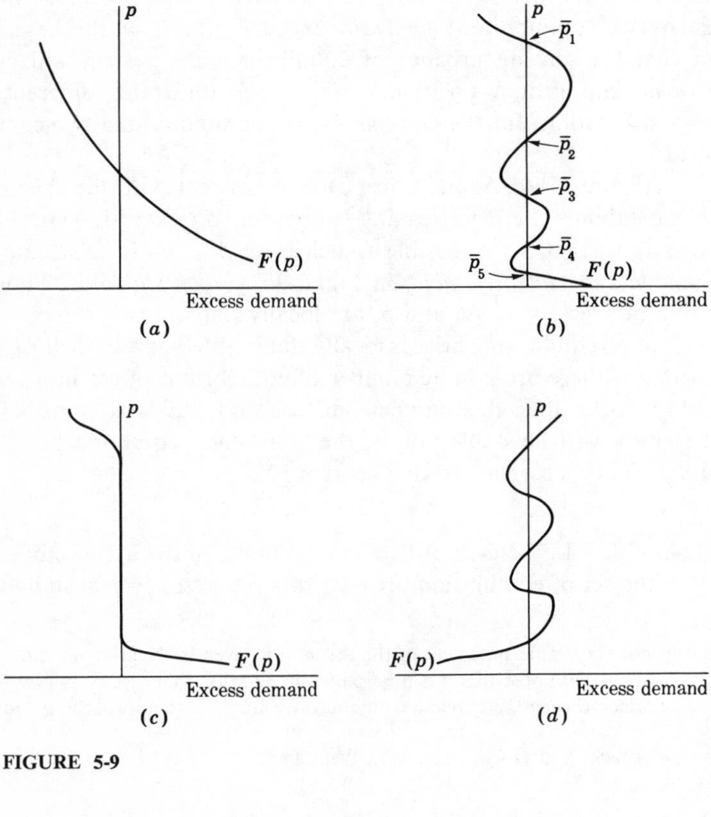

FIGURE 5-9

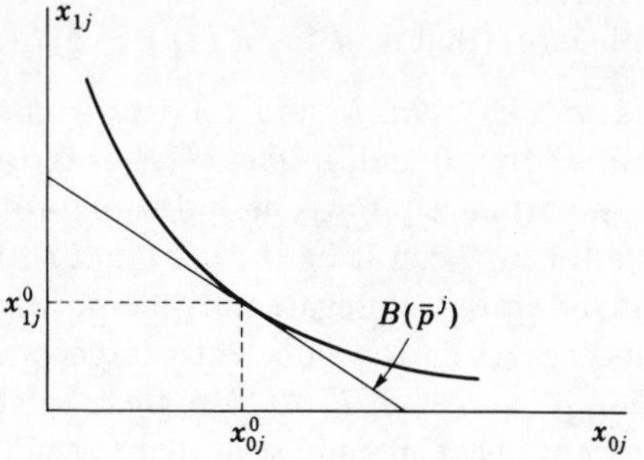

FIGURE 5-10

Denoting excess demand for commodity 1 by the jth individual by $f^j(p)$, it thus follows that for some unique $\bar{p}^j$, $0 < \bar{p}^j < \infty$, $f^j(\bar{p}^j) = 0$. Because the equilibrium is globally stable (Theorem 7), it must be that $(p - \bar{p}^j)z^j < 0$ for any $p \neq \bar{p}^j$, where $z^j = f^j(p)$. (This simply asserts that if price is above equilibrium, excess demand is negative, and if price is below equilibrium, excess demand is positive.)

In generalizing to the case of many individuals, Arrow and Hurwicz distinguish between two situations: (1) For each j, $\bar{p}^j = 0$; (2) for some j_0, $\bar{p}^{j_0} > 0$. (Because free disposal is assumed throughout the Arrow-Hurwicz paper, prices for all commodities can be taken to be nonnegative.) To say that the jth individual is in equilibrium at $\bar{p}^j$ in the m-individual case means exactly what is meant in the one-individual case, that is, $f^j(\bar{p}^j) = 0$—at $\bar{p}^j$ the jth individual is at his most preferred position, when his final holdings equal his initial holdings.

In situation 1 ($\bar{p}^j = 0$ for each $j = 1, \ldots, m$), the argument of the one-individual economy carries over almost in its entirety. For each individual, equilibrium is stable, so that $(p - \bar{p}^j)z^j < 0$ for $p \neq \bar{p}^j = 0$ for each j, which implies that $f^j(p) < 0$ for $p > 0$. [And $f^j(p) = 0$ for $p = 0$.] Thus aggregate excess demand $F(p) = \sum_{j=1}^{m} f^j(p)$ satisfies $F(p) = 0$ for $p = 0$, and $F(p) < 0$ for $p > 0$, which is the global stability criterion, i.e., the unique equilibrium position associated with $p = 0$ is globally stable.

If, for some individual(s), the equilibrium position is one for which $\bar{p}^j > 0$, a somewhat more complicated proof is required. Let $\hat{p}$ denote the largest of the equilibrium prices. [For each individual, the equilibrium price $\bar{p}^j$ exists and is unique; since there are only a finite number of individuals ($= m$), the maximum of the equilibrium prices for individuals exists. This does not mean that the number of market equilibrium prices is finite, as Fig. 5-8 has already shown.] Because each individual's demand function is characterized by the condition $f^j(p) < 0$ for $p > \bar{p}^j$, this means that for p sufficiently large (that is, $p > \hat{p}$), $F(p) = \sum_{j=1}^{m} f^j(p) < 0$. (Note the situations depicted in Fig. 5-9*a*, *b*, and *c*.) By a continuity argument, it is established that $F(0) > 0$ and, in fact, $F(\epsilon) > 0$, for some sufficiently small ϵ, $\epsilon > 0$. [In particular, if j_0 is an individual for whom $\bar{p}^{j_0} > 0$, then $f^{j_0}(0) > 0$, while for no j can it be the case that $f^j(0) < 0$.] We thus have that excess demand in the aggregate must be positive for a sufficiently small value of p and negative for a sufficiently large value of p. Now consider any price p^0, $0 < p^0 < \infty$. If $F(p^0) > 0$, there exists some $\bar{p} > p^0$ such that $F(\bar{p}) = 0$, since we have already seen that for sufficiently large p, $F(p) < 0$ and F is assumed continuous. Then, because $dp/dt = F(p)$, p rises until it reaches some equilibrium price. Similarly, if p^0 is such that $F(p^0) < 0$, there exists an equilibrium price $\bar{p}$ where $\bar{p} < p^0$, and the price adjustment mechanism will drive price toward some equilibrium. What has thus been established is that the system of equilibrium prices in the two-commodity case (this system perhaps consisting of an infinite number of equilibria) possesses system stability.

5-8 EXAMPLES OF UNSTABLE EQUILIBRIUM POSITIONS

In a certain sense, the results presented above are somewhat disappointing; as contrasted with the rather general conditions under which the existence and optimality of competitive equilibrium can be guaranteed, stability of equilibrium (in any of the senses of the term) has been established for only a handful of cases. While further work in the analysis of the *tâtonnement* mechanism will no doubt lead to an extension of the class of cases summarized above, examples of globally unstable equilibrium positions constructed by Scarf and Gale indicate some of the limitations to the scope of stability of the *tâtonnement* mechanism in a competitive environment.[1]

The cases of unstable equilibria discovered by Scarf and Gale have the same fundamental characteristic—at equilibrium, the law of demand does not hold, i.e., an increase in the price of a commodity (holding other prices constant) does not lead to a fall in the quantity demanded of the commodity. In one of the Scarf examples, quantity demanded for any good is completely insensitive to its own price, while the Giffen's paradox case ($F_{ii} > 0$) is involved in Scarf's other examples and in Gale's work. Thus far, no one has constructed an example of an equilibrium possessing

[1] Herbert Scarf, Some Examples of Global Instability of Competitive Equilibrium, *International Economic Review*, vol. 1, 1960; David Gale, A Note on the Global Instability of Competitive Equilibrium, Department of Mathematics, Brown University, Providence, R.I. (multilithed).

Hicksian stability that is unstable in the dynamic sense, so the example cited in Sec. 5-5 has yet to be connected directly to the competitive mechanism.

Scarf's famous example of instability assumes perfect complementarity in the utility functions of three consumers in a three-commodity world (as he remarks, however, the class of examples he works with can be extended to a larger number of consumers and commodities). The initial holdings of consumers 1, 2, and 3 are taken to be (1,0,0), (0,1,0), and (0,0,1), respectively. The utility function for Mr. 1 is written as $u_1 = \min(x_{11}, x_{21})$, for Mr. 2 as $u_2 = \min(x_{22}, x_{32})$, and for Mr. 3 as $u_3 = \min(x_{13}, x_{33})$, where x_{ij} is the amount of the ith commodity obtained by Mr. j; $i = 1, 2, 3$, $j = 1, 2, 3$. Mr. 1 treats commodities 1 and 2 as perfect complements and has no use for commodity 3; Mr. 2 treats commodities 2 and 3 as perfect complements and has no use for commodity 1; and Mr. 3 treats commodities 1 and 3 as perfect complements and has no use for commodity 2. Let p_1, p_2, and p_3 denote the prices of the three commodities. Then, for example, Mr. 1 maximizes u_1 subject to the constraint $p_1(x_{11} - 1) + p_2(x_{21}) + p_3(x_{31}) = 0$. Clearly, to maximize utility, Mr. 1 chooses an equal number of units of commodities 1 and 2 and no units of commodity 3; thus we have $x_{11} = x_{21}$, $x_{31} = 0$, and solving for x_{11} from the budget constraint ($p_1x_{11} - p_1 + p_2x_{11} = 0$), we obtain $x_{11} = p_1/(p_1 + p_2)$ $(= x_{21})$. Denoting excess demand by Mr. j for commodity i by z_{ij} ($z_{ij} = x_{ij} - x^0_{ij}$), we have the following excess demand functions holding for Mr. 1:

$$z_{11} = \frac{-p_2}{p_1 + p_2}$$

$$z_{21} = \frac{p_1}{p_1 + p_2}$$

$$z_{31} = 0$$

Performing the same operations with respect to the utility functions for Mr. 2 and Mr. 3, Scarf obtains the excess demand functions:

$$z_{12} = 0 \qquad z_{13} = \frac{p_3}{p_3 + p_1}$$

$$z_{22} = \frac{-p_3}{p_2 + p_3} \qquad z_{23} = 0$$

$$z_{32} = \frac{p_2}{p_2 + p_3} \qquad z_{33} = \frac{-p_1}{p_3 + p_1}$$

Aggregate excess demand functions are then given by

$$F_1 = z_{11} + z_{12} + z_{13} = \frac{-p_2}{p_1 + p_2} + \frac{p_3}{p_3 + p_1}$$

$$F_2 = z_{21} + z_{22} + z_{23} = \frac{p_1}{p_1 + p_2} + \frac{-p_3}{p_2 + p_3}$$

$$F_3 = z_{31} + z_{32} + z_{33} = \frac{p_2}{p_2 + p_3} + \frac{-p_1}{p_3 + p_1}$$

The unique equilibrium position for this system of equations is given by $p_1 = p_2 = p_3$. [If one price, say p_1, is chosen as 1 (commodity 1 is *numéraire*), then (1,1,1) is the unique normalized equilibrium price vector.]

The differential equation system (with speeds of adjustment all equal to 1) is given by $\dot{p}_i = F_i$ for 1, 2, 3. Further, since Walras' law holds $\left(\sum_{i=1}^{3} \dot{p}_i p_i = 0\right)$, we have $\sum_{i=1}^{3} \dot{p}_i p_i = 0$, which implies $\sum_{i=1}^{3} p_i^2 = \text{constant}$. Scarf shows that any solution to the differential-equation system must take the form $p_1 p_2 p_3 = \text{constant}$. This is done by noting that since p_i is a function of t for each i,

$$\frac{d(p_1 p_2 p_3)}{dt} = F_1 p_2 p_3 + F_2 p_1 p_3 + F_3 p_1 p_2 = p_3(p_1 - p_2) + p_2(p_3 - p_1) + p_1(p_2 - p_3)$$

which is identically zero; thus any solution to the differential-equation system must be such that $p_1 p_2 p_3$ is a constant. In particular, choose p_1, p_2, p_3 such that $p_1^2 + p_2^2 + p_3^2 = 3$. Then equilibrium occurs when $p_1 = p_2 = p_3 = 1$. But if the initial values of p_1, p_2, p_3 are taken to be different from 1, it cannot be the case that the system converges to this equilibrium, since $p_1 p_2 p_3$ cannot equal 1 given these initial values, and thus the equilibrium position (1,1,1) is not on the time path of the price vector. [The only set of values for p_1, p_2, p_3 consistent with both $p_1^2 + p_2^2 + p_3^2 = 3$ and $p_1 p_2 p_3 = 1$ are the values (1,1,1). Thus the equilibrium position is globally unstable.]

Scarf's other examples involve Giffen's paradox commodities, A general theorem concerning these is stated by Gale:

Assume that the economy consists of two individuals, one (C) a consumer and the other (P) a producer. Mr. C possesses stocks of a commodity G_0, and Mr. P produces amounts of two goods G_1 and G_2. Commodity G_0 is taken to be *numéraire*. Mr. P is assumed to be a profit maximizer, i.e., his utility function is strictly increasing with respect to *numéraire* G_0, while commodities G_1 and G_2 provide no utility for Mr. P at all. Mr. C is assumed to possess a nondecreasing, continuous concave utility function $u(x_{1C}, x_{2C})$ defined over all nonnegative amounts of commodities G_1 and G_2, where x_{1C} is the amount of the ith commodity held by

Mr. C, $i = 1, 2$. (Mr. C is thus assumed to regard only goods G_1 and G_2 as desirable—*numéraire* possesses no utility for Mr. C.) Gale's theorem is as follows:

If $u(x_{1C}, x_{2C})$ is twice differentiable at equilibrium, and if the Giffen effect obtains there, then for a range of values of speeds of adjustment of prices, the unique equilibrium point is antistable, i.e., given any initial set of prices (other than the equilibrium set), the price vector will not converge to equilibrium over time. (By the Giffen effect is meant simply that the partial derivative of excess demand for some commodity is positive with respect to its own price.)

The proof of Gale's theorem will not be presented here, but it might be pointed out that (1) Gale constructs an example of a utility function satisfying his hypothesis, i.e., for at least one commodity, the Giffen effect obtains; thus the theorem is nonvacuous, and (2) given the presence of the Giffen effect with respect to one commodity, it should be clear that it is always possible to find speeds of adjustment of markets k_1 and k_2 such that the following matrix has real part of at least one characteristic root nonnegative:

$$\begin{bmatrix} k_1F_{11} & k_1F_{12} \\ k_2F_{21} & k_2F_{22} \end{bmatrix}$$

where F_{ir} is the partial derivative of excess demand for the ith commodity with respect to the rth price. (In terms of this notation, the Giffen effect prevails if $F_{11} > 0$ or $F_{22} > 0$.)

Gale's paper, plus the related examples of Scarf, shows that stability of competitive equilibrium under the *tâtonnement* process is closely tied up with the absence of strongly inferior goods. Scarf remarks on this property of the *tâtonnement* process that in evaluating the cases of unstable equilibrium, one may take the position that the process does a good job of describing the real-life adjustment patterns of markets and therefore instability of the market mechanism should be expected in the case of strongly inferior goods. Alternatively, it might be the case that the dynamic mechanism is in fact unrealistic—too simplified—and that the stable behavior of markets we think we observe must in fact be described by a more complicated dynamic mechanism. Finally, it might be the case that, in fact, the assumptions employed to generate the examples of instability are "unrealistic," at least over the entire market, so that the unstable examples are of only theoretical interest.

5-9 REMARKS ON NON-*TÂTONNEMENT* PROCESSES

In the *tâtonnement* adjustment process, trading takes place only when an equilibrium price vector is announced; consequently the initial holdings of all participants in the market remain fixed during the time the adjustment process is in operation. In contrast, under non-*tâtonnement* processes, trading takes place at each announced value of the price vector, so that the endowments of the market participants change continually as the adjustment of prices goes on. Since, at nonequilibrium prices, supply is not equal to demand in some markets, this means that it is not possible for all consumers to actually attain their most preferred positions by trading at nonequilibrium prices; instead, some sort of arbitrary allocation device such as "first come, first serve" or rationing must be used, with unsatisfied demands spilling over into other markets. Figure 5-11 illustrates the problem of allocation of commodities in a non-*tâtonnement* process.

Given the initial-holdings point $\mathbf{X}^0$, a price vector $\mathbf{p}$ is announced. Mr. A is assumed to maximize utility subject to his constraint $B(\mathbf{p})$, which implies that Mr. B cannot attain his most preferred position; instead, trading between Mr. A and Mr. B occurs in such a way that the joint-holdings point $\mathbf{X}'$ is achieved. Since there is excess demand for commodity 1 at $\mathbf{X}'$ (Mr. B is willing to give up units of commodity 2 for commodity 1), the price of commodity 1 is increased. Following the new announcement of a price vector, trading takes place on the basis of the rule promulgated, and, if the adjustment process is stable, convergence to some point on the contract curve eventually occurs. It will be noted that the movement toward equilibrium is a movement in a "Pareto-superior" direction in the

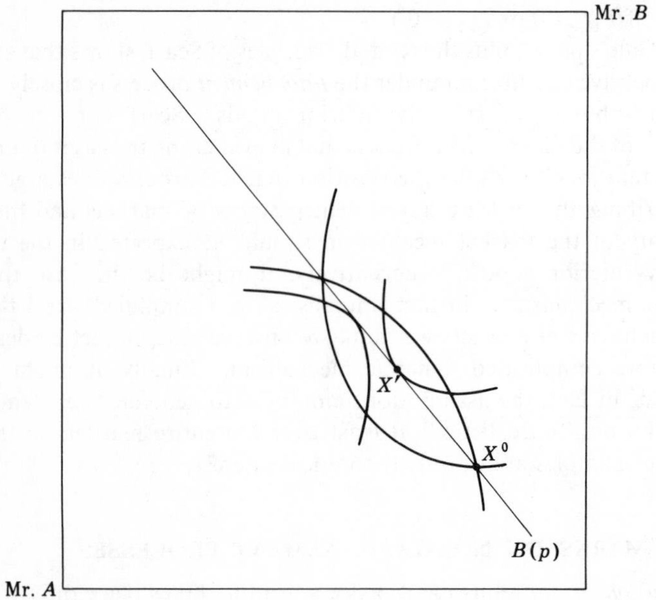

FIGURE 5-11

sense that each new joint-holdings point is Pareto-superior to the point achieved in the previous step. Further, the equilibrium position finally attained is determined both by the initial-holdings point and by the time path of prices "called out," not simply by the initial-holdings point, as is the case in the *tâtonnement* process (if equilibrium is unique for the initial-holdings point).

Hahn and Negishi have shown that if a mild condition on the relationship between individual and aggregate excess demand functions is satisfied, then given the existence of single-valued individual excess demand functions and, roughly, differentiable aggregate excess demand functions, the non-*tâtonnement* process converges from an arbitrary initial-holdings point to *some* equilibrium position.[1] Thus, when the rules governing trade at nonequilibrium prices are relaxed, the possibility of attaining equilibrium, given a disturbance, increases. Because of the dependence of the equilibrium position attained on the time path of trading, however, the role played by stability in comparative statics analyses of the competitive equilibrium model is essentially eliminated in non-*tâtonnement* processes. In the next chapter, we review the results available concerning the comparative statics of general equilibrium, utilizing in most cases a *tâtonnement* mechanism.

[1] Frank Hahn and Takashi Negishi, A theorem on Non-Tâtonnement Stability, *Econometrica*, vol. 30, no. 3, pp. 463–469, 1962. The condition imposed is that the trading occurs in such a way that the sign of excess demand for any commodity for any individual is the same as the sign of excess demand for that commodity in the aggregate; e.g., the case depicted in Fig. 5-11 satisfies this rule.

SIX

COMPETITIVE EQUILIBRIUM: COMPARATIVE STATICS

6-1 INTRODUCTION

Comparative statics is that branch of economic theory concerned with determining the effects on the equilibrium values of economic variables brought about by changes in the environment of the model under study. Most of what might be termed the body of traditional economic theory consists of theorems of comparative statics; for example, Slutsky's equation in consumer theory; the theorems that demand functions for inputs are downward sloping and supply functions for outputs are upward sloping in production theory; and the many policy-oriented results of macroeconomics are comparative statics theorems. In this chapter we are interested in summarizing those theorems of comparative statics that have been established concerning equilibrium positions of a competitive economy. The work of Hicks and Samuelson has been especially important in deriving these theorems.[1] We first summarize the general nature of the comparative statics problem:

Assume that in an economic model, there are n endogenous variables (*economic variables*) with values given by $x_1, \ldots, x_n$, and m exogenous variables (*shift parameters*) with values given by $a_1, \ldots, a_m$. A particular set of values for the exogenous variables will be said to constitute an *environment* for the model. It is further assumed that there are n single-valued functional relationships linking the economic variables to the shift parameters, the ith of these being written as $f_i(\mathbf{x};\mathbf{a}) = z_i$ for

[1] J. R. Hicks, *Value and Capital*, 2d ed., Oxford University Press, London, 1946, and Paul A. Samuelson, *The Foundations of Economic Analysis*, Harvard University Press, Cambridge, Mass., 1955.

$i = 1, \ldots, n$, where $\mathbf{x}$ and $\mathbf{a}$ are n- and m-dimensional vectors of economic variables and shift parameters, respectively.

An *equilibrium position* of the model for a given environment $\mathbf{a}^0 = (a_1^0, \ldots, a_m^0)$ is defined as a set of values $\bar{\mathbf{x}} = (\bar{x}_1, \ldots, \bar{x}_n)$ for the economic variables such that

$$f_i(\bar{\mathbf{x}};\mathbf{a}^0) = 0 \qquad \text{for } i = 1, \ldots, n \tag{1}$$

Given that an equilibrium position exists for the economic model with the environment specified by $\mathbf{a}^0$, in comparative statics analysis we are concerned with determining the changes that occur in $\bar{\mathbf{x}}$ if the environment changes from $\mathbf{a}^0$ to $\mathbf{a}^1$ (again assuming that equilibrium exists in the new environment specified by $\mathbf{a}^1$). In most of this chapter we shall restrict our attention to the *local* comparative statics properties of the competitive model. Morishima's work on the *global* comparative statics properties of the gross substitute case is noted in Sec. 6-5, however.[1]

The local analysis of the comparative statics properties of an economic model deals with the impact of "small" changes in the environment of the model on the equilibrium values of economic variables of the model. In particular, assume that in some sufficiently small neighborhood of the equilibrium position defined by (1), each of the f_i functions possesses a total differential. Then, for a given change in the vector $\mathbf{a}$, the effects on $\bar{\mathbf{x}}$ can be determined from the relationships

$$df_i = \sum_{r=1}^{n} f_{ir}\, d\bar{x}_r + \sum_{s=1}^{m} f_{ia_s}\, da_s = 0 \qquad \text{for } i = 1, \ldots, n \tag{2}$$

where

$$f_{ir} = \frac{\partial f_i}{\partial x_r} \qquad f_{ia_s} = \frac{\partial f_i}{\partial a_s}$$

these partial derivatives being evaluated at the point $(\bar{\mathbf{x}};\mathbf{a}^0)$. In (2), $df_i = 0$ for every i because the changes in the endogenous variables are constrained by the fact that the system must be at some equilibrium before and after the change in $\mathbf{a}$; that is, $f_i = 0$ for every i both before and after the change in $\mathbf{a}$; thus $df_i = 0$ for every i.

Rewriting (2) in matrix notation, we have

$$\begin{bmatrix} f_{11} & f_{12} & \cdots & f_{1n} \\ \cdots & \cdots & \cdots & \cdots \\ f_{n1} & f_{n2} & \cdots & f_{nn} \end{bmatrix} \begin{bmatrix} d\bar{x}_1 \\ \vdots \\ d\bar{x}_n \end{bmatrix} = - \begin{bmatrix} \sum_{s=1}^{m} f_{1a_s}\, da_s \\ \vdots \\ \sum_{s=1}^{m} f_{na_s}\, da_s \end{bmatrix} \tag{3}$$

[1] Michio Morishima, *Equilibrium Stability and Growth*, Oxford University Press, London, 1964.

so that, letting $\mathbf{A} = [f_{ir}]$ for $i, r = 1, \ldots, n$; $\mathbf{d\bar{x}} = [d\bar{x}_r]$ for $r = 1, \ldots, n$; and $\mathbf{b} = \left[\sum_{s=1}^{m} f_{ia}\, da_s\right]$ for $i = 1, \ldots, n$, the comparative statics system becomes

$$\mathbf{A d\bar{x}} = -\mathbf{b} \tag{4}$$

If the f_i functions are completely specified and the differentiability assumptions are satisfied, the solution to the comparative statics problem of determining values for the elements of the vector $\mathbf{d\bar{x}}$ for given values of the elements of $\mathbf{da}$ presents "merely" the computational problem of solving (4) explicitly. In most problems in economic theory, however, we are not faced with situations in which the f_i functions are completely specified; instead, typically it is assumed that only certain general properties of these functions are known, e.g., qualitative characteristics such as the sign pattern (+,—,0) of the matrix **A** and the vector **b** or quantitative characteristics such as those specified by the symmetry of **A**, the definiteness of **A**, or perhaps the stability of **A**.

In our discussion of the local comparative statics properties of economic models, we shall restrict our attention to models for which total differentials as given in (4) lead to unique solutions. Thus we shall only deal with cases in which the matrix **A** is nonsingular, that is, $|\mathbf{A}| \neq 0$, so that the solution to (4) may be written as

$$\mathbf{d\bar{x}} = -\mathbf{A}^{-1}\mathbf{b} \tag{5}$$

where $\mathbf{A}^{-1}$ is the inverse of **A** and is calculated by the formula

$$\mathbf{A}^{-1} = \frac{1}{|\mathbf{A}|} [\Delta_{ir}]' \tag{6}$$

where Δ_{ir} is the cofactor of f_{ir} in **A** so that $\Delta_{ir} = (-1)^{i+r}$ times the determinant formed by eliminating the ith row and rth column of **A** and $[\Delta_{ir}]'$ is the transpose of $[\Delta_{ir}]$.

In many of the applications of comparative statics analysis in economics, it is possible to work with the special assumption that only a restricted subset of the shift parameters is changing values; in particular we shall concentrate on the case where $da_s = 0$ for every s except a single s', so that the elements of **b** are no longer summations but rather single elements. In all that follows (unless otherwise noted) we shall make this assumption, and, for simplicity of notation, we shall write a typical element of **b** as $f_{ia}\, da$.

Because economic theory is concerned with problems in which the f_i functions are not completely specified, in general it is not possible to determine precise quantitative magnitudes for the elements of the vector $\mathbf{d\bar{x}}$ from (5) for a given value of da. Instead, less specific theorems concerning the sign pattern taken on by the elements of $\mathbf{d\bar{x}}$ for given incomplete specifications of **A** and **b** are often the most that can be achieved in comparative statics studies. We shall adopt the following terminology:

Comparative statics information is said to be available concerning the system whose solution is given by (5) if it is possible to solve for the sign (+,−,0) of one or more of the elements of $\mathbf{d\bar{x}}$ in (5). *Complete comparative statics information* is available in (5) if it is possible to solve for the sign (+,−,0) of each element of $\mathbf{d\bar{x}}$.

It is clear from the form of (5) that, from a purely mathematical point of view, the problem of comparative statics in essence boils down to that of deriving characteristics of $\mathbf{A}^{-1}$ from whatever information is assumed available concerning **A**. Samuelson's treatment of comparative statics in the *Foundations* was the first to give prominence to this basic similarity in mathematical structure of the problems taken up in comparative statics analysis.

The thesis of the *Foundations* is that essentially all of the comparative statics theorems of traditional economic theory are derived from one or more of the following fundamental hypotheses concerning equilibrium positions:

1. That equilibrium positions may be viewed as regular maximum or minimum positions of some criterion function such as utility, profits, welfare, or costs.
2. That equilibrium positions are stable.
3. That qualitative information is available to the economist concerning the characteristics of equilibrium, particularly with respect to the sign patterns of **A** and **b**.

Hypothesis 1 is particularly important in the comparative statics analysis of individual economic units such as households or firms, but has only limited applicability to the analysis of economic models involving relationships among aggregates such as occurs in macroeconomics or general equilibrium theory. The special cases of general equilibrium theory in which (1) is of interest are taken up in Sec. 6-2.

Stability of equilibrium positions occupies a special place in the study of comparative statics. This is because comparative statics theorems, which are statements about changes in the equilibrium values of economic variables when equilibrium is disturbed, have no predictive content if equilibrium is dynamically unstable. In the case of a globally unstable equilibrium position, for example, a change in the environment will lead to time paths of economic variables that do not converge to equilibrium, hence any statements about changes in equilibrium values in response to a disturbance will provide at best only misleading information. In brief, the assumption that equilibrium is stable is a theoretical necessity if the comparative statics analysis of a model is to have predictive content. Figure 6-1 illustrates this aspect of comparative statics analysis.

For $a = a^0$, excess demand $F(p,a^0)$ is zero at $p = \bar{p}^0$; when a change in the environment from a^0 to a^1 occurs, shifting $F(p,a^0)$ to $F(p,a^1)$, a new equilibrium occurs at $p = \bar{p}^1$, where $\bar{p}^1 < \bar{p}^0$. Assume a Walrasian *tâtonnement* adjustment process governs the time path of p. Following the change from a^0 to a^1, there is positive excess demand at $p = \bar{p}^0$, which implies that p rises; hence the system does not regain equilibrium when disturbed. In fact, price moves over time in a direction opposite to that predicted by the comparative statics result concerning *equilibrium* price.

The hypothesis that equilibrium is stable plays an additional role in comparative statics analysis, however. What Samuelson asserts in the *Foundations* is that there exists what he terms a "correspondence principle" linking stability of equilibrium and comparative statics theorems in the sense that, corresponding to stable equilibrium positions of an economic model, there are, at least in certain situations, restrictions implied about the comparative statics properties of the model; i.e., from the stability hypothesis, comparative statics theorems can be derived. Section 6-3 is concerned with the scope of a qualitative approach to comparative statics. In Sec. 6-4, we investigate the scope of the comparative statics properties of the correspondence principle.

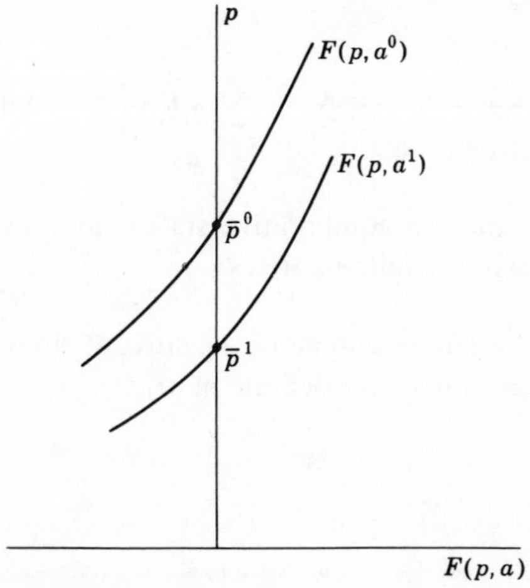

FIGURE 6-1

6-2 MAXIMIZATION AND COMPARATIVE STATICS

As noted in Sec. 2-4, equivalent conditions for regular unconstrained maximization of a real-valued function are given by the following:

Let $\mathbf{x}$ be an n-dimensional vector and let $\psi(\mathbf{x})$ be a real-valued function with continuous first- and second-order partial derivatives

$$\psi_i = \frac{\partial \psi}{\partial x_i} \text{ and } \psi_{ij} = \frac{\partial^2 \psi}{\partial x_i \, \partial x_j} \; (\psi_{ij} = \psi_{ji}) \qquad i, j = 1, \ldots, n$$

Then necessary and sufficient conditions for the existence of a regular maximum of $\psi(\mathbf{x})$ at a point $\mathbf{x}^0$ are the following:

1. $\psi_i = 0$ for $i = 1, \ldots, n$.
2. $[\psi_{ij}]$ is negative definite, that is, $\mathbf{h}'[\psi_{ij}]\mathbf{h} < 0$ for any nonzero vector $\mathbf{h}$. (All partial derivatives are evaluated at $\mathbf{x}^0$.)

Similarly, $\psi(\mathbf{x})$ attains a regular constrained maximum at a point $\mathbf{x}^0$ subject to the constraint $g(\mathbf{x}) = 0$ if and only if, when $L = \psi + \lambda g$, the following conditions are satisfied:

1′. $L_i = \psi_i + \lambda g_i = 0$ (where $g_i = \partial g/\partial x_i$), $i = 1, \ldots, n$.

2′. $\left[\begin{array}{c|c} L_{ij} & g_i \\ \hline g_j & 0 \end{array}\right]$ is negative definite subject to constraint, that is,

$$\mathbf{h}'\left[\begin{array}{c|c} L_{ij} & g_i \\ \hline g_j & 0 \end{array}\right]\mathbf{h} < 0$$

for any nonzero vector $\mathbf{h}$ satisfying $\sum_{i=1}^{n} g_i h_i = 0$. (All partial derivatives are evaluated at $\mathbf{x}^0$.)

Of particular importance to comparative statics analysis are the following theorems on negative definite matrices:

THEOREM 1: Assume $\mathbf{A} = [a_{ij}]$ is a symmetric negative definite matrix. Then $\mathbf{A}^{-1}$ is a symmetric negative definite matrix.

THEOREM 2: Assume

$$\mathbf{A}^* = \left[\begin{array}{c|c} a_{ij} & c_i \\ \hline c_j & 0 \end{array}\right] \qquad i, j = 1, \ldots, n$$

is a symmetric matrix negative definite subject to the constraint that $\sum_{i=1}^{n} c_i h_i = 0$. Then in

$$\mathbf{A}^{*-1} = \left[\begin{array}{c|c} \bar{a}_{ij} & \bar{c}_i \\ \hline \bar{c}_j & \bar{d} \end{array}\right]$$

the submatrix $[\bar{a}_{ij}]$ $(i, j = 1, \ldots, n)$ is symmetric and negative semidefinite of rank $n - 1$.†

To indicate the application of these theorems to the comparative statics analysis of competitive equilibrium, consider the case of a pure trade world in which there is no trade at equilibrium (e.g., the one-consumer case, the case of identical consumers, the case where the initial resource endowments are Pareto-optimal, etc.). In Chap. 5 the Arrow-Hurwicz proof of stability of equilibrium in this case was given. Let a be a parameter that shifts demand away from the *numéraire* commodity to commodity 1, but does not shift demand directly for any other commodity. The system of equations characterizing equilibrium is the following:

$$F_i(\bar{p}_0, \ldots, \bar{p}_n, a) = 0 \qquad \text{for } i = 0, \ldots, n \tag{7}$$

Differentiating these excess demand functions totally and dropping the equation relating to the *numéraire* commodity, we obtain

$$\mathbf{A}d\bar{\mathbf{p}} = -\mathbf{b} \qquad \text{where } \mathbf{A} = [F_{ir}],\ i, r = 1, \ldots, n,\ d\bar{\mathbf{p}} = [d\bar{p}_i] \quad \text{for } i = 1, \ldots, n \tag{8}$$

and

$$\mathbf{b} = \begin{bmatrix} F_{1a}\,da \\ 0 \\ \cdot \\ \cdot \\ \cdot \\ 0 \end{bmatrix}$$

† See Samuelson, *Foundations*, especially appendix A. Similar theorems exist for positive definite matrices or matrices positive definite under constraint. Such theorems are identical to Theorems 1 and 2 except that "positive definite" replaces "negative definite" everywhere in the statement of the theorems.

A symmetric matrix A is said to be negative semidefinite if for any nonzero vector $\mathbf{h}$, $\mathbf{h}'\mathbf{A}\mathbf{h} \leq 0$, and for some nonzero vector $\mathbf{h}^*$, $\mathbf{h}^{*\prime}\mathbf{A}\mathbf{h}^* = 0$. $\mathbf{A}$ is of rank $n - 1$ if $n - 1$ rows (columns) of $\mathbf{A}$ are linearly independent, while $|\mathbf{A}| = 0$. Necessary and sufficient conditions for an $n \times n$ symmetric matrix $\mathbf{A}$ to be negative semidefinite of rank $n - 1$ are that the principal minors of $\mathbf{A}$ alternate in sign, with $|\mathbf{A}| = 0$.

A typical element of **A** may be written as

$$F_{ir} = \sum_{j=1}^{m} \frac{\partial x_{ij}}{\partial p_r} = \sum_{j=1}^{m} S_{ir}^{j} - \sum_{j=1}^{m} (x_{rj} - x_{rj}^{0}) \frac{\partial x_{ij}}{\partial I^j}$$

Because there is no trade at equilibrium, $x_{rj} - x_{hj}^0 = 0$ for every $r = 1, \ldots, n$ and $j = 1, \ldots, m$. Because of the negative definite property of the substitution-term matrix for any one consumer (which follows from Theorem 2 when the *numéraire* commodity is eliminated), **A** is a negative definite matrix.

Hence, in solving (8) to obtain

$$\mathbf{d\bar{p}} = -\mathbf{A}^{-1}\mathbf{b} \tag{9}$$

by Theorem 1, $\mathbf{A}^{-1}$ is negative definite, which in turn implies that every diagonal element in $\mathbf{A}^{-1}$ is negative. Solving for $d\bar{p}_1$, we obtain

$$d\bar{p}_1 = -\frac{\Delta_{11}}{|\mathbf{A}|} F_{1a}\, da \tag{10}$$

Since $\Delta_{11}/|\mathbf{A}|$ is a diagonal element of $\mathbf{A}^{-1}$, it is negative. F_{1a} is positive by assumption, and thus we obtain the following comparative statics theorem:

COMPARATIVE STATICS THEOREM 1: In a pure trade world, if there is no trade at equilibrium, a shift away from the *numéraire* commodity to commodity i (no other excess demand functions being shifted) leads to an increase in the equilibrium price of commodity i. Further, since equilibrium is stable under any speeds of adjustment of prices, the limiting value of the time path of p_i approaches the new (higher) equilibrium value.

In general, if, for any reason, the matrix **A** is symmetric negative definite, the same result holds. Beyond this case, there is apparently no other comparative statics theorem concerning general equilibrium models that is derivable from the maximization hypothesis alone.

6-3 QUALITATIVE ECONOMICS

Assume that in the system of equations $\mathbf{A}\mathbf{d\bar{x}} = -\mathbf{b}$ the only information available to the economist is the knowledge of the signs (+,−,0) of the entries in **A** and **b**. Then what are necessary and sufficient conditions on these sign patterns so that it is possible to solve for the signs of the entries of $\mathbf{d\bar{x}}$? We refer to a model in which only knowledge of the signs of the entries in **A** and **b** is available as a *purely qualitative* model. In this section we examine the comparative statics properties of such purely qualitative models.

While Samuelson has a brief discussion of purely qualitative models in the *Foundations*, it remained for Lancaster and Gorman to determine equivalent conditions for complete comparative statics information in a purely qualitative model.[1] The problem of deriving comparative statics theorems in a purely qualitative environment may be illustrated by considering the following example:

Let $\mathbf{A}$ have sign pattern $\begin{bmatrix} + & - \\ + & + \end{bmatrix}$ and let $\mathbf{b}$ have sign pattern $\begin{bmatrix} + \\ 0 \end{bmatrix}$ so that $\mathbf{A}d\bar{\mathbf{x}} = -\mathbf{b}$ can be written as

$$\begin{bmatrix} + & - \\ + & + \end{bmatrix} \begin{bmatrix} \dfrac{d\bar{x}_1}{da} \\ \dfrac{d\bar{x}_2}{da} \end{bmatrix} = \begin{bmatrix} - \\ 0 \end{bmatrix} \tag{11}$$

where we have divided through on both sides by da.

To solve (11), $\mathbf{A}^{-1}$ must be evaluated. It will be noted that $|\mathbf{A}| > 0$ for any values of the entries in $\mathbf{A}$. Thus $\mathbf{A}^{-1}$ exists and the solution to (11) is given by

$$\begin{bmatrix} \dfrac{d\bar{x}_1}{da} \\ \dfrac{d\bar{x}_2}{da} \end{bmatrix} = \frac{1}{|\mathbf{A}|} \begin{bmatrix} \Delta_{11} & \Delta_{21} \\ \Delta_{12} & \Delta_{22} \end{bmatrix} \begin{bmatrix} - \\ 0 \end{bmatrix} = \begin{bmatrix} + & + \\ - & + \end{bmatrix} \begin{bmatrix} - \\ 0 \end{bmatrix} \tag{12}$$

Thus, on the basis of the sign patterns of $\mathbf{A}$ and $\mathbf{b}$ alone, it is possible to state that sign $d\bar{x}_1/da < 0$ and sign $d\bar{x}_2/da > 0$. Hence complete comparative statics information as defined above is available concerning the system (11) under the sign patterns assumed. It is easy to verify that if the 0 entry in the $\mathbf{b}$ vector is replaced by either $+$ or $-$, it is not possible to solve unambiguously for the signs of both $d\bar{x}_1/da$ and $d\bar{x}_2/da$.

Gorman's theorem giving necessary and sufficient conditions for complete comparative statics information in a purely qualitative model was reformulated by Lancaster in terms of what he refers to as a "partitionable" standard form. It is still not known, however, whether the

[1] W. M. Gorman, More Scope for Qualitative Economics, *Review of Economic Studies*, vol. 31, pp. 65–68, 1964; K. J. Lancaster, The Scope of Qualitative Economics, *Review of Economic Studies*, vol. 29, pp. 99–123, 1962; K. J. Lancaster, Partitionable Systems and Qualitative Economics, *Review of Economic Studies*, vol. 31, pp. 69–72, 1964.

partitionable form exhausts the class of all systems providing complete comparative statics information. The partitionable form is the following:

Let $\mathbf{C} = [\mathbf{A};\mathbf{b}]$; that is, $\mathbf{C}$ is a matrix with n rows and $n + 1$ columns, the entries in the first n columns of $\mathbf{C}$ being those appearing in $\mathbf{A}$, with entries in the $(n + 1)$st column of $\mathbf{C}$ being those of the vector $\mathbf{b}$. $\mathbf{C}$ is said to be partitionable if, by interchanges of rows or columns of $\mathbf{C}$ or by multiplication of rows or columns of $\mathbf{C}$ by (-1), $\mathbf{C}$ can be brought into the form

$$\begin{bmatrix} \mathbf{a}_1 & \mathbf{b}_1 \\ \mathbf{A}_2 & \mathbf{0}_2 \\ \mathbf{0}_3 & \mathbf{A}_3 \end{bmatrix}$$

where $\mathbf{a}_1$ is of dimension $1 \times k$; $\mathbf{b}_1$ is of dimension $1 \times (n + 1 - k)$; $\mathbf{A}_2$ is $(k - 1) \times k$; $\mathbf{0}_2$ is $(k - 1) \times (n + 1 - k)$; $\mathbf{0}_3$ is $(n - k) \times k$; and $\mathbf{A}_3$ is $(n - k) \times (n + 1 - k)$. All the elements in $\mathbf{a}_1$ are nonnegative (and at least one element is positive); all the elements in $\mathbf{b}_1$ are nonpositive (and at least one element is negative); all the elements in $\mathbf{0}_2$ and $\mathbf{0}_3$ are zero. Further, $\mathbf{A}_2$ and $\mathbf{A}_3$ are partitionable into the same pattern that characterizes the matrix above, the partitioning continuing until rows with only one negative and one positive entry are reached.

The basic theorem concerning purely qualitative models is the following:

COMPARATIVE STATICS THEOREM 2 (GORMAN-LANCASTER): A purely qualitative model $\mathbf{A}d\bar{\mathbf{x}} = \mathbf{b}$ may be solved to obtain complete comparative statics information if the matrix $\mathbf{C} = [\mathbf{A};\mathbf{b}]$ can be brought into partitionable form.

An alternative to the Lancaster-Gorman approach is provided by the use of the concepts of "cycles" and "chains" of matrices. Given any matrix $\mathbf{B} = [b_{ij}]$, a *chain* in $\mathbf{B}$ (of length $r - 1$) is a product of the form $b_{i_1i_2}b_{i_2i_3} \cdots b_{i_{r-1}i_r}$, where $i_1, i_2, \ldots, i_r$ are distinct integers. A *cycle* in $\mathbf{B}$ (of length r) is a product of the form $b_{i_1i_2}b_{i_2i_3} \cdots b_{i_{r-1}i_r}b_{i_ri_1}$, where $i_1, i_2, \ldots, i_r$ are distinct integers.[1] Then comparative statics theorem 2′ holds:

COMPARATIVE STATICS THEOREM 2′ (BASSETT-MAYBEE-QUIRK): A purely qualitative model $\mathbf{A}d\bar{\mathbf{x}} = \mathbf{b}$ may be solved to obtain complete

[1] See J. Maybee, Remarks on the Theory of Cycles in Matrices, Purdue University, Lafayette, Ind., 1965 (mimeographed); L. Bassett, H. Habibagahi, and J. Quirk, Qualitative Economics and Morishima Matrices, *Econometrica* (in press); L. Bassett, J. Maybee, and J. Quirk, Qualitative Economics and the Scope of the Correspondence Principle, Purdue University, Lafayette, Ind., 1966 (mimeographed).

comparative statics information if and only if by interchanging of equations and/or renumbering of variables or multiplying equations and/or variables by (-1), the system can be brought into the form $\hat{\mathbf{A}}\mathbf{dw} = \hat{\mathbf{b}}$, $\hat{\mathbf{b}} \geq \mathbf{0}$, where $\hat{\mathbf{A}}$ satisfies (1) all diagonal elements are negative and (2) all nonzero cycles are negative. $\hat{b}_j > 0$ implies all nonzero chains of $\hat{\mathbf{A}}$ terminating at an element in the jth column of $\hat{\mathbf{A}}$ are positive. (Under these conditions, the solution vector $\mathbf{dw}$ satisfies $\mathbf{dw} \leq \mathbf{0}$.)

The application of either Theorem 2 or 2′ to the example given in (11) involves some manipulation, but is relatively straightforward. In the context of general equilibrium theory, where the matrix $\mathbf{A}$ is a matrix of partial derivatives of excess demand functions with respect to prices; the vector of unknowns is $\mathbf{d\bar{p}}$, changes in equilibrium prices; and the elements of $\mathbf{b}$ reflect the effects of changes in the environment (e.g., tastes) in shifting excess demand functions, the Gorman-Lancaster theorem (or Theorem 2′) gives sufficient conditions for obtaining complete comparative statics information in a qualitative environment. However, as the form of the conditions relating to purely qualitative systems indicates, the field of application of the theorems to problems of general equilibrium theory is severely limited. In particular, there are strong "independence" conditions imposed on excess demand functions if the theorems are to be applied, i.e., a substantial number of zeros must appear as entries in $\mathbf{A}$. From an even more basic point of view, a further difficulty with these theorems is that they are stated independently of any reference to the stability properties of the qualitative model. As was mentioned earlier, this makes it impossible to judge whether any comparative statics theorems derived under the conditions stated are consistent with the limiting values of the time paths of the economic variables as determined by the adjustment mechanism.

If a *tâtonnement* mechanism is assumed to operate in a purely qualitative environment, with adjustment equations given by

$$\dot{\mathbf{x}} = \mathbf{DA}(\mathbf{x} - \bar{\mathbf{x}}) \qquad \dot{\mathbf{x}} \equiv \left[\frac{dx_r}{dt}\right] \qquad (\mathbf{x} - \bar{\mathbf{x}}) \equiv [(x_r - \bar{x}_r)] \tag{13}$$

where $\mathbf{D}$ is a positive diagonal matrix of speeds of adjustment, then stability of (13) on the basis of the sign pattern of $\mathbf{A}$ alone occurs if and only if Theorem 5 of Chap. 5 holds. This means that every indecomposable diagonal block of $\mathbf{A}$ must have every diagonal element nonpositive (and at least one diagonal element negative), off-diagonal elements must satisfy $a_{ij}a_{ji} \leqq 0$ $(i \neq j)$, no nonzero cycle of length greater than two in $\mathbf{A}$ can exist, and at least one term in the expansion of the determinant of $\mathbf{A}$ must be nonzero. These conditions for sign stability of $\mathbf{A}$ are, in general, even less appealing than the Gorman-Lancaster conditions, but unless they are satisfied, the comparative statics theorems of any purely qualitative model have unknown predictive content.

While the conditions for sign stability are admittedly extremely strong, nonetheless they do guarantee that any comparative statics theorems derived when the conditions hold will be consistent with the limiting values of the variables of the model. For one special case, a comparative statics theorem utilizing the sign-stability conditions has been proved:

COMPARATIVE STATICS THEOREM 3 (QUIRK-RUPPERT):[1] Assume that $\mathbf{A} = [F_{ir}]$ is sign-stable and indecomposable. Further assume that all diagonal entries in **A** are negative. Then, if there is a shift away from the *numéraire* commodity to commodity i (no other excess demand functions being shifted), the equilibrium price of commodity i will increase and the change in the equilibrium value of every other price may be determined (in sign) unambiguously. Since equilibrium is stable under any speeds of adjustment of prices, the limiting values of the time paths for all p_i approach the new equilibrium values.

The need to impose conditions as strong as those stated in the theorem above arises at least in part because not all of the features of equilibrium positions of a competitive economy have been exploited; in particular, the quantitative restrictions imposed by Walras' law and homogeneity of excess demand functions have not been incorporated into the analysis. While there appears at present to be some (limited) scope for purely qualitative analysis in the derivation of predictive comparative statics results in such fields as macroeconomics, the above discussion indicates that its applicability to general equilibrium models is slight.[2]

6-4 THE CORRESPONDENCE PRINCIPLE

Of the three hypotheses of the *Foundations* mentioned earlier, both the hypothesis that equilibrium is attained as the regular maximum of a

[1] J. Quirk and R. Ruppert, Qualitative Economics and the Stability of Equilibrium, *Review of Economic Studies*, vol. 32, pp. 311–326, 1965. An extension of this appears in Bassett, Maybee, and Quirk, *op. cit.*

[2] In particular, in all of the purely qualitative theorems involving negative diagonal elements, the existence of comparative statics results requires asymmetry (in sign) of the matrix **A**, which in turn requires strongly asymmetric income effects to prevail; while this can occur in general equilibrium models, it is not the "usual" case investigated in the literature.

criterion function and the hypothesis that qualitative information is available concerning equilibrium turn out to have disappointingly little by themselves to offer in the way of comparative statics theorems concerning general equilibrium theory. There remains Samuelson's hypothesis 2, the assumption that equilibrium is stable. When taken in conjunction with other assumptions of a qualitative or quantitative nature, the stability hypothesis turns out to be the most important tool of the economist interested in the comparative statics properties of systems involving relationships among aggregates. Further, as the above comments make clear, it is an indispensable assumption if the comparative statics theorems derived are to have predictive content.

We shall examine the implications of the stability hypothesis under the assumption that a *tâtonnement* process governs the time path of prices, that is,

$$\dot{\mathbf{p}} = \mathbf{BA}(\mathbf{p} - \bar{\mathbf{p}}) \qquad \mathbf{B} \text{ a positive diagonal matrix, } \mathbf{A} = [F_{ir}] \tag{14}$$

Stability of (14) means the real parts of the characteristic roots of **BA** are negative; in studying the correspondence principle, we are interested in the implications of stability of (14) for the derivation of theorems concerning the qualitative and/or quantitative properties of $\mathbf{d\bar{p}}$ as given by

$$\mathbf{d\bar{p}} = -\mathbf{A}^{-1}\mathbf{b} \tag{15}$$

To illustrate the use of the stability hypothesis, consider the two-equation model

$$\begin{bmatrix} F_{11} & F_{12} \\ F_{21} & F_{22} \end{bmatrix} \begin{bmatrix} d\bar{p}_1 \\ d\bar{p}_2 \end{bmatrix} = -\begin{bmatrix} F_{1a}\,da \\ 0 \end{bmatrix} \tag{16}$$

where a is assumed to shift only the excess demand function of commodity 1.

Assume that qualitative information is available concerning the entries in $\mathbf{A} = [F_{ir}]$ and concerning F_{1a}, that is, the signs (+,−,0) of these terms are known. If the Gorman-Lancaster conditions are satisfied, then the signs of $d\bar{p}_1/da$ and $d\bar{p}_2/da$ may be determined. However, if stability is assumed, then the signs of $d\bar{p}_1/da$ and $d\bar{p}_2/da$ can be calculated whatever the sign pattern of **A**. This follows because if **BA** is stable, then $|\mathbf{BA}| \equiv |\mathbf{B}| \cdot |\mathbf{A}|$ has sign $(-1)^n$; thus since $|\mathbf{B}| > 0$, $|\mathbf{A}|$ has sign $(-1)^n$ (e.g., by the Routh-Hurwitz theorem of Sec. 5-4). For the case under consideration ($n = 2$), $|\mathbf{A}| > 0$ and, given the signs of the entries in **A**, the signs of all the elements in $\mathbf{A}^{-1}$ are known. This clearly implies that the signs of $d\bar{p}_1/da$ and $d\bar{p}_2/da$ are known, if **b** contains only one nonzero element. We formalize this in

COMPARATIVE STATICS THEOREM 4: If there are three commodities (including *numéraire*), if qualitative information is available concerning the entries in **A** and in **b**, and if equilibrium is locally stable under some set of speeds of adjustment of prices, then if there is a shift in tastes away from the *numéraire* commodity to some other commodity (other excess demand functions being unchanged), the signs of $d\bar{p}_1/da$ and $d\bar{p}_2/da$ are known, and for the given speeds of adjustment of prices, the time paths for all p_i approach the new equilibrium values.

Unfortunately, this theorem does not generalize to higher-dimensional cases, and the precise relationship among qualitative information, stability, and the properties of $\mathbf{A}^{-1}$ is not known when the systems (14) and (15) involve more than two equations. Even more fundamentally, it is not known for what class of cases involving qualitative information the stability hypothesis is nonvacuous. For example, in the case considered above, if A has sign pattern $\begin{bmatrix} + & 0 \\ 0 & + \end{bmatrix}$, then **A** is not stable for any values of entries that preserve the sign pattern of **A**, since, by the Routh-Hurwitz theorem, at least one of the diagonal entries of A must be negative. The following limited results in the study of stability of qualitative matrices are easily established:[1]

Given any real $n \times n$ matrix **A**, let $Q_{\mathbf{A}}$ denote the set of matrices with sign similar to **A**, that is, if $\mathbf{A}^* \in Q_{\mathbf{A}}$, then the sign pattern $(+,-,0)$ of $\mathbf{A}^*$ is the same as that of **A**. **A** will be said to be a *potentially stable* matrix if there exists a matrix $\mathbf{A}^* \in Q_{\mathbf{A}}$ such that $\mathbf{A}^*$ is stable (the real parts of the characteristic roots of $\mathbf{A}^*$ are all negative).

THEOREM 3: If **A** has all diagonal entries negative, then **A** is potentially stable. (For example, choose $\mathbf{A}^*$ with diagonal elements sufficiently large in absolute value that $\mathbf{A}^*$ is a dominant diagonal matrix, hence stable.)

THEOREM 4: Let **A** be a matrix with some diagonal elements positive and let **C** be a matrix with the same sign pattern as **A** except that the positive diagonal elements in **A** are replaced by zeros in **C**. Then **A** is potentially stable if and only if **C** is potentially stable. (The proof is based on a simple continuity condition concerning characteristic roots.)

THEOREM 5: A necessary condition that an $n \times n$ matrix **A** be potentially stable is that at least one term in the expansion of a principal minor

[1] See J. Quirk, The Correspondence Principle: A Macroeconomics Application, *International Economic Review* (in press).

of **A** of order i have sign $(-1)^i$ for $i = 1, \ldots, n$ (from the Routh-Hurwitz theorem).

Because of our lack of knowledge of equivalent conditions for potential stability, it is impossible to establish truly general theorems relating to the scope of Samuelson's correspondence principle in comparative statics. However, in the negative diagonal case, where Theorem 3 guarantees potential stability, a considerable amount is now known about the implications of the stability hypothesis for the properties of $\mathbf{A}^{-1}$ and thus for comparative statics theorems.[1] On the other hand, in the most general case, the following extremely weak result represents apparently the furthest extent to which the correspondence principle provides comparative statics results:

COMPARATIVE STATICS THEOREM 5: Assume $\mathbf{A} = [F_{ir}]$ is stable; then if a_i shifts upward the ith excess demand function (and leaves other excess demand functions unchanged) ($i = 1, \ldots, n$), there exists a k such that $d\bar{p}_k/da_k > 0$.†

This theorem follows directly from the Routh-Hurwitz conditions. If **A** is stable, then $|\mathbf{A}|$ has sign $(-1)^n$, and some $(n-1)$st-order principal minor of **A** must have sign $(-1)^{n-1}$. But the diagonal elements of $\mathbf{A}^{-1}$ are ratios of $(n-1)$st-order principal minors of **A** to $|\mathbf{A}|$; hence at least one of the diagonal elements of $\mathbf{A}^{-1}$ must be negative. For that diagonal element, under the conditions of the theorem above, $d\bar{p}_k/da_k > 0$.

Stronger results may be obtained if we strengthen our stability requirement; in particular, if we insist that equilibrium must be stable for all (positive) speeds of adjustment, then **A** is *D*-stable (see Sec. 5-4 above). **A** *D*-stable implies that **A** is "almost Hicksian," i.e., every even-order principal minor of **A** is nonnegative and every odd-order principal minor of **A** is nonpositive, and at least one nonzero principal minor of **A** of every order must exist. This leads into the following theorem:

COMPARATIVE STATICS THEOREM 6: Assume that equilibrium is locally stable under all positive speeds of adjustment of prices. Then if there is a shift in tastes away from the *numéraire* commodity to commodity i, all other excess demand functions being unchanged, the equilibrium value of the ith price cannot fall. (For some k, the equilibrium value of the kth price actually rises when excess demand for that commodity is increased by the shift parameter.)

[1] See Bassett, Maybee, and Quirk, *op. cit.*

† It will be noted that there are n a_i's, one such shift parameter for each F_i.

Similarly, based on the comments in Sec. 5-4,

COMPARATIVE STATICS THEOREM 7: Assume that equilibrium is *totally stable*, i.e., equilibrium is locally stable under any nonnegative speeds of adjustment of prices. Then if there is a shift in tastes away from the *numéraire* commodity to commodity i, all other excess demand functions being unchanged, the equilibrium value of the ith price increases.

This result holds because if **A** is totally stable, then **A** is Hicksian, which implies that every $(n - 1)$st-order principal minor of **A** has sign opposite to that of $|\mathbf{A}|$, from which the theorem follows directly.

Again, because equivalent conditions for neither D stability nor total stability are known, the theorems above are of somewhat limited usefulness. It is obvious, however, that the assumption of D stability (or of total stability) is not vacuous if the matrix **A** has a negative diagonal.

We shall return to a discussion of the scope and limitations of Samuelson's correspondence principle following the discussion in the next section of the one special case in which stability provides essentially all of the information needed for comparative statics studies.

6-5 THE GROSS SUBSTITUTE CASE AND THE MORISHIMA CASE

Assume that for every pair of distinct commodities i and r, an increase in the price of commodity i, other prices being held fixed, leads to an increase (or at least not a fall) in excess demand for commodity r. This case, already discussed in Chap. 5, is termed the "weak gross substitute" case. In the matrix **A**, all the off-diagonal entries are nonnegative and the diagonal entries are negative, given any choice of *numéraire*, under the weak gross substitute assumptions. In Chap. 5 it was noted that given Walras' law and/or homegeneity of excess demand functions, together with an indecomposability condition (each indecomposable diagonal block of **A** must have associated with it a nonzero entry in some corresponding row or column entry referring to the *numéraire* commodity), the weak gross substitute case exhibits stability in both the local and global senses. The local comparative statics properties of the gross substitute case follow from the following fundamental theorem on nonnegative indecomposable matrices:

THEOREM 6 (PERRON-FROBENIUS):[1] Let **M** be an indecomposable $n \times n$ real matrix with all entries nonnegative. Then there exists a

[1] For a proof of Theorem 6, see Gerard Debreu and I. N. Herstein, Non-negative Square Matrices, *Econometrica*, pp. 597–607, 1953.

maximal characteristic root λ^* of $\mathbf{M}$ with the following properties:

1. λ^* is simple, real, and positive.
2. $\lambda^* \geqq |\lambda|$ for every characteristic root λ of $\mathbf{M}$.
3. $\lambda^* > m_{ii}$ for every $i = 1, \ldots, n$, where m_{ii} is the ith diagonal entry of $\mathbf{M}$.
4. In the characteristic equation $\mathbf{Mx}^* = \lambda^*\mathbf{x}^*$, the characteristic vector $\mathbf{x}^*$ associated with λ^* can be chosen strictly positive, and it is the only characteristic vector of $\mathbf{M}$ with that property.

Further, given $\mathbf{A} = \mathbf{M} - c\mathbf{I}$, let A_{ij} denote the cofactor of the element in the ith row and jth column of $\mathbf{M} - c\mathbf{I}$, and let $|\mathbf{A}|$ denote $|\mathbf{M} - c\mathbf{I}|$. Then $c > \lambda^*$ implies $A_{ij}/|\mathbf{A}| < 0$ for every i, j, and $c > \sum_{j=1}^{n} m_{ij}$ for every $i = 1, \ldots, n$ implies $A_{ij} > A_{ii}$ for every $i \neq j$.

The Frobenius theorem is applied to the gross substitute case through the following result:

THEOREM 7: Let $\mathbf{M}$ be an $n \times n$ indecomposable nonnegative matrix with maximal characteristic root λ^*. Then $\mathbf{M} - c\mathbf{I}$ is a stable matrix if and only if $c > \lambda^*$.†

PROOF: Let μ be a characteristic root of $\mathbf{M} - c\mathbf{I}$ so that μ satisfies $|\mathbf{M} - c\mathbf{I} - \mu\mathbf{I}| = 0$, that is, $|\mathbf{M} - (c + \mu)\mathbf{I}| = 0$. Thus if λ is a root of $\mathbf{M}$ we have $\lambda = c + \mu$ and $R(\lambda) = c + R(\mu)$. Stability of $\mathbf{M} - c\mathbf{I}$ occurs if and only if $R(\mu) < 0$ for every μ, that is, $R(\lambda) - c < 0$ for every λ. By the Frobenius theorem, $\lambda^* \geqq |\lambda|$ for every λ; hence $\mathbf{M} - c\mathbf{I}$ is stable if and only if $c > \lambda^*$.

Because $\lambda^* > m_{ii}$ for every i, $c > \lambda^*$ implies that in $\mathbf{M} - c\mathbf{I}$, diagonal terms are negative and off-diagonal terms are nonnegative, i.e., we have the gross substitute case.

Other conditions equivalent to stability in the gross substitute case are the following:

THEOREM 8 (METZLER):[1] Let $\mathbf{A}$ be an $n \times n$ indecomposable matrix with negative diagonal and nonnegative off-diagonal terms; then $\mathbf{A}$ is stable if and only if $\mathbf{A}$ is Hicksian (principal minors alternate in sign).

† *Ibid.*

[1] L. Metzler, Stability of Multiple Markets: The Hicks Conditions, *Econometrica*, vol. 13, pp. 277–292, 1945. In the context of Leontief models this is referred to as the Hawkins-Simon condition.

THEOREM 9 (MC KENZIE):[1] Let **A** be an $n \times n$ indecomposable matrix with negative diagonal and nonnegative off-diagonal terms; then **A** is stable if and only if **A** is quasidominant diagonal, i.e., there exist positive numbers $d_1, \ldots, d_n$ such that

$$d_i\,|a_{ii}| > \sum_{j \neq i} d_j\,|a_{ij}| \qquad i = 1, \ldots, n$$

or there exist positive numbers $b_1, \ldots, b_n$ such that

$$b_i\,|a_{ii}| > \sum_{j \neq i} b_j\,|a_{ji}| \qquad i = 1, \ldots, n$$

We next consider the gross substitute case in the context of general equilibrium theory. It will be recalled that the system of comparative statics relations was written as

$$\mathbf{d\bar{p}} = -\mathbf{A}^{-1}\mathbf{b} \qquad \text{where } \mathbf{A} = [F_{ij}],\ \mathbf{b} = \left[\frac{\partial F_i}{\partial a}\,da\right],\ i, j = 1, \ldots, n$$

where a is a shift parameter; the dynamic system of relations was given by

$$\dot{\mathbf{p}} = \mathbf{BA}[\mathbf{p} - \mathbf{p}] \qquad \text{where } \mathbf{B} \text{ is a positive diagonal matrix.}$$

The gross substitute assumptions state that $F_{ij} = \partial F_i/\partial p_j$ satisfies $F_{ij} \geqq 0\ (i \neq j)$, $F_{ii} < 0\ (i = 0, \ldots, n)$; further assume **A** is indecomposable. Under Walras' law $\left[\sum_{i=0}^{n} F_{ij}p_i = 0\ (j = 0, \ldots, n)\right]$ or homogeneity $\left[\sum_{j=0}^{n} F_{ij}p_j = 0\ (i = 0, \ldots, n)\right]$ with $F_{0j} > 0$ for some $j \neq 0$ or $F_{i0} > 0$ for some $i \neq 0$, it is known that equilibrium is totally stable; hence by the theorems above, $\mathbf{A}^{-1}$ is composed solely of negative terms, **A** is a Hicksian matrix, **A** is a quasidominant diagonal matrix, and $A_{ij} > A_{ii}$ for every $i \neq j$.

Assume now that **b** has one positive entry in the ith position with zeros elsewhere, i.e., a shifts demand from the *numéraire* commodity to commodity i and does not directly affect excess demand for any other commodity. Then the following three "laws," first noted by Hicks, hold:[2]

COMPARATIVE STATICS THEOREM 8 (THE THREE HICKSIAN LAWS OF COMPARATIVE STATICS): Given the gross substitute assumptions, a shift in demand away from the *numéraire* commodity to commodity i

[1] Lionel W. McKenzie, The Matrix with Dominant Diagonal and Economic Theory, *Proceedings of a Symposium on Mathematical Methods in the Social Sciences*, Stanford University Press, Palo Alto, Calif., 1960, pp. 277–292.

[2] Hicks, *op. cit.* J. Mosak, *General Equilibrium Theory and International Trade*, Principia Press, Bloomington, Ind., 1944.

(other excess demand functions being unchanged) leads to the following results:

1. $\bar{p}_i$, the equilibrium price of commodity i, increases.
2. $\bar{p}_j$ increases for every $j \neq 0$.
3. $\bar{p}_i$ increases proportionately more than $\bar{p}_j$ $(j \neq 1)$.

Further, because equilibrium is totally stable, the limiting values of the time paths of prices approach the new equilibrium values for any nonnegative speeds of adjustment of prices.

The Hicksian laws hold in the gross substitute case because under Walras' law and/or homogeneity of excess demand functions, local stability of equilibrium occurs, which means the relevant portions of the Perron-Frobenius theorem can be applied to the problem of determining the qualitative and semiquantitative properties of the elements of $\mathbf{A}^{-1}$. It should also be noted that Morishima has shown that the Hicksian laws hold in the large as well, i.e., the laws hold for disturbances of arbitrary magnitude, while global stability of equilibrium implies these global comparative statics results have predictive content.[1]

A further generalization of these results is the so-called "Morishima case," already mentioned in Sec. 5-5. We refer to a matrix $\mathbf{C} = [c_{ij}]$ as a *Morishima matrix* if it has the property that by identical row and column permutations, $\mathbf{C}$ can be brought into the form

$$\mathbf{C} = \begin{bmatrix} \mathbf{C}_{11} & \mathbf{C}_{12} \\ \mathbf{C}_{21} & \mathbf{C}_{22} \end{bmatrix}$$

where $\mathbf{C}_{11}$ and $\mathbf{C}_{22}$ are square blocks, $\mathbf{C}_{11} \geqq 0$, $\mathbf{C}_{22} \geqq 0$, $\mathbf{C}_{12} \leqq 0$, $\mathbf{C}_{21} \leqq 0$, and $\mathbf{C}$ is indecomposable. If $c_{ij} \neq 0$ for every i, j, then an equivalent statement is that $c_{ii} > 0$ for every i, sign c_{ij} = sign c_{ji} for every i, j, and sign c_{ij} = sign $c_{ik}c_{kj}$, i, j, k distinct. Morishima has proved the following:

THEOREM 10 (GENERALIZED FROBENIUS THEOREM):[2] Assume $\mathbf{C}$ is a Morishima matrix. Then there exists a maximal characteristic root λ^* of $\mathbf{C}$

[1] Morishima, *op. cit*,.

[2] Michio Morishima, On the Laws of Change of the Price System in an Economy Which Contains Complementary Commodities, *Osaka Economic Papers*, vol. 1, pp. 101–113, 1952.

with the properties that:

1. λ^* is simple, real and positive.
2. $\lambda^* \geq |\lambda|$ for every characteristic root λ of **C**.
3. $\lambda^* > c_{ii}$ for every i, where c_{ii} is the ith diagonal entry in **C**.

Further when **C** is reindexed into the form of the preceding paragraph, in the matrix $\mathbf{G} = [\mathbf{C} - c\mathbf{I}]^{-1}$, $c > \lambda^*$ implies that every element in the blocks in **G** corresponding to $\mathbf{C}_{11}$ and $\mathbf{C}_{22}$ is negative and every element in the blocks of **G** corresponding to $\mathbf{C}_{21}$ and $\mathbf{C}_{12}$ is positive.

In particular it will be noted that when $\mathbf{C}_{12}$ and $\mathbf{C}_{21}$ are empty, the Morishima case reduces to the gross substitute case. In the context of general equilibrium theory, the Morishima case is one in which commodities are assumed to obey the rules "substitutes of substitutes are substitutes, complements of complements are substitutes, and complements of substitutes and substitutes of complements are complements."

The similarity between the gross substitute case and the Morishima case carries over to stability conditions. Let $\mathbf{A} = \mathbf{C} - c\mathbf{I}$, where **C** is a Morishima matrix. Then **A** is a stable matrix if and only if any one of the following holds:

1. $c > \lambda^*$.
2. **C** is a Hicksian matrix.
3. **C** is a quasidominant diagonal matrix.

The following comparative statics theorem holds in the Morishima case.[1]

COMPARATIVE STATICS THEOREM 9: Assume $\mathbf{A} = \mathbf{C} - c\mathbf{I}$, where **C** is a Morishima matrix and $\mathbf{A} = [F_{ij}]$. Then if **A** is a stable matrix, a shift in demand from the *numéraire* commodity to commodity i (no other excess demand functions being shifted) has the following results:

1. $\bar{p}_i$ increases.
2. $\bar{p}_j$ increases $(j \neq i)$ if j and i are substitutes, and $\bar{p}_j$ decreases $(j \neq i)$ if j and i are complements.

[1] Morishima, "On the Laws . . . ." *op. cit.*

As contrasted with our other comparative statics theorems, it is not true, in general, that the competitive assumptions imply **A** is stable in the Morishima case; in fact, if all commodities (including *numéraire*) obey the Morishima conditions, and if we exclude the gross substitute case, equilibrium is not locally stable; if we relax the condition on the *numéraire* commodity, still for no case is it possible to *prove* local stability of equilibrium under the Morishima conditions on the basis of the sign pattern alone, except in the gross substitute case.[1] Stability in the Morishima case occurs, if at all, only for particular quantitative magnitudes of the elements of **A**.

This result is somewhat disappointing because, in connection with the question raised in the previous section concerning the scope of Samuelson's correspondence principle, the following holds:[2]

THEOREM 11: Assume **A** is a stable matrix with all diagonal elements negative and with $a_{ij} \neq 0$ for every i, j. Then $\mathbf{A}^{-1}$ is of known sign pattern, given only these conditions and a knowledge of the sign pattern of **A**, if and only if

1. **A** is a 2×2 matrix or
2. $\mathbf{A} = \mathbf{C} - c\mathbf{I}$, where **C** is a Morishima matrix and $c > \lambda^*$.

Because "signing" the inverse of **A** is so closely tied in with the derivation of comparative statics theorems and because of the status of stability in the Morishima case under the competitive assumptions, it appears that there is, after all, perhaps only a rather limited scope for the correspondence principle in general equilibrium theory. The next section completes our discussion of this problem.

6-6 CONCLUDING REMARKS

While the issue of the scope of Samuelson's correspondence principle remains unresolved, certain further results extending Theorem 11 in the negative diagonal case are known.[3] However, because these conditions under which the inverse may be signed given the stability hypothesis are

[1] See Kenneth J. Arrow, H. Block, and Leonid Hurwicz, The Stability of the Competitive Equilibrium II, *Econometrica*, vol. 27, pp. 82–109, 1959, and Bassett, Habibagahi, and Quirk, *op. cit.*

[2] Bassett, Habibagahi, and Quirk, *op. cit.*

[3] Bassett, Maybee, and Quirk, *op. cit.*

difficult to interpret in economic terms, their usefulness remains conjectural. One particular result of some interest, however, should be mentioned:[1]

THEOREM 12: In the system $\mathbf{Ay} = \mathbf{b}$, where $\mathbf{A}$ is nonzero and is an $n \times n$ real matrix, assume that the sign patterns of $\mathbf{A}$ and $\mathbf{b}$ are known, that $a_{ii} < 0$ for $i = 1, \ldots, n$, and $b_i = 0$ for every $i \neq i'$. Then the system $\mathbf{Ay} = \mathbf{b}$ can be solved for the sign pattern of $\mathbf{y}$ when $\mathbf{A}$ is assumed to be a stable matrix if and only if the system $\mathbf{Ay} = \mathbf{b}$ can be solved for the sign pattern of $\mathbf{y}$ when $\mathbf{A}$ is assumed to be a Hicksian matrix.

For the special case covered by Theorem 12, a correspondence principle based on dynamic stability thus has the same scope as one based on Hicks' notion of stability.

[1] *Ibid.*

NAME INDEX

SUBJECT INDEX